MUNICIPAL
PRODUCTIVITY

MUNICIPAL PRODUCTIVITY

A Comparison of Fourteen High-Quality-Service Cities

David N. Ammons

PRAEGER

PRAEGER SPECIAL STUDIES • PRAEGER SCIENTIFIC

New York • Philadelphia • Eastbourne, UK
Toronto • Hong Kong • Tokyo • Sydney

Library of Congress Cataloging in Publication Data

Ammons, David N.
  Municipal productivity.

  Bibliography: p.
  Includes index.
  1. Municipal services--United States--Management.
2. Municipal government--United States.   I. Title.
HD3887.A55   1984   352.073   83-17821
ISBN 0-03-069387-X (alk. paper)

Published in 1984 by Praeger Publishers
CBS Educational and Professional Publishing,
a Division of CBS Inc.
521 Fifth Avenue, New York, NY 10175 USA

56789 052 987654532

Printed in the United States of America
on acid-free paper

To Cindy

CONTENTS

LIST OF TABLES AND FIGURES

ACKNOWLEDGMENTS

I am grateful to many persons who contributed in different ways to this book. Guidance was received from several faculty members at the University of Oklahoma, where I prepared the dissertation from which the book developed. The many suggestions of David R. Morgan were especially helpful. I also want to thank F. Ted Hebert, Hugh G. MacNiven, Kenneth J. Meier, and B. G. Schumacher, all of the University of Oklahoma, and Ted Robinson, University of San Francisco. In addition I wish to express appreciation to William Lyons, University of Tennessee, for reviewing and commenting on two critical chapters.

Several persons outside of academia also took an interest in this project and encouraged its completion. M. Lyle Lacy III and Joseph C. King, practicing municipal administrators, were especially helpful sounding boards. The contributions of professors and practitioners are gratefully acknowledged, but I retain the responsibility for any errors that may remain.

Several agencies made relevant information available without which the project would have suffered. The Insurance Services Office was especially generous with data instrumental in the screening process. Officials from cities throughout the nation supplied requested service-quality information. The fourteen study cities provided revenue and expenditure details. Furthermore, four city officials in each of the study cities graciously responded to individual questionnaires, permitting an analysis of factors that would have been inaccessible otherwise. I am indebted to each of them.

I owe a special debt of gratitude to Faith M. Frykman, who typed the final manuscript and most of its earlier drafts. She was assisted on some of the drafts of the initial chapters by Rebecca K. Brown. In addition, Jane D. Longendorfer provided special computer programming assistance that was most helpful during the city-screening stage of the project. Kenneth E. McCoy provided artwork. Their efforts are gratefully acknowledged.

Finally, I want to express deepest appreciation to my wife, Cindy, and my children, Drew, Alicia, and Paige. Their patience, encouragement, and even enthusiasm for "the book" that consumed so many evenings and weekends made the difference.

ACKNOWLEDGMENTS

MUNICIPAL PRODUCTIVITY

1

INTRODUCTION

Government productivity has been likened to the Loch Ness monster: there have been numerous reported sightings, but according to the analogy, nothing has been confirmed.[1] Despite the size and economic significance of the public sector, relatively little beyond subjective impressions is known about governmental efficiency or effectiveness—and less still is known about the factors that positively or negatively affect the pursuit of efficiency and effectiveness objectives. The "monster" remains in large measure a mystery.

The focus of this study is upon productivity in municipal government. The need for an increased understanding of productivity—what it means, techniques designed to improve it, how it can be measured, common barriers to improvement efforts, and factors that influence it—is no less pressing at the local level than at other levels of government. The public's simultaneous desires for increased quantity and improved quality of public services and modest rates of taxation create serious problems for public service providers. Improved public sector productivity is espoused by many as the logical answer to the perplexing quandary in which many officials find themselves, yet the signals from productivity proponents are confused and sometimes contradictory. Techniques that appear useful in one instance fail in others. The bases for judging productivity gains are often ill-defined and subjective. It is no wonder that some local officials are not certain what productivity means or how best to pursue it.

Productivity improvement is not a new concept, but events of the past several years have helped to renew theoretical and practical interest in it. Fiscal stress, the term used to describe the resource scarcity plaguing many cities, has altered the outlook and management style of U.S. municipal governments. The mood of the cities in the emergent 1970s was one of confidence in community growth and

1

concomitant tax-base expansion, leading city officials to prize their skills in development of new programs as among their most important talents.[2] Local budgetary strategies were generally predicated upon the apparent certainty of incremental revenue growth derived from a developing tax base.[3]

The frailty of the growth assumption, however, became increasingly evident as U. S. cities moved through the 1970s. Growing public dissatisfaction with levels of taxation perceived to be excessive and levels of service thought to be inadequate spurred the exodus of businesses, industries, and middle-class and upper-class residents from many cities; brought at least a few municipalities menacingly close to bankruptcy; and led some observers, including the Future Horizons Committee of the International City Management Association (ICMA), to predict that a strategy of "holding the line indefinitely" would replace the assumption of inevitable growth.[4]

Economic and demographic problems merged with citizen demands for additional services, intolerance with tax increases, and impatience with poor performance to create a milieu of frustration for both the service recipient and the service provider. Part of the problem was of the local officials' own making, as they repeatedly followed the popular course of service expansion over more prudent choices, acceded to employee and constituent demands despite adverse long-term consequences, and devoted less attention than warranted to matters of service efficiency. Much of the problem, however, was generated elsewhere. Social and economic conditions realistically beyond the local officials' control placed many hurdles in their path. State and federal program mandates and pressure for new services from a more articulate clientele exacerbated an already strained revenue-expenditure mismatch.[5] Worse still, the voice of the citizenry was not uniform but instead was contradictory in its disparate demands and priorities.

By the mid-1970s—and perhaps much earlier—the aggregate mood, despite the demands of special interest groups, supported governmental deceleration. Surveys conducted by the Advisory Commission on Intergovernmental Relations (ACIR) indicate general public support for a go-slow policy on taxes and spending since 1975.[6] Popular reluctance to expand public services may be explained in part by the public's low regard for governmental performance. In a 1974 Lou Harris poll performed for the National Commission on Productivity, respondents more frequently rated government workers as having below average productivity than any of the seven other categories of workers included in the survey.[7] In ranking categories of workers with above average productivity, respondents placed government workers next to last.

Ominous signs of public dissatisfaction with performance were articulated in the 1970s through increasingly vociferous public resistance to increased taxation. Bond referenda for schools and other public facilities were defeated in instance after instance, as were tax referenda of all kinds. Reacting to the public mood, officials anxiously sought ways to lighten the local burden through increases in intergovernmental revenues or other shifting mechanisms, hoping to avoid testing the limits of taxpayer tolerance for fear of a "disastrous explosion of public wrath."[8]

Popular dissatisfaction with local taxes is revealed in the results of eight ACIR surveys conducted from 1972 to 1982 on fairness of taxes. In five of the ten surveys, the public perceived the local property tax to be less fair than the federal income tax, the state income tax, or the state sales tax. In only five instances, including the four most recent surveys (1979, 1980, 1981, and 1982), was the local property tax ranked as favorably as second worst.[9] Dissatisfaction with local taxes reached a crescendo in California on June 6, 1978, when the voters of that state enacted Proposition 13 by a wide margin. Enactment of the measure limited local property tax collections to no more than 1 percent of market value, restricted the magnitude and timing of future assessment increases, and established difficult legislative and popular consent hurdles for new tax levies. The California measure was followed by tax-restricting action in other states, with at least 37 states cutting taxes or imposing spending limits in 1979, perhaps helping to explain the improvement in public sentiment toward the local property tax reported in the ACIR surveys of 1979 and 1980.[10]

Unusual pressures, such as those produced by citizens simultaneously demanding more services and restricting revenue availability, require unusual countermeasures. Continued reliance on an assumption of revenue growth and the ultimate durability of public entities and continued inattention to the ramifications of income-expenditure imbalance are, at best, administratively and politically naive and, at worst, potentially devastating to a municipality's financial health. Dan Cordtz asserts that persons involved in the public sector, from employees to supervisors to elected officials, have subscribed to a general attitude that public services by their very nature must continue and that the taxpayer must provide whatever resources are necessary to employ whatever number of workers is necessary to perform the job without increasing individual work loads.[11] Public resistance to increased taxation demonstrates the fallacy of this belief and provides the backdrop for urban observers who contend that productivity improvement must be a key element in efforts to cope with the problems plaguing U.S. cities.

The purpose of this study is to examine some of the major community, administrative, and political variables that help to explain productivity differences between municipalities. For reasons that will be explored in Chapter 3, this examination will focus upon a relatively small number of cities that provide high-quality services in multiple functional areas.

In Chapter 4, service-quality standards will be described for seven municipal functions and a screening process will be applied from which only 14 U.S. cities will emerge designated as high-quality, full-service cities. In Chapter 5, a method for assessing differences in the relative productivity of municipalities providing a similar scope and quality of services will be described and applied to the 14 study cities. Common barriers to productivity improvement, accounting for much of the difficulty encountered in productivity-improvement programs and for some of the productivity differences among U.S. cities, will be examined in some detail in Chapter 6. Some of these barriers will be included among the organizational and community characteristics examined in Chapter 7 to identify the relevance of such characteristics to relative productivity in high-quality, full-service cities. An effort will be made in Chapters 7 and 8 to describe the linkages or the apparent absence of linkages between socioeconomic, demographic, financial, administrative, and political factors and municipal productivity.

Before turning our attention to these topics, however, it is important to place this study in perspective by reviewing the concept of productivity and some of the important work done to date. Chapter 2 is devoted to an overview of municipal productivity including its definition, its significance, the distinctive environment in which public sector operations are conducted, barriers to productivity-improvement programs, a sample of productivity-improvement programs undertaken to date, popular approaches utilized or identified, and a review of relevant research.

NOTES

1. J. D. Hodgson, "Worker Productivity Key Element in Government and Business," Defense Management Journal 8 (October 1972): 5.

2. Richard J. Stillman II, The Rise of the City Manager: A Public Professional in Local Government (Albuquerque: University of New Mexico Press, 1974), p. 73.

3. Charles H. Levine, "Organizational Decline and Cutback Management," Public Administration Review 38 (July-August 1978): 316.

4. "Final Report of the I.C.M.A. Committee on the Future Horizons of the Profession," excerpted in Elizabeth K. Kellar, ed., Managing with Less: A Book of Readings (Washington, D.C.: International City Management Association, 1979), pp. 2-7.

5. See, for example, Frances Fox Piven and Richard A. Cloward, Regulating the Poor: The Functions of Public Welfare (New York: Random House, 1971), pp. 281-82. The authors suggest that Great Society programs of the 1960s utilized relatively limited funding in some cases to stimulate minority protests over local service inadequacies. The complaint articulation skills learned in the 1960s were not forgotten in the 1970s.

6. Advisory Commission on Intergovernmental Relations, Changing Public Attitudes on Governments and Taxes, 1982 (Washington, D.C.: U.S. Government Printing Office, 1982), p. 7. In a 1982 survey that reflected a pattern similar to other ACIR surveys since 1975, 36 percent of the respondents desired a decrease in government services and taxes; 42 percent preferred to keep taxes and services about where they were; 8 percent wanted an increase in services and taxes; and 14 percent had no opinion. A preference for either decreasing services and taxes or keeping them where they were was stated by 78 percent of all respondents (91 percent of those who expressed an opinion).

7. John S. Thomas, So, Mr. Mayor, You Want to Improve Productivity (Washington, D.C.: U.S. Government Printing Office, 1974), p. 31.

8. Peter G. Peterson, "Productivity in Government and the American Economy," Public Administration Review 32 (November-December 1972): 746.

9. ACIR, Changing Public Attitudes, p. 4.

10. John Herbers, "Nationwide Revolt on Taxes Showing No Sign of Abating," New York Times, August 5, 1979, pp. 1, 38.

11. Dan Cordtz, "City Hall Discovers Productivity," Fortune 84 (October 1, 1971): 96.

2

PRODUCTIVITY
IMPROVEMENT IN
CITY GOVERNMENT

Productivity is like pornography . . . I can't define it, but I
know it when I see it.

Unidentified city manager*

Although recent survey results indicate that most local government administrators associate the concepts of efficiency and effectiveness with productivity, many, like the city manager quoted above,
have only a vague sense of what the term means.[1] There is clearly
a lack of unanimity among local officials on any single definition of
productivity. Lack of definitional unanimity (of a somewhat different
nature) prevails among academicians as well. Absent a strong consensus on the meaning of productivity, it is hardly surprising that
sharply differing levels of commitment to productivity improvement
exist among local governments and local officials—according perhaps
to the meanings they ascribe to it—and that programs often subjectively
judged to have improved productivity in one sense of the term may be
ridiculed as valueless or even counterproductive in another sense.

In this chapter, different definitions of productivity and other
topics pertaining to local government productivity will be examined:
its importance, the factors that distinguish the public sector from
the private sector insofar as productivity is concerned, barriers to
improvement, recent productivity-improvement program efforts,
and current thinking regarding techniques likely to produce favorable
results.

---

*Quotation by unidentified city manager in "NLC's SPEER Unit
Is Co-sponsoring Productivity Training," Nation's Cities Weekly 3
(May 26, 1980): 12.

DEFINITION OF PRODUCTIVITY

Productivity has been defined narrowly as the ratio between the output of an activity and the input of resources necessary to achieve that output. In popular usage, it has been defined broadly at times to mean anything that cuts costs and at other times to mean everything associated with good management.[2] The appropriateness of the narrow definition, with its strict emphasis upon production efficiency, has been challenged in attempted public sector applications; a broad definition, on the other hand, is too vague and all-encompassing to be of real value.

Private sector use of the output-to-input ratio as its primary measure of productivity is well established and is reported routinely by the Bureau of Labor Statistics. Output of goods and services is measured against inputs required to obtain that output. The input measure may include all resources associated with the output (labor, capital, energy, and other necessary elements), or it may reflect only a single element, typically production man-hours. The emphasis of such measures is upon the product rather than simply upon activities.[3] Productivity improvement, in this view, is achieved by altering outputs and/or inputs to achieve a more favorable ratio.

The use of the ratio of outputs to inputs as a performance gauge clearly indicates the importance of efficiency in a given operation; however, effectiveness is also an important element of performance. Stated simply, effectiveness is the degree to which objectives are being accomplished. Included in the concept of effectiveness are considerations of quality of service and the contribution of a given service toward achieving objectives. Jerome Mark notes that the distinction between efficiency and effectiveness is more pronounced in the public sector than in the private sector owing to the presence in the latter of competition and market forces that tend to elevate quality and cost considerations simultaneously.[4]

Although some productivity definitions applied to the public sector exclude specific mention of quality of service or effectiveness and a few explicitly deny the appropriateness of encumbering productivity measurement with effectiveness considerations, most analysts of public sector productivity either state explicitly the relevance of effectiveness or define productivity in terms that may be construed to include quality-of-service considerations.[5] Productivity definitions that stress more services for a given quantity of tax dollars or the same services at a reduced cost may be interpreted so that more and same have qualitative as well as quantitative connotations.[6] Quality of service, though presumed to be present, is less explicit in such definitions than in many others.

Productivity definitions generally found to be most acceptable in the public sector incorporate both efficiency and effectiveness.

Effectiveness in such uses may encompass quality of service, the relationship between output and goals, compliance with standards of
performance, considerations of equity in service provision, and in
some instances, factors of social value.[7] The following definition,
advanced by Nancy S. Hayward, shall be used in this study:

> Governmental productivity is the efficiency with which re-
> sources are consumed in the effective delivery of public ser-
> vices. The definition implies not only quantity, but also quality.
> It negates the value of efficiency, if the product or service it-
> self lacks value. It relates the value of all resources con-
> sumed—human, capital, and technological—to the output of pub-
> lic services or results achieved.[8]

This definition permits the use of the output-to-input ratio for measuring productivity only if some means is devised to account for differences in output quality or effectiveness.

Once defined, a natural question regarding productivity is "How
can it be improved?" Marc Holzer notes four ways.[9] First, the
output-to-input ratio is improved if outputs remain constant while inputs are reduced. Second, it improves if output increases while inputs remain constant. Third, the productivity ratio is improved if
outputs increase while inputs decline. Fourth, productivity may be
improved with an increase in both output and input if output grows at
a faster rate than input. A fifth possibility for productivity improvement, not included in Holzer's listing, would involve a reduction of
both output and input, with input declining at a faster rate than output.
Application of these approaches to productivity improvement in a manner in keeping with the Hayward definition requires that the term output connote quality of output as well as quantity and that the analyst
attempting to assess productivity changes have some means of measuring the qualitative as well as quantitative aspects of productivity.

The simple productivity formula of output divided by input, used
in the above examples, is vulnerable to criticism for its failure to
account explicitly for variation in quality of service or effectiveness.
Various alternate formulas have been suggested, but most have proved
to be unsatisfactory for one reason or another. The following have
been among the formulas suggested:

- Productivity = $(O/I) + (O/S)$ where O = outputs, I = inputs, and S =
degree to which outputs are deemed satisfactory.[10]

- Productivity = (W/R) $(Q_1 \times Q_2)$ where W = work load; R = resources;
Q_1 = quality, defined as percentage of consumer satis-

faction; and Q_2 = quantity, defined as percentage of community need satisfied. [11]

- Productivity = $100E \cdot \sqrt{(c^2 + s^2)}d$ where E = efficiency index, c = consistency, s = user satisfaction, and d = employee dependability. [12]

- P = A/(pU + cE) where P = process quality productivity, A = number of acceptable units, U = number of units processed, E = number of units that have been corrected, p = processing cost per unit, and c = cost per unit for correction processing. [13]

Efforts to measure public sector productivity at all—much less to combine the concepts of efficiency and effectiveness in a single productivity measure—are complicated by a series of factors that, if present in the private sector, are magnified in the public sector. Jesse Burkhead and Patrick Hennigan list the five fundamental problems in public sector productivity analysis as the absence of discrete units of public sector output; the absence of a clearly specified production function that, for example, expresses the contribution of capital facilities to public sector output; the presence of multiple and sometimes competing objectives; the presence of reciprocal externalities through which one department's performance is dependent on that of others; and the absence of an adequate data base. [14] Despite such constraints, attempts have been made to analyze public sector productivity. Mark identifies the two primary approaches employed as, first, productivity inferences based upon changes in cost per unit of service over time and, second, specification of work load and costs of inputs as independent variables to the dependent expenditure variable with productivity inferences based upon a residual term taken to represent changes in productivity and quality of service. He points out, however, that even these approaches are constrained by problems in defining the population served and lack of availability of a suitable data base. [15] Some fairly major efforts, including that of the Joint Financial Management Improvement Program, have relied for the sake of simplicity upon the traditional productivity formula (P = O/I) and have attempted to measure efficiency while holding quality of service constant over the period of examination. [16]

SIGNIFICANCE OF PUBLIC SECTOR PRODUCTIVITY

Diminished growth of U.S. productivity has been a cause of concern to economic analysts. In terms of overall productivity, the United States enjoys a leadership role. In terms of rate of productivity growth, however, the United States is being outpaced by its major industrial counterparts, placing its overall productivity lead in jeopardy. Symptomatic of the nation's economic problems, the U.S. balance of trade in 1971 showed a deficit for the first time since 1893. The rate of exportation increases and productivity improvement by major industrial competitors has far exceeded U.S. percentage gains.

The average annual rate of productivity growth of U.S. businesses has declined from 3.3 percent in the 1947–65 period to 0.7 percent during 1973–82 (Table 2.1). A similar decline has been registered

TABLE 2.1

Average Annual Rates of U.S. Labor Productivity Growth:
Output per Hour of All Persons
(in percent)

Period	Business	Nonfarm Business
1947–65	3.3	2.7
1965–73	2.4	2.1
1973–82	0.7	0.6

Source: U.S., Department of Labor, Bureau of Labor Statistics, unpublished material.

by nonfarm businesses. Despite a slowdown in productivity growth, however, the wages of U.S. workers have continued to rise. Until the mid-1960s, wage increases had generally been matched or exceeded by productivity gains.[17] After that point, productivity gains began to lag behind.

Productivity is viewed not only as a means of improving the U.S. posture in world trade but also as a means of breaking the syndrome of inflation in which wages and prices pursue one another in an ever upward spiral.[18] Sufficiently increased worker productivity would interrupt the spiral by permitting wage increases without causing escalation of unit cost and its attendant pressure on prices. Burton Malkiel explains the relationship between productivity and inflation in the following manner:

Indeed, the slowdown of productivity growth may well have contributed to our current stagflation condition. If labor groups have become accustomed to, and thus insist on, increases in real wages larger than the present growth in productivity, their living standards will increase only at the expense of others. Only productivity growth can provide the increases in real output per person that make possible overall gains in real living standards. Without such growth, the resulting struggle over income shares leads directly to inflation. [19]

Moreover, productivity is perceived to hold the key to reductions in unemployment, since average unemployment rates have been lower during periods of rapid productivity growth than during times of slow increases. [20]

As a large and growing component of the national economy, the public sector is a factor both in the nation's current economic condition and also in the likelihood for improvement. Although an optimist might view improved public sector performance as a potential contributor to increased national productivity, most analysts would appear to be satisfied if the public sector would simply keep pace with private sector growth and cease being a "drag on the productivity of the society as a whole."[21] Government waste and inefficiency and slow productivity gains among most service-providing entities in general, public and private, restrict the availability of capital for more productive uses. [22] Calculations by the Tax Foundation have indicated that direct and indirect federal, state, and local taxes consume the equivalent of the average worker's income for the first 121 days of the year, thereby claiming a major quantity of resources otherwise available for other purposes. [23]

Despite its national economic importance, little is known about public sector productivity in general or that of local government in particular. The public sector is essentially ignored in most studies of aggregate productivity. In gross national product (GNP) data, for instance, public sector output is valued at factor cost; that is, the value of the output is simply taken as the cost of the input. By this approach, public sector productivity is locked in a static position: there is no possibility for improvement or decline. As the public sector grows in size and importance to the national economy, such an interpretation of performance has an increasingly distorting effect.

To demonstrate the importance of the public sector in overall national productivity considerations, Mark computed the national productivity improvement rate under various assumptions regarding federal, state, and local rates of productivity growth (Table 2.2 .[24] If, for example, the private rate of productivity growth were 3.1 percent; the federal rate, 1.9 percent; and the state and local rate, 2.0 percent; the overall national rate of productivity growth would be 2.9 percent. With an assumption of no growth in public sector productivity, the national rate would be much less.

TABLE 2.2

Effect on Total National Productivity Growth of Alternate Rates of
State and Local Government Productivity
(in percent)

Private Rate (less government enterprises), 1950–71	Assumed Federal Rate	Assumed State and Local Rate	Implied National Rate
3.1	1.9	0.0	2.7
3.1	1.9	1.0	2.8
3.1	1.9	2.0	2.9
3.1	1.9	3.0	3.0
3.1	1.9	4.0	3.1

Source: Jerome A. Mark, "Progress in Measuring Productivity in Government," Monthly Labor Review 95 (December 1972): 5.

A major problem in public sector productivity analysis is the difficulty in measuring outputs. The absence of direct pricing for public sector outputs has led to the practice of estimating output quantity and quality based upon estimates of inputs, consequences, or direct outputs. As noted by John Ross and Jesse Burkhead, each method has its drawbacks and even the preferred direct–output approach suffers from an inability to address changes in quality as well as a more fundamental problem of the typical absence of necessary data. [25]

Although critics tend to be harsh in their judgment of local government productivity, the paucity of hard data led two Urban Institute researchers to a more cautious conclusion.

> The main thing to be said about the productivity of local governments in the United States is that little is known about it. Little factual data is currently available to show the current level of productivity of local governments in the United States or to indicate whether it has been rising or falling, and at what rates. Escalating costs and escalating urban problems suggest it has been falling; however, the nation has little in the way of hard facts to go on. [26]

Although rising costs suggest the likelihood of a poor record of productivity improvement in local government, such evidence is inconclusive. Cost increases in excess of the rate of inflation may be caused by service expansion, quality-of-service improvements, declining productivity, or some combination of these factors. Service expansion by local government, both in terms of additional services per client and in terms of added clientele, is perhaps the most easily documented of the factors.[27] Municipal service quality has improved markedly over the past century but may have declined in some functions and some communities in recent years. Trends in municipal productivity are more difficult to gauge, but a serious urban observer could hardly miss the major advances over the past century in performance techniques in selected functional areas of local service, which presumably have had a favorable impact on productivity.[28]

Despite notable technological advances in such areas as street maintenance, water and sewer facilities, and public safety communications, popular notions of governmental performance suggest that such advances have not been sufficient to offset an otherwise dismal productivity-improvement record. Abundant superficial evidence indicates that local government productivity is not keeping pace with that of the private sector. Such evidence portends serious consequences when viewed in the context of the conclusions drawn by William Baumol, forecasting a scenario of decline known as Baumol's disease.[29] Baumol constructs a model of unbalanced growth in which he depicts the economy divided into two sectors: one that is technologically progressive, quick to innovate, and characterized by constantly increasing productivity, and the other that is tied to labor, not as a means to an end but as an end in itself, in which productivity increases are only sporadic. He suggests that education and the performing arts are among the activities that are heavily, if not toally, dependent upon labor with little means of effective capital substitution. He further suggests that a large proportion of municipal services falls into this relatively nonprogressive sector of the economy. The growing urban crisis, Baumol contends, is tied to the likelihood that wages in both sectors will vary together and that wages—and unit costs—in the nonprogressive sector will be carried upward by productivity-based wage gains in the progressive sector. Assuming the ratio of outputs between the sectors to remain constant, Baumol predicts from his model that the labor component in the progressive sector will continually decline while that of the less productive sector will expand, thereby exacerbating many of the problems associated with the urban crisis. At an extreme, the overwhelming majority of society's resources would move from the more-productive to the less-productive sector, according to Baumol's scenario.

In general support of Baumol's theory, D. F. Bradford, R. A. Malt, and W. E. Oates found that local governments had not "been able to offset the rising costs of inputs, notably manpower, by cutting back on the use of these inputs through significant cost-saving advances in techniques of production. Improvements in quality of output have certainly occurred," they note, "but they seem, if anything, to have stimulated rather than reduced levels of public spending."[30] Analysis by others indicates substantial growth in the service sector, partly as a result of the low rate of service-sector productivity gains and partly because of increased demand for services owing to growth in real income per capita as a result of productivity increases in other areas of the economy.[31]

Whether owing to factors outlined in Baumol's thesis or to others, the recent growth in state and local government has been dramatic. The General Accounting Office (GAO) reports that state and local government expenditures increased by more than 600 percent from the mid-1950s to the mid-1970s because of population increases, rising public service demands, increasing governmental involvement in welfare and regulation, and rising costs.[32] By 1976 state and local government expenditures accounted for 15.1 percent of the nation's GNP, with federal expenditures accounting for another 22.5 percent. Nowhere is the growth more dramatically demonstrated than in increased public sector employment.

At the turn of the century, 1 out of every 24 workers was employed in a public sector job; the comparable figure today is 1 out of 6.[33] From 1869 to 1969, governmental employment grew from 3.7 percent to 18.1 percent of the U.S. work force.[34] From 1957 to 1976, compensation costs for state and local personnel rose 204 percent, compared with a Consumer Price Index increase of 102 percent during the same period.[35] The long-term productivity trend in the private service sector, perhaps a suitable proxy for public sector performance, is revealing: from 1919 to 1948, the private sector services industries recorded a productivity growth rate of only 1.6 percent compared with an overall rate for the private domestic economy of 2 percent; and from 1948 to 1969, the service industry productivity growth rate was 1.8 percent compared with 2.3 percent overall.[36]

Arguments popular in the 1950s that government workers' pay was adjusted simply to keep pace with that of industrial workers may have lost validity in more recent years. There is some evidence, in fact, that the situation has been reversed. "Try as they will," writes James Kuhn, "industrial unions have not been able to outrace tax and price increases. And rising taxes and prices primarily reflect a great increase in the cost of public and private services, which has been the most important inflationary force in the economy."[37] From 1953 to 1973 state and local government compensation increased 188 percent, while wages in wholesale and retail, manufacturing, mining, contract construction, private nonagricultural, and the service industries rose 132 percent, 141 percent, 163 percent, 154 percent, 141 percent, and 171 percent, respectively.[38]

Critics of public sector productivity frequently advocate an expanded federal role in the development of productivity improvement techniques, productivity measurement, productivity funding assistance, research and development, and information dissemination. Justification for federal involvement in state and local productivity improvement is expressed both in terms of the state and local impact on the national economy and the federal interest in the efficiency and effectiveness with which federally initiated programs are carried out by state and local governments. [39] Although various federal efforts over the past century designed to rationalize governmental operations and decision making as well as, more recently, to measure governmental productivity have been directed primarily at the federal level, the federally established National Commission on Productivity identified governmental productivity improvement—including the state and local levels—as one of six targets of opportunity in 1971. The commission attempted, among other things, to humanize the concept of productivity. Television and magazine advertisements, as well as billboards, asked "Would you hire you?" and stressed the importance of workmanship, showing, for example, proud street center-line painters signing their work. [40] In 1975 the Congress created the National Center for Productivity and Quality of Working Life, but the center's coordinative efforts were found to be "minimal in scope and ineffective due to its insufficient staff, lack of top management support, and lack of leverage over federal agencies." [41] The National Center was terminated in 1978 and the Office of Personnel Management was thereafter designated as the focal point for federal productivity improvement efforts.

Public sector productivity is significant because of the impact of that sector upon the economy as a whole and because of the importance of the services provided by public agencies. Maximization of the output-to-input ratio addresses both points of significance.

PUBLIC SECTOR-PRIVATE SECTOR COMPARISONS

The public sector generally fares poorly when its productivity is compared empirically or anecdotally with that of the private sector. The Committee for Economic Development (CED) reports "little clear evidence that productivity in state and local government has kept pace with productivity in the private sector." [42] Private sector operations consistently appear to outperform their public sector counterparts, even when providing essentially identical services. E. S. Savas, for instance, reports that public refuse collection in New York City has been found to be twice as costly as private collection. [43] Numerous such examples tend to solidify a public sector image of waste, substandard performance, and mismanagement.

But the environment in which public sector managers operate is much different than the private sector. David Rogers lists ten basic constraints on public sector efficiency.

1. The lack of measurability of the public sector's service, or "product" . . . ;
2. The consequent absence of any clear pricing or market test as an outside control on performance and accountability;
3. The monopolistic market situation of many local agencies, which limits their incentive to innovate or adapt;
4. The existence of a complex and often turbulent public sector "politics," which makes decision makers, especially elected officials, highly vulnerable to pressures from outside publics;
5. The unique role of the civil service in limiting administrative flexibility, employee motivation and performance, efficiency, innovation, and accountability;
6. The existence of a fragmented intergovernmental production system that limits local autonomy and flexibility;
7. Financing arrangements that reflect such an intergovernmental system and have the same constraining effects;
8. A reversal of the pattern of staff (expert)-line (manager) relationships that prevails in business which reinforces a pattern of "insider rule" by professional practitioners and downgrades management to a secondary or means activity;
9. The short term of office and high turnover of top agency officials . . .; and
10. The consequent time horizons of government officials, which tend to be generally more short-term than those of top management in the private sector.[44]

Walter Balk perhaps identifies more fundamental constraints when he notes basic philosophical differences in attitudes toward and within the two sectors. For example, corporate growth is thought to be the mark of success in the private sector, but the public mood toward government expansion is currently quite negative. Furthermore, competition is thought to be appropriate among businesses but is unacceptable among public agencies.[45]

Robert Yin and coauthors suggest that both private and public sector organizations pursue a variety of self-interest goals including growth, status, and survival. For private sector organizations, attainment of such goals is likely to be dependent upon organizational efficiency and effectiveness for successful market performance. For public sector organizations, attainment of self-interest goals is more likely dependent upon bureaucratic and political factors.[46]

Decision-making processes differ markedly between public sector organizations and their private sector counterparts. The basic unit of decision making in the private sector is the individual producer or individual consumer; the basic unit of decision making in the public sector is more generally a group. The mechanism of resource acquisition and expenditures in the private sector is the marketplace; in the public sector, it is the budget process. Products in the private sector are divisible among consumers; in the public sector, products are frequently indivisible. Finally, for most public sector products, consumers almost surely do not get what they pay for—they either pay more or less than the value received. [47]

The absence of competition and profit motives is a common theme among observers attempting to explain poor public sector performance. [48] In contrast with the private sector, where competitive market pressures reward the most productive enterprises, weed the least productive from the economy, induce cost-saving rather than cost-increasing innovations, and force producers to match their products to consumer preferences, public sector operations more often have the luxury of growing comfortable in the status quo. [49] A recent GAO report emphasizes the importance of competition.

> Among the many explanations proffered for subpar State-local productivity growth, the absence of private sector incentives in the public sector is most important. Whereas increased output per worker in the private sector improves profits, increased output per worker in the public sector may not bring commensurate economic gains. Furthermore, the monopoly enjoyed by State and local governments removes the discipline of competition that forces private firms to cut costs or increase services in order to stay in business. As a result, there is little incentive for State or local governments to compare their performance rates with other jurisdictions. [50]

Recognition of the advantages of competition has led a few cities to manufacture a competitive environment in municipal service delivery where none existed before. For example, some cities have established separate geographical zones for purposes of employing both public and private sector residential refuse collection agencies. Based upon a seven-city study, Savas has concluded that competitive systems offer the advantages of "increased efficiency; decreased vulnerability to employee actions; decreased vulnerability to contractor failures; protection against monopolistic behavior of contractors and of municipal employees; dual yardsticks for measuring and comparing performance; and more substantive knowledge and understanding of service delivery." [51]

Attainment of the private sector goal of profitability requires attention to both effectiveness and efficiency. Without the former, product demand will decline; without the latter, the product stands to be priced out of the market. In marked contrast, several authors note the tendency for public sector analyses to virtually ignore efficiency measures and concentrate entirely on measures of effectiveness.[52]

Another major distinction between public and private sector operations is the more present possibility of bankruptcy for the latter. Private sector managers contemplating the risks of innovation must also consider the risks of failure to innovate and the organizational consequences that may follow. Few public sector managers experience a directly analogous circumstance. As stated by Robert Wood, public sector officials, "unlike those of a private corporation, expect with some confidence that dissolution will not result if, by some parallel circumstance, costs exceed revenue. Other sources of revenue will ultimately be found."[53]

According to Charles Wise, private sector productivity improvement may occur through any of three factors: process factors, including primarily work simplification, improved organizational arrangements, and technological improvements; product factors, involving such things as economies of scale and product improvement and diversification; and personnel factors, involving improvements in working conditions and professional development.[54] A. W. Steiss and Gregory Daneke note that private sector productivity gains have focused primarily upon process factors owing to the capital-intensive nature of industry and that labor-intensive public sector operations are more likely to have to focus upon personnel factors for productivity improvement to occur.[55]

The labor-intensive nature of most public sector operations has caused productivity-improvement attention frequently to be focused upon employee-related aspects of governmental performance. Some critics have simplistically blamed public employees for poor performance, promoting a public employee stereotype of high security consciousness and low concern for self-actualization.[56] Others have leveled their criticism at public personnel management in general and at civil service practices and procedures in particular. In some instances, evidence has been presented that suggests that municipal civil service is not only meritless but that its processes are actually dysfunctional, leading to the hiring of less capable job candidates.[57] Furthermore, insider domination in municipal hiring and promotions is seen as a severely limiting factor, with organizations in need of managerial talent unable or unwilling to go outside the organization to get it.[58]

A general indictment of civil service is provided by Rogers in the following:

Civil service has created an independent, insider-dominated, countervailing power group of long-term career officials who often defy top administrators, the latter being political appointees who only serve for short terms. The career civil servants can always wait them out and are in that sense often a major stumbling block to management efficiency, to innovation, and to agency flexibility in adapting to changing conditions. Examinations often have no relationship to skills required on the job; the requirement of rigid adherence to civil service lists and seniority prevents top agency officials from bringing in competent outsiders, engendering instead a tradition of "promotion from within"; the use of seniority as an automatic basis for promotion breeds much mediocrity, limiting employee motivation to innovate or excel; and with no standards for defining competence, there can be no quality control and no incentive to improved performance. Finally, civil service, often masquerading under the guise of professionalism, actually promotes highly nonprofessional practices, by protecting government personnel from demands for accountability and protecting the upward-mobility opportunities of those who already have access to agency jobs and control over examination procedures as well. Without some system that—unlike civil service—recognizes and rewards good performance, it is difficult to have efficient or effective management. [59]

To remedy government's assorted maladies, periodic efforts have been directed toward making its operation more businesslike. Principal movements of the twentieth century have emphasized efficiency and professional administration in government. [60] Frederick Taylor's Principles of Scientific Management, [61] published in 1911, captured the attention of early advocates of greater efficiency by espousing the concepts of rationality, planning, specialization, quantitative measurement, one best way of doing a job, and the development of standards and standardization. [62] Reformers on the local level promoted the council-manager plan as a means of separating administrative duties assigned to an appointed city manager from the policy responsibilities of the city council, with anticipated benefits of greater efficiency and a reduced likelihood of political corruption. [63]

The quest for greater rationality in government was reflected in proposals for structural change, such as the council-manager form of government, and in changing management practices exemplified, perhaps, by the evolution of budgetary techniques. The succession from line-item budgeting to performance budgeting, planning-programming-budgeting systems (PPBS), and zero-based budgeting (ZBB) was motivated by the desire to make decision making more rational. [64]

Changes at the national level influenced similar changes in management practices at the local level as more and more cities established budget offices and adopted executive budgets modeled after the latest techniques.

The importance placed at various times upon the adoption of businesslike techniques by local governments has led fairly naturally to attempts to transfer private management techniques. In addition to the rather standard practice of hiring private consultants for particular projects, some cities have borrowed private sector help through feeless, cooperative arrangements. [65] Scott Fosler notes that private sector assistance has worked best in local government functions most akin to business operations, having clear, quantifiable objectives, and has been less satisfactory in politically sensitive areas. [66]

The use of advanced managerial techniques is limited in the public sector because of a variety of factors already cited, including the short time horizons of local officials and the absence of the competitive incentives of a market environment. Rogers, moreover, points to the "underlying values of many government administrators" as a fundamental difference that works against the adoption of many advanced techniques. According to Rogers,

> These administrators are much more concerned with effectiveness—with the delivery of more (and hopefully better) services to clients—than with efficiency. They tend to be . . . practitioner professionals who see in any undue emphasis on economic efficiency an assault on their ideals and mores. Those in human resources or other people-serving agencies often find efficiency approaches particularly irritating, seeing them as dehumanizing their clients and as basically trivial by comparison with their broader concerns with improving programs, responding to the needs of all of their constituents, and redressing inequities that the wider society has imposed on minority populations. The goal of administrators in the public sector, then, is not to cut costs, but rather to keep expanding services. Such administrators rarely consider whether they might be more effective in serving clients if they managed their agencies in a more efficient way. [67]

Touching upon the same theme, but in a less harsh tone, the GAO reports that

> another major reason for alleged State-local productivity lag may reside in the nature of public sector goals and services. Often, the effectiveness or efficiency of public services is secondary to policymakers who are primarily concerned with the

traditional distributional question of a democratic political society: Who gets what, when, why, how, and where? In the policy process, considerations of equity and the need to develop political consensus may result in less efficient or effective programs, but may nevertheless be rational to those concerned with the stability and responsiveness of the political system.[68]

MAJOR BARRIERS TO PUBLIC SECTOR PRODUCTIVITY

Many of the barriers to public sector productivity improvement have been discussed in the comparison of the public and private sectors.* A more complete list, however, includes several factors not previously described. A review of the public sector productivity literature reveals the following productivity-improvement obstacles:

- Insufficient analytical skills or analytic staffing
- Political factors that influence decision making
- Inadequate research, development, and experimentation
- Requirement of a large initial investment for productivity efforts
- Inadequate information dissemination and reluctance to use what is known
- Inadequate information on intracity and intercity performance
- Tendency of federal grant programs to impose excessive red-tape requirements, restrict administrative flexibility, and provide no reward-penalty mechanism for productive-unproductive local use of federal funds
- Lack of public appreciation for productivity benefits and ease of public mobilization against change
- Tendency for productivity-improvement programs to lack political appeal
- Lack of accountability in the public sector
- Union resistance
- Fragmentation of local government
- Civil service restrictions
- Reward system that encourages staff expansion and large budgets
- Legal restrictions against some types of motivational programs
- Ambiguous public sector objectives and lack of performance measurement
- Perpetuation of costly myths regarding what is required for adequate public services

---

*Chapter 6, "Common Barriers to Productivity Improvement," includes a more thorough discussion of this topic.

- Reluctance to abandon ineffective programs once they are initiated
- Short time horizon for politicians hoping for reelection and for top administrative officials, requiring rapid payoff on productivity projects
- Absence of adequate performance evaluation
- Frustration brought on by overselling productivity
- Dominant social class preference of the status quo
- Productivity's commonly perceived threat to job security
- Absence of market pressures
- Inadequate management commitment to productivity
- Unwillingness to take risks and, more generally, the attraction of persons with high risk avoidance into public sector employment
- Tendency for top-level administrators to be more frequently judged on the basis of quality of policy recommendations than on productivity performance indicators
- Bureaucratic socialization processes
- Managerial tendency to use commonly perceived productivity barriers as an excuse for inaction rather than exercise available authority in often unpleasant tasks
- Absence of personal rewards for innovation and productivity
- Barriers to monetary incentive plans, including legal, civil service, political, and funding restrictions and employee opposition
- Bureaucratic rigidities and fragmented authority
- Tendency of public sector professionals to overemphasize effectiveness to the point of virtually ignoring efficiency
- Supervisory resistance

The factors inhibiting public sector productivity are substantial. Although many are of a general administrative nature, a report prepared by the GAO contends that the political barriers are greater than the technical ones.[69] As noted by Frederick Hayes, "The cards are stacked against new ideas" in local government.

> There will rarely be strongly supportive forces in the community. The inertial drag of the system will make internal progress slow and difficult. The political risks are substantial.
> Those who would improve productivity in local government must overcome these deficiencies. They must increase the political rewards and reduce the political risks of change. They must increase the likelihood that changes will be successful. They must establish a favorable climate for performance improvement with the public, the civil servants, and the city council. They must find means to either make the government system responsive to the new needs or to subvert system constraints. They must, in other words, create artificially a

milieu that is equivalent, in effect, to the role of profit and competition in the private economy. [70]

PROGRAM EFFORTS

Many programs designed to improve municipal productivity have reported success. Many others have apparently failed to achieve the intended results. A brief listing of some of the more publicized efforts follows.

Dallas, Texas: The city of Dallas has pursued productivity advances in a relatively unstructured format. Operational improvements have come largely at the initiative of departmental managers with encouragement from the city manager's office and technical assistance, if needed, from the Office of Management Services. Hayes characterizes the Dallas productivity strategy as "unstructured, opportunistic, pragmatic, and adaptive rather than systematic and comprehensive. The city has 'picked its spots,' concentrating its productivity efforts on opportunities with a high potential payoff and low departmental resistance."[71]

Detroit, Michigan: The city of Detroit established the Detroit Productivity Center in 1974 as the formal focal point for its productivity efforts. With first-year funding of $225,000 from the city of Detroit and the Ford Foundation, potential savings of $1.5 million were projected for fiscal year 1976. The anticipated savings, however, were not secured and the effort generally has been considered a failure. Cited as reasons for failure have been lack of strong support from the mayor and inadequate staff training and development.[72] Ironically, the most frequently cited productivity improvement by the city of Detroit occurred prior to the establishment of the center. In 1972 the city's sanitation union agreed to the use of new, larger-volume refuse trucks under a plan for sharing productivity savings. Savings of almost $570,000, shared between the city and employees, were realized in the 1976/77 operating year.[73] A similar program of shared savings was established in Flint, Michigan.

Fairfax County, Virginia: The local government of Fairfax County established decentralized field offices for its inspection operation in an effort to reduce travel time and costs. However, an economic recession coinciding with program implementation struck a severe blow to the construction industry, altered inspection activity, and made program gains imperceptible.[74]

Honolulu, Hawaii: Elaborate productivity efforts have been undertaken in the parks and public works operations of the city and county of Honolulu. In the area of parks maintenance, for example, mobile finishing crews, created to supplement a reduced corps of grounds-keepers, reportedly enabled the parks department to increase its manpower efficiency and improve park appearance. [75]

Kansas City, Missouri: The establishment of work standards in the Kansas City streets division yielded mixed results. While employees presumably gained a better understanding of what was expected of them and found the standards generally acceptable, friction between supervisors and work-measurement analysts developed and the degree of top-management confidence in and utilization of the program was reportedly unclear. [76]

Lake Charles, Louisiana: In 1969 Lake Charles established a program whereby its 75 refuse collectors were allowed to leave work upon completion of specified routes under a task-system arrangement. For two and one-half years the program reportedly worked well, but thereafter quality-of-service decline accompanied increasing collection pace. Some routes were completed in as little as four hours, but increases in noise, spillage, missed stops, and accidents resulted in program discontinuation in 1973. [77]

Little Rock, Arkansas: Engineered work standards have been applied to the sanitation and custodial maintenance departments of the city of Little Rock. Although only 50 percent of the preengineered sanitation routes were completed on time, 98 percent were completed on time following the establishment of work standards and route equalization. Citizen complaints declined from 24 per day to 1.5 per day shortly following the change, and unauthorized absences declined by 81 percent. Performance improvements allowed the city of Little Rock to achieve savings of 21 percent of the previously budgeted sanitation personnel costs. The application of work standards for custodial maintenance led the city to a decision to contract for services upon finding that city custodians were performing at 45 percent of standard and that a contractor would produce at 116 percent of standard, reducing city costs by almost 50 percent. [78]

Los Angeles, California: Application of computer technology to the activities of the sanitation bureau permitted analysis of daily crew activities and the forecasting of collection requirements, thereby minimizing overhiring. As a result, "Los Angeles has cut the man-hours required to collect a ton of refuse from 2.68 in 1958 to 1.67."[79] Los Angeles County has established a work-measurement and methods-improvement program credited with saving $35 million per year since 1965. [80]

New York, New York: The first major municipal productivity program to be labeled as such was formally established in New York

City in 1972 by Mayor John V. Lindsay. Its less formal beginnings may be traced to December 1970 when the Mayor's Labor Policy Committee announced contract negotiation guidelines allowing no salary increases beyond cost-of-living adjustments unless they were based upon productivity gains. This insistence on performance for pay coupled with an elaborate system of quarterly performance targets initiated in 1972 set the tone of the New York City productivity program that Lindsay relied upon to help the city cope with its pressing financial difficulties. Hayes reports that

> the Lindsay productivity program resulted in few direct reductions in the budget, although it certainly aided in the adjustment to the budget reductions required in the 1970-1972 period. The Mayor's primary concern was effectiveness, not efficiency. In Sanitation, for example, the productivity improvement in refuse collection made it possible to both meet collection schedules and to release manpower for street sweeping; the chief result was cleaner streets although by the end of 1973 the force had been reduced by about half the 1500 men added in 1970 just before the productivity effort began. [81]

According to Hayes, most experiences with productivity bargaining in New York City fell short of success, and little of the overall productivity program was successfully institutionalized, a shortcoming exposed upon the departure of the analysts recruited by the Lindsay administration. However, substantial productivity gains were recorded in some areas, and important union concessions were achieved. [82] A single example provides insight into gains in at least one area. Upon investigation, analysts discovered that the productivity rate of New York City mechanics was approximately 50 percent of the private garage standard. Despite insistence by mechanics that their job differed from that of their private sector counterparts, new mechanics hired to fill 60 vacancies were organized as an isolated repair unit with instructions that performance at private sector standards would be evidence of meeting probationary requirements. After six months, nearly all of the work-load standards had been met by most of the probationary mechanics. [83]

North Charleston, South Carolina: Recognizing that police calls are frequently clustered in the evening hours rather than spread evenly throughout a 24-hour period, North Charleston adopted a police schedule featuring overlapping shifts and a 10-hour work day. Each 24-hour day includes three 10-hour shifts: 6 a.m. to 4 p.m., 4 p.m. to 2 a.m., and 8 p.m. to 6 a.m. An overlap occurs between 8 p.m. and 2 a.m., during which time calls for police service are generally at their greatest and the police department is double-staffed to handle them. The plan, variants of which have been implemented in several cities, including Huntington Beach, California, was adopted by North Charleston in 1973.[84]

Orange, California: In 1973 the city of Orange and the local Police Association agreed to an incentive plan whereby pay increases above a base adjustment were tied to the targeted reduction of four types of crime: rape, robbery, burglary, and auto theft.[85] Achievement of the first-year target provided officers with an extra 2 percent incentive wage increase on March 1, 1974; achievement of the second-year target produced another 3 percent above the basic adjustment. During the 20-month period of the program, an overall reduction of 5.6 percent in the reported rate of the targeted crimes was achieved. Special efforts by the Crime Prevention Bureau and general community-education efforts were credited for much of the success. Follow-up evaluation produced ambiguous evidence regarding the plan's impact on quality of service, providing evidence of increased job satisfaction and improved teamwork on the one hand and some indications of harsher treatment of suspects on the other. Despite apparent overall success, critics note the plan's potential vulnerability to misreporting of crime statistics.[86] The combined rate of the targeted crimes increased rapidly following termination of the plan.

Palo Alto, California: Palo Alto's productivity program took the form of an elaborate management-information system designed for budgetary and evaluation purposes and called the Service Management System (SMS). Introduced in 1973, it met immediate resistance from department managers apprehensive about additional data-collection requirements and budgetary impact. The basic elements of the system were to be departmental goals, objectives, and performance criteria—all to be developed by the second year under the system. By 1974, the implementation timetable had been adjusted to a five-year period. By 1975, the five-year timetable had been scrapped. Departmental resistance to evaluation and organizational revision was epitomized by the declaration of public works as off limits to SMS staff upon the insistance of an irate director of public works following the elimination of one public works position subsequent to SMS analysis.[87]

Phoenix, Arizona: Following the 1969 recommendations of the consulting firm of Booz, Allen and Hamilton, the city of Phoenix established within its budget and research department two productivity-improvement work units—one involved in the improvement of work methods via industrial engineering techniques and the other involved largely in improvement of program effectiveness. The former operated under the Work Planning and Control System (WPC); the latter, under Program Analysis and Review (PAR). A major thrust of WPC was the establishment of work-performance standards for most city jobs. By October 1975, standards had been developed for more than 3,200 positions. [88]

Among the major budgetary economies in Phoenix attributable to special analytical efforts were reported savings of $94,000 through reduction of the size of street-repair crews; $124,000 through reduction of the size of refuse-collection crews; and $130,000 in travel-time savings by authorizing building inspectors to take city cars home and report directly to job sites. A benefit-cost ratio of 4.5 to 1 has been calculated for the Phoenix program. [89]

San Jose, California: San Jose saved substantial funds through the adoption of relatively simple practices. For example, recapped tires were found to be both cheaper and more satisfactory than new tires on the rear axles of fire emergency vehicles; more than $30,000 in maintenance costs were eliminated with the removal of street fire-alarm boxes; and $175,000 in personnel costs were saved when the police department began sending notification of warrants by mail rather than assigning officers to make personal deliveries. [90]

Savannah, Georgia: The city of Savannah adopted a Responsive Public Services Program (RPSP), which utilized trained observers, citizen surveying, and other techniques in an effort to improve public service delivery. [91]

Scottsdale, Arizona: Municipal performance in Scottsdale has received acclaim in several functional areas, particularly refuse collection and fire services. Scottsdale was among the pioneers in mechanized refuse collection with the introduction of the single-operator vehicle Godzilla. Fire services are provided under contract with Rural/Metro Fire Department Inc., which operates using its own full-time employees supplemented by city employees cross-trained in fire-fighting skills. The Rural/Metro performance record has been judged approximately equal to that of public fire departments in three neighboring cities, but is achieved at approximately half the cost of its counterparts. [92] A similar program, modeled after the Scottsdale approach but utilizing exclusively public sector employees, has been established with an annual savings greater than 10 percent in the fire department of Oak Ridge, Tennessee. [93]

Tacoma, Washington: Perhaps two factors above all others distinguish Tacoma's productivity efforts: an extensive cooperative effort with the private sector (Boeing) and rather elaborate emphasis upon technology (a characteristic shared in many respects with Scottsdale, Arizona). In an examination of the Tacoma program, Hayes found no centralized productivity program but instead a city-manager-fostered atmosphere conducive to innovation. Few department heads

were willing to be excluded from the group that climbed aboard the
city manager's innovation bandwagon, but some embraced change
much less enthusiastically than did others. Hayes concluded that "the
listing of the city's numerous technological projects suggests that the
impact was marginal; the skeptics and standpatters were inched along,
some more than others, but they did not become innovators."[94]

Productivity-improvement efforts of varying formality, structure, and magnitude in cities of varying size, governmental form,
and economic condition have met with widely differing levels of success. The above list is only a small sample and assuredly underrep-
resents the vast number of special projects undertaken even in the
cities named. Prominent among the examples are programs dealing
with refuse collection and fire services. Such functions, particularly
the former, have been the frequent focal point of productivity-improvement efforts. As noted by Hayes, "If we were to eliminate refuse
collection from the list of productivity improvements, the accomplish-
ment of the typical productivity program would shrink to half its size.
It is one of the curiosities of local government that in the first half
of the 1970s so many cities elected to take on the garbage collectors."[95]

MAJOR PRODUCTIVITY-IMPROVEMENT APPROACHES
UTILIZED OR IDENTIFIED

Local government officials who have recognized the need for
productivity improvement and have attempted to overcome the numerous obstacles have collectively established a wide array of productivity-improvement approaches. The tactics employed may be adver-
sarial or cooperative. Analysis may be performed and recommendations developed on an in-house basis or by an outside consultant.
The local government may originate a tailor-made solution or it may
adapt something developed in the private sector or by another public
sector agency. Within this array of options in overall strategy, numerous techniques or approaches of a more specific nature have been
used or recommended as means of improving productivity. Among
such techniques and approaches are the following:

- Utilization of improved technology[96]
- Improvement of operating procedures[97]
- Sharing of productivity-improvement information through clearing-
  houses or interorganizational networks
- Modification of organizational structures[98]
- Improved communications[99]

- Improvement of employee skills at various organizational levels[100]
- Improved working conditions[101]
- Promotions of economies of scale through such means as annexation, consolidation, metropolitan government, and federation[102]
- Greater decentralization, citizen participation, public choice[103]
- Civilianization, especially of police activities not requiring a sworn officer[104]
- Greater use of volunteerism[105]
- Improved matching of service levels with citizen preference in order to avoid overproduction and eliminate unnecessary services[106]
- Encouragement of self-help as an alternative to growing reliance on government[107]
- Improved specification of objectives[108]
- Performance monitoring through use of productivity measurement[109]
- Application of analysis and evaluation techniques[110]
- Total Performance Management (TPM)[111]
- Increased accountability through dissemination of information comparing unit cost and effectiveness of governments, reporting degree of citizen and employee satisfaction, and reporting consideration given to adopting the best practices used elsewhere[112] and, at the individual level, through increased public attribution of the employee responsible for a given assignment[113]
- Revision of personnel management policies, such as those affecting retirement and pensions, allowable sick leave accumulations, health insurance, wage-setting formulas, disability payments, and longevity payments, in order to maximize productivity in the use of public resources[114]
- Centrally mandated cost reductions or cutback strategies, such as across-the-board allocation cuts, hiring freezes, and delays in hiring and expenditures[115]
- Tying services to user fees in an effort to match service quality with demand and minimize overproduction[116]
- Productivity bargaining[117]
- Establishment of performance standards or performance targets[118]
- Privatization or contracting[119]
- Monetary incentives, such as gainsharing plans and performance-based bonuses or wage increases[120]
- Other incentive or motivational programs, such as educational incentives, attendance incentives, task systems, variations in working hours, suggestion awards, and safety incentives[121]
- Worker participation[122]
- Organizational Development (OD)[123]
- Job restructuring or job enrichment[124]
- Job rotation[125]
- Utilization of less costly but equally appropriate service alternatives (for example, in the criminal justice system, diversion of first-time

offenders to rehabilitation programs rather than formal criminal prosecution)[126]
- Prioritization of services, placing greatest emphasis on those considered most important[127]
- Work distribution analysis[128]
- Siting and development of capital facilities with consideration given to long-term operating costs
- Improved matching of community facility operating hours to times when utilization justifies operation[129]
- Adoption of intergovernmental service agreements[130]
- Shifting responsibilities to the private sector (for example, more stringent sprinkler-system requirements, prohibition of disposable bottles and cans, and so forth)[131]
- Targeting of prime productivity opportunities based upon likelihood of payoff, minimal political or employee opposition, and/or ease of solution[132]

The administrator's view of productivity lacks a great deal of the precision of the economist's definition. To the administrator, productivity improvement may include more than improved efficiency and effectiveness; it may also include the achievement of conditions less susceptible to work disruption and unrest within the organization and more conducive to low rates of turnover, low absenteeism, and citizen satisfaction.[133] A wide assortment of improvement approaches is the natural product of a broad definition of productivity improvement.

KEYS TO SUCCESS: RECENT RESEARCH

Literature on municipal productivity research is surprisingly scanty given the magnitude and importance of municipal operations. The general material that is available on the topic is often subjective or inconclusive. Despite limitations in quantity and quality, however, some research (much of it based upon the private sector) is relevant to serious consideration of municipal productivity.

The relationship of productivity, motivation, and job satisfaction has important implications for productivity-improvement strategies. In an analysis of previous research primarily involving the private sector, Raymond Katzell and Daniel Yankelovich found evidence that tends to dispel a popular myth regarding that relationship. Contrary to the belief common to both labor and management that improvement in worker satisfaction will lead to productivity gains (that is, that a happy worker is a productive worker), Katzell and Yankelovich found no direct linkage between the two ideals. While various approaches have been found to be effective in improving either job satisfaction or productivity, an approach that consistently improves both has been more elusive. Some analysts have argued, in fact, that some techniques make gains in one only at the expense of the other. In short, "job satisfaction and productivity do not necessarily follow parallel paths."[134]

In a review of the literature on job enlargement, job enrichment, and job redesign, Katzell and Yankelovich found instances of employee job-attitude improvement and no productivity gain, improvement in both job attitude and productivity, and improvement in neither. They conclude that the success of such efforts may depend on a variety of factors pertaining to employee characteristics, such as security needs, desire for self-expression and growth, age, cultural background, and type of job.[135]

Rensis Likert also reports inconsistent evidence in various studies regarding the relationship between employee attitudes and productivity as well as the effect of varying leadership or management styles on each.[136] His own research indicates that organizations adopting a more participative, as opposed to authoritative, management style tend within three to five years to experience "long-range improvement in productivity, labor relations, costs, and earnings."[137] A note of caution, however, is sounded by Katzell and Yankelovich regarding assumptions about the direction of causality between organizational productivity and worker participation and the extent of egalitarianism advisable in an organization adopting a participative style. They note that where workers throughout the organization "exercise greater control over what goes on in the organization," organizations tend to have more highly motivated and satisfied employees and to be more productive.[138] Such findings, however, may easily be misinterpreted or misapplied. It is possible that worker participation in organizational affairs may favorably impact both job satisfaction and productivity through its positive effect upon the linkage of employee motivation—but the direction of causality is not a certainty. It is also possible that organizations with highly motivated (and hence, productive) employees may be more inclined to permit worker participation. Katzell and Yankelovich's review of relevant studies furthermore suggests moderation in the degree of worker participation. Katzell and Yankelovich's review of relevant studies furthermore suggests moderation in the degree of worker participation. Greater control by employees does not necessarily mean equal control with management. They found that where control is equally shared by various echelons of the work force, greater worker satisfaction is not necessarily accompanied by greater productivity.[139]

The important employee ingredient for organizational productivity appears to be motivation, which is not the same as satisfaction.

To the extent that factors such as increased participation lead to greater employee motivation, productivity should be enhanced. In actual application in local government settings, however, techniques such as job enrichment, designed to enhance satisfaction and performance, may be falling short of their goal. Greiner and coauthors report that the results of job-enrichment efforts on public sector job satisfaction have been mixed. Of the 365 state and local job-enrichment efforts they reviewed, 56 had been terminated. Many jurisdictions reported only modest effectiveness or efficiency improvements and no single type of approach appeared to be effective on a consistent basis.[140]

Somewhat better results, though still mixed, have been reported for flextime, yet another program that increases employee control in the work setting. Based upon a review of pertinent studies, Robert Golembiewski and Carl Proehl provide a cautious endorsement of the use of flextime in the public sector. Although many of the reported findings are of a subjective and ambiguous nature, attitudinal impact seems generally to be positive, as does the evidence regarding absenteeism, tardiness, turnover, overtime, costs, and productivity.[141]

According to Katzell and Yankelovich, the principal factors leading simultaneously to high motivation, job satisfaction, and high productivity appear to be adequate recognition and meaningful rewards for effective performance. Effective rewards may be financial, psychological, or both, as long as they are meaningful to the employee. "The key to having workers who are both satisfied and productive is motivation, i.e., arousing and maintaining the desire and will to work effectively—having workers who are productive not because they are coerced, but because they are committed."[142]

Katzell and Yankelovich found the following relationships regarding compensation:

Better job satisfaction, less absenteeism, and less turnover were positively associated with relatively well-paid employees. Such employees also tend to have higher motivation and productivity if pay is based on performance;

Satisfaction with pay is greater when it is performance based;

Employees who perceive their pay to be inequitable are less satisfied than those who believe their pay to be fair; and

Improved compensation plans that adversely impact other working conditions—such as job security or social relationships—tend to negate productivity gains.[143]

Although pay for performance was found by the authors to have a positive impact on productivity, "absolute amount of pay, in and of itself, is not related to performance."[144]

Such findings point up the importance of effective incentive plans. While the development of such plans is made difficult by factors such as task interdependency, problems in specifying comprehensive performance criteria, task complexity, and intraorganizational mistrust, the reported effectiveness of such plans, particularly at the individual level, indicates that efforts directed toward their development are well placed. Limited evidence suggests an effectiveness hierarchy, with individual incentives most effective and group incentives less effective than individual incentives but more effective than no incentives at all. [145]

The establishment of performance targets is often incorporated in incentive programs. Evidence regarding the use of performance targeting in local governments, however, is not particularly encouraging. To obtain information on public sector performance targeting, Greiner and coauthors interviewed officials in 25 cities. Most officials expressed positive opinions about targeting but had little, if any, objective bases for their opinions. Of the 25 jurisdictions surveyed, 23 had used a management by objectives (MBO) system and 17 were reportedly using performance targets—although most targets were of the work-load or due-date variety rather than geared toward effectiveness or efficiency. Almost half of the 17 jurisdictions using performance targets reported at least some negative effects of the system. [146]

Lack of consistent success is common in public sector programs featuring performance targeting, performance incentives, or opportunities for greater employee control. In fact, the National Center for Productivity and Work Quality reported the existence of no "specific type of incentive with a history of consistently successful implementation in state or local government."[147] Katzell and Yankelovich contend that it is too much to expect a limited job-enrichment, employee participation, or incentive program to improve both productivity and job satisfaction; it is more reasonable for such programs to be included as ingredients in a comprehensive system designed to achieve such goals. [148]

Useful productivity research has also been directed toward economies of scale in service delivery, contracting for services, and alternate service-delivery approaches. For example, considerable debate has focused upon the contention that larger organizations are normally in a better position to provide more effective services at a lower unit cost than are small organizations. Elinor Ostrom and associates, however, found that compared with large police departments, small police departments function at equivalent or greater levels of effectiveness, to cite but one contradictory example. [149]

Considerable debate has also centered upon the advantages and disadvantages of contracting or privatization. Although private service providers must pay taxes and maintain a profit margin in order to remain in business, proponents of increased contracting contend that the productivity-inducing nature of the private sector market more than offsets such additional cost elements. For example, private provision of paramedic services has reportedly been found to be one-half to one-third as costly as public provision.[150] Contract refuse-collection service has also been found to be less expensive than public provision, especially in cities of more than 50,000 population, with public agencies costing 29 to 37 percent more than their private sector counterparts for the same level of service.[151] Additionally, advantages accruing from a competitive market situation have been found for the districting of large cities into sections of 50,000 population for purposes of dividing solid waste collection services between public employee and contract service providers. Furthermore, a survey of National Institute of Governmental Purchasing members from cities of less than 50,000 population revealed overall strong agreement among respondents that an improved quality of service can be obtained by contracting for services and, somewhat less strongly, that contracting provides a lower-cost option.[152]

Various means of organizing the work force and delivering public services have been suggested as methods of improving public sector productivity. For example, the assignment of total responsibility for a complete operation has yielded some successful results, as when police officers given total responsibility for their cases increased case closures by 80 percent.[153] Favorable results have also been claimed for team policing, another approach to personnel deployment. Conflicting information on total responsibility and team policing, however, is provided by Peter Greenwood and Jean Petersilia, who conclude that information supplied by the victim is the most important factor in solving a crime and that "the method by which police investigators are organized (i.e., team policing, specialists versus generalists, patrolmen-investigators) cannot be related to variations in crime, arrest, and clearance rates."[154] Moreover, Greiner and co-authors report no instances of cost savings attributed to team policing despite claims of greater efficiency.[155]

Still another popular service delivery variant, the much-touted four-day workweek, or four-forty plan, offers advantages of extended service hours at no additional personnel costs and, in some instances, improved morale and decreased overtime and absenteeism; but research has also indicated shortcomings in such plans. Four-day workweeks have been found to cause problems, particularly in small cities, in scheduling, communications, and crosstraining of employees to fill in for one another during the nonuniform workweek.[156]

Productivity improvement requires change from the organizational status quo. Although not directed specifically toward productivity improvement, research into public sector innovation is relevant nevertheless for the light such research sheds on organizational change processes. Not all organizational changes produce productivity gains, but major productivity improvement never occurs without organizational change. The literature on innovation generally contends that innovation is positively related to organizational and community size and wealth, degree of urbanization, high occupational and educational level of citizens, and stable population turnover rate and that develop-ment of innovative ideas is negatively related to organizational centralization and strict emphasis on hierarchy of authority, while im-plementation is positively related to centralization.[157] Furthermore, the likelihood of implementation appears to be enhanced under conditions of client participation and when the aim is to improve services rather than merely to reduce costs.[158]

George W. Downs, Jr., found that the initiative for innovation, if it exists at all, tends to rest not with the environment in the form of demand for innovation but rather within the organization itself. According to Downs, socioeconomic homogeneity tends to produce an environment that permits but does not force bureaucratic innovation. Such findings tend to emphasize the importance of the bureaucrat as an innovator. Based upon the work of John Loy, Everett Rogers, and Floyd Shoemaker, Downs developed a list of innovator attributes: educational status, social status, achievement motivation, undogmatic attitude, intelligence, venturesomeness, imaginativeness, sociableness, cosmopolitanism, and dominance.[159] These individual characteristics are believed to be positively related to innovation.

The work of numerous researchers and local government commentators, only some of whom have been cited above, would suggest the following keys to local government productivity improvement:[160]

- Genuine support for productivity improvement from the chief executive
- At least modest support from the legislative body and senior management
- Adequate resources
- Sufficient analytic capability assigned to productivity improvement and situated prominently within the organization
- Recognition of a performance gap and a desire to close it
- Managerial and employee accountability
- General organizational strength
- Support, or at least neutrality, of employees, unions, and citizen groups
- At least modest support from department heads and middle management
- A performance measurement system for monitoring progress and identifying productivity-improvement opportunities

- Adequate means of gauging citizen desires and level of satisfaction with services
- Ability to overcome bureaucratic rigidities, such as are commonly found in civil service systems and other organizational activities
- Awareness of state-of-the-art service-delivery methods and experimentation in other cities
- Employee input
- Attention to professional development at all organizational levels
- Adequate communication with employees and, in the case of unionization, with their organizations
- Employee pay based upon performance and productivity
- Employee perception of a work situation capable of meeting their needs
- A work opportunity that fully utilizes employee abilities
- Adequate hygiene conditions, including such factors as adequate pay, job security, and working conditions
- Reliance upon attrition for any employee reductions made possible by productivity improvement
- Careful nurturing of employee motivation

It is unlikely that many local government organizations possess all of the elements in the foregoing list. It is equally unlikely that organizations deficient in most of them can experience prolonged productivity improvement.

SUMMARY

Among the many productivity definitions offered, perhaps the one that best states the importance of efficiency and effectiveness in public sector service delivery is provided by Hayward. "Governmental productivity is the efficiency with which resources are consumed in the effective delivery of public services."[161] Productivity improvement is not the single-minded pursuit of cost savings. The concept of productivity emphasizes the importance of quantity and quality of output as well as quantity of resource input.

The public sector constitutes a major segment of the U.S. economy. Government productivity, therefore, is important to the nation's well-being; but government productivity at all levels, including municipal government, appears to be lagging behind that of the private sector. Lacking the competition and profit motive of the private sector and burdened by numerous productivity barriers unique to the public sector, local government officials seemingly have few incentives to attempt to alter the status quo. Yet, productivity-improvement efforts have been undertaken in many cities, often with reportedly favorable results.

Various approaches have been recommended for local government productivity improvement, including improved operating procedures, volunteerism, self-help, increased accountability, improved personnel management, productivity bargaining, use of performance standards, contracting for services, greater use of incentives, worker participation, organizational development, and job enrichment. Research regarding the effectiveness of various approaches, however, is limited. That which is available suggests the importance of motivation as a key element for sustained productivity improvement and reports mixed results for many of the currently popular productivity-improvement techniques.

NOTES

1. David N. Ammons and Joseph C. King, "Productivity Improvement in Local Government: Its Place among Competing Priorities," Public Administration Review 43 (March–April 1983): 113-20.

2. See, for example, Frederick O'R. Hayes, Productivity in Local Government (Lexington, Mass.: D. C. Heath, Lexington Books, 1977), p. 3; Neal R. Peirce, "State-Local Report/'Productivity' Is Slogan for Taming Spiraling Expenses," National Journal Reports 7 (April 12, 1975): 540; Brian Usilaner and Edwin Soniat, "Productivity Measurement," in Productivity Improvement Handbook for State and Local Government, ed. George J. Washnis (New York: John Wiley & Sons, 1980), p. 91; and Washnis, Productivity Improvement Handbook, pp. 87-88. For the distinction between the productivity perspectives of the economist, the industrial engineer, and the practicing manager, see Robert E. Quinn, "Productivity and the Process of Organizational Improvement: Why We Cannot Talk to Each Other," Public Administration Review 38 (January–February 1978): 41-45.

3. See, for example, Joint Financial Management Improvement Program, Implementing a Productivity Program: Points to Consider (Washington, D.C.: U.S. Government Printing Office, 1977), p. 1; Jerome A. Mark, "Meanings and Measures of Productivity," Public Administration Review 32 (November–December 1972): 748; John P. Ross and Jesse Burkhead, Productivity in the Local Government Sector (Lexington, Mass.: D. C. Heath, Lexington Books, 1974), pp. 11-12; and Clair F. Vough, Productivity: A Practical Program for Improving Efficiency (New York: Amacom, 1979), p. 4.

4. Jerome A. Mark, "Measuring Productivity in Government: Federal, State and Local," Public Productivity Review 5 (March 1981): 22-23; and U.S., Congress, Joint Economic Committee, Measuring and Enhancing Productivity in the Federal Sector, 92nd Cong., 2d sess., 1972, quoted in Jerome A. Mark, "Progress in Measuring

Productivity in Government," Monthly Labor Review 95 (December 1972): 6.

5. Osbin L. Ervin, "A Conceptual Niche for Municipal Productivity," Public Productivity Review 3 (Summer-Fall 1978): 20-22. Despite the author's contention that productivity "is concerned only with efficiency," he acknowledges the need to make adjustments for quality change, rendering the strength of his argument somewhat questionable.

6. See, for example, Eckhard Bennewitz, "Mass Transit," in Productivity Improvement Handbook, ed. Washnis, p. 785; Vincent Ostrom, The Intellectual Crisis in American Public Administration (University: University of Alabama Press, 1974), p. 45; and John S. Thomas, So, Mr. Mayor, You Want to Improve Productivity (Washington, D.C.: U.S. Government Printing Office, 1974), p. 5.

7. See, for example, Walter L. Balk, "Why Don't Public Administrators Take Productivity More Seriously?" Public Personnel Management 3 (July-August 1974): 318-19; idem, "Decision Constructs and the Politics of Productivity," in Productivity Improvement Handbook, ed. Washnis, pp. 176-77; Edward C. Baumheier and Patricia Barry, "Welfare, Vocational Rehabilitation, and Social Services," in Productivity Improvement Handbook, ed. Washnis, p. 1195; Ralph C. Bledsoe, Dennis R. Denny, Charles D. Hobbs, and Raymond S. Long, "Productivity Management in the California Social Services Program," Public Administration Review 32 (November-December 1972): 799-800; Frederick O'R. Hayes, "Leadership and Politics of the Productivity Process," in Productivity Improvement Handbook, ed. Washnis, p. 16; Mark E. Keane, "Why Productivity Improvement?" in Productivity Improvement Handbook, ed. Washnis, pp. 7-10; Selma J. Mushkin and Frank H. Sandifer, Personnel Management and Productivity in City Government (Lexington, Mass.: D. C. Heath, Lexington Books, 1979), p. 57; Urban Institute and the International City Management Association, Improving Productivity Measurements and Evaluation in Local Governments, reprinted in Marc Holzer, ed., Productivity in Public Organizations (Port Washington, N.Y.: Kennikat Press, 1976), p. 120; and numerous publications by the Urban Institute.

8. Nancy S. Hayward, "The Productivity Challenge," Public Administration Review 36 (September-October 1976): 544. Reprinted with permission from Public Administration Review, ©1976 by The American Society for Public Administration, 1225 Connecticut Avenue, N.W., Washington, D.C. All rights reserved.

9. Holzer, Productivity in Public Organizations, p. 6.

10. Walter L. Balk, "Technological Trends in Productivity Measurement," Public Personnel Management 4 (March-April 1975): 130.

11. Rackham S. Fukuhara, "Productivity Improvement in Cities," The Municipal Year Book 1977, vol. 44 (Washington, D.C.: International City Management Association, 1977): 193-94.

12. This formula, developed in Nassau County, N.Y., is reported in Hayes, Productivity in Local Government, pp. 84-85.

13. Everett E. Adam, Jr., James C. Hershauer, and William A. Ruch, "Developing Quality Productivity Ratios for Public Sector Personnel Services," Public Productivity Review 5 (March 1981): 47.

14. Jesse Burkhead and Patrick J. Hennigan, "Productivity Analysis: A Search for Definition and Order," Public Administration Review 38 (January-February 1978): 34-35.

15. Mark, "Measuring Productivity in Government," pp. 40-41.

16. Donald C. Kull, "Productivity Programs in the Federal Government," Public Administration Review 38 (January-February 1978): 6.

17. Peter G. Peterson, "Productivity in Government and the American Economy," Public Administration Review 32 (November-December 1972): 743-45.

18. Herbert Stein, "The Meaning of Productivity," in Holzer, Productivity in Public Organizations, p. 83.

19. Burton G. Malkiel, "Productivity: The Problem behind the Headlines," Harvard Business Review 57 (May-June 1979): 82.

20. John W. Kendrick, Understanding Productivity: An Introduction to the Dynamics of Productivity Change (Baltimore: Johns Hopkins University Press, 1977), p. 6.

21. Peterson, "Productivity in Government," p. 747.

22. See, for example, Kendrick, Understanding Productivity, pp. 108-9; and Robert W. Poole, Jr., Cutting Back City Hall (New York: Universe, 1980), p. 21.

23. Tax Foundation, "Tax Freedom Day is May 2, One Day Earlier than 1982" (news release, April 15, 1983).

24. Mark, "Progress in Measuring Productivity," p. 5.

25. Ross and Burkhead, Productivity in the Local Government Sector, p. 58.

26. Harry P. Hatry and Donald M. Fisk, Improving Productivity and Productivity Measurement in Local Governments (Washington, D.C.: Urban Institute, 1971), p. vii. Reprinted with permission.

27. Consider, for example, the lengthening of the typical school year from 99 days in 1900 to 155 days by mid century and the burgeoning demand for urban services owing to the national migration from the farm to the city, as reported in Solomon Fabricant, The Trend of Government Activity in the United States since 1900 (New York: National Bureau of Economic Research, 1952), pp. 86-118.

28. See, for example, O. W. Wilson and Roy Clinton McLaren, Police Administration (New York: McGraw-Hill, 1972), pp. 8-9, for a description of the police evolution from horse patrol to modern transportation, communication, and crime detection techniques.

For a contrary view, see Vernon E. Palmour, Donald W. King, and R. Boyd Ladd, "Public Library Services," in Washnis, Productivity Improvement Handbook, ed. Washnis, p. 1447, in which the authors suggest that labor productivity in library services has been at a virtual standstill since the Industrial Revolution.

29. William J. Baumol, "Macroeconomics of Unbalanced Growth: The Anatomy of Urban Crisis," American Economic Review 57 (June 1967): 415-26.

30. D. F. Bradford, R. A. Malt, and W. E. Oates, "The Rising Cost of Local Public Services: Some Evidence and Reflections," National Tax Journal 22 (June 1969): 188-89.

31. See, for example, Kendrick, Understanding Productivity, p. 50.

32. General Accounting Office (GAO), State and Local Government Productivity Improvement: What Is the Federal Role? (Washington, D.C.: U.S. Government Printing Office, 1978), pp. 4-5.

33. Robert C. Wood, 1400 Governments: The Political Economy of the New York Metropolitan Region (Cambridge, Mass.: Harvard University Press, 1961), p. 8.

34. Kendrick, Understanding Productivity, pp. 43, 117-18.

35. GAO, State and Local Government Productivity Improvement, pp. 4-5.

36. Kendrick, Understanding Productivity, p. 41.

37. James W. Kuhn, "The Riddle of Inflation: A New Answer," Public Interest 27 (Spring 1972): 67.

38. Committee for Economic Development (CED), Improving Productivity in State and Local Government (New York: CED, 1976), p. 37.

39. GAO, State and Local Government Productivity Improvement, pp. i-ii.

40. "Speaking Out for Better Output," Nation's Business 61 (November 1973): 62.

41. GAO, State and Local Government Productivity Improvement, p. 58. See also "Speaking Out for Better Output," p. 62 for a report of congressional impatience with the National Commission on Productivity.

42. CED, Improving Productivity, p. 28.

43. Sig Gissler, "Productivity in the Public Sector: A Summary of a Wingspread Symposium," Public Administration Review 32 (November-December 1972): 846.

44. Reprinted with permission of Macmillan Publishing Company from Can Business Management Save the Cities? The Case of New York by David Rogers, p. 15. Copyright © 1978 by the Free Press, a Division of Macmillan Publishing Company.

45. Walter L. Balk, "Toward a Government Productivity Ethic," Public Administration Review 38 (January-February 1978): 46.

46. Robert K. Yin, Karen A. Heald, and Mary E. Vogel, Tinkering with the System: Technological Innovations in State and Local Services (Lexington, Mass.: D. C. Heath, Lexington Books, 1977), p. 90.

47. The distinction between public and private decision-making processes is described more fully in Wood, 1400 Governments, especially pp. 17-22.

48. See, for example, Steve Carter, "Trends in Local Government Productivity," The Municipal Year Book 1975, vol. 42 (Washington, D. C.: International City Management Association, 1975), p. 180; and Poole, Cutting Back City Hall, pp. 22-23.

49. See Crist H. Costa, "Elementary and Secondary Education," in Productivity Improvement Handbook, ed. Washnis, pp. 1144-45; Kendrick, Understanding Productivity, p. 109; and Ostrom, The Intellectual Crisis, pp. 62, 122.

50. GAO, State and Local Government Productivity Improvement, p. 6.

51. E. S. Savas, "Intracity Competition between Public and Private Service Delivery," Public Administration Review 41 (January-February 1981): 50.

52. See, for example, Ross and Burkhead, Productivity in the Local Government Sector, p. 16; Patrick E. Haggerty, "Productivity: Industry Isn't the Only Place Where It's a Problem," Forbes 107 (February 1, 1971): 43-45; and Rogers, Can Business Management Save the Cities?, pp. 25-26.

53. Wood, 1400 Governments, p. 21. See also Vough, Productivity, p. 189.

54. Charles R. Wise, "Productivity in Public Administration and Public Policy," in Public Administration and Public Policy, ed. H. George Frederickson and Charles R. Wise (Lexington, Mass: D. C. Heath, Lexington Books, 1977), pp. 177-78.

55. Alan Walter Steiss and Gregory A. Daneke, Performance Administration: Improved Responsiveness and Effectiveness in Public Service (Lexington, Mass.: D. C. Heath, Lexington Books, 1980), p. 220.

56. For recent research findings challenging the stereotype, see John W. Newstrom, William E. Reif, and Robert M. Monczka, "Motivating the Public Employee: Fact vs. Fiction," Public Personnel Management 5 (January-February 1976): 67-72.

57. E. S. Savas and Sigmund G. Ginsburg, "The Civil Service: A Meritless System?" Public Interest 32 (Summer 1973): 70-85.

58. Samuel J. Bernstein and Leon Reinharth, "Management, The Public Organization and Productivity: Some Factors to Consider," Public Personnel Management 2 (July-August 1973): 261-62; and Rogers, Can Business Management Save the Cities?, p. 65.

59. Rogers, Can Business Management Save the Cities?, pp. 20-21.

60. Frederick C. Mosher, Democracy and the Public Service (New York: Oxford University Press, 1968), pp. 54-55. See also Rogers, Can Business Management Save the Cities?, pp. 7-10, for a description of the history of the business-management-in-government movement.

61. Frederick W. Taylor, Principles of Scientific Management (New York: Harper & Row, 1911).

62. Mosher, Democracy and the Public Service, pp. 72-73.

63. Richard J. Stillman II, The Rise of the City Manager: A Public Professional in Local Government (Albuquerque: University of New Mexico Press, 1974), p. 17.

64. For a review of the evolution of budgeting, see Nicholas Henry, Public Administration and Public Affairs (Englewood Cliffs, N.J.: Prentice-Hall, 1975), pp. 158-65. An introduction to ZBB is provided in George W. Reinhart, "Zero-Base Budgeting: How to Do It," Management Information Service Report (September 1978), reprinted in Elizabeth K. Kellar, ed., Managing with Less: A Book of Readings (Washington, D.C.: International City Management Association, 1979), pp. 139-48.

65. See, for example, Rogers, Can Business Management Save the Cities?; Lee J. Stillwell, "The Niagara Falls Experiment," Public Management 59 (August 1977): 6-10; Wes McClure, "Cost-Saving Ideas for Cities," Management Information Service Occasional Paper (December 1978), reprinted in Kellar, Managing with Less, pp. 73-80; Hayes, Productivity in Local Government, p. 185; and H. Gene Walker, "The McAlester, Oklahoma, C.O.S.T. Review Program," Municipal Management: A Journal 3 (Summer 1980): 2-6.

66. R. Scott Fosler, "State and Local Government Productivity and the Private Sector," Public Administration Review 38 (January-February 1978): 22.

67. Rogers, Can Business Management Save the Cities?, pp. 25-26.

68. GAO, State and Local Government Productivity Improvement, pp. 6-7.

69. Ibid., p. 23.

70. Reprinted by permission of the publisher from Productivity in Local Government by Frederick O'R. Hayes (Lexington, Mass.: Lexington Books, D. C. Heath and Company, copyright 1977, D. C. Heath and Company), p. 13.

71. Ibid., p. 35.

72. Ibid., pp. 42, 50-51; and Mark Holzer, David Tatge, and John Jay, "Educating and Training for Productivity," Public Productivity Review 2 (Fall 1977): 3.

73. GAO, State and Local Government Productivity Improvement, pp. 21-22.

74. National Center for Productivity and Quality of Working Life, Improving Governmental Productivity: Selected Case Studies (Washington, D. C.: U.S. Government Printing Office, 1977), p. 20.

75. Ibid., pp. 46-54.

76. National Commission on Productivity and Work Quality, Employee Incentives to Improve State and Local Government Productivity (Washington, D. C.: U.S. Government Printing Office, 1975), p. 125.

77. Ibid., p. 100.

78. Roger Lubin, "The Little Rock Custodial Make-Buy Study . . . A Transferable Technology," Public Productivity Review 3 (Summer-Fall 1978): 61-72.

79. Dan Cordtz, "City Hall Discovers Productivity," Fortune 84 (October 1, 1971): 127.

80. GAO, State and Local Government Productivity Improvement, p. 10.

81. Reprinted by permission of the publisher from Productivity in Local Government by Frederick O'R. Hayes (Lexington, Mass.: Lexington Books, D. C. Heath and Company, copyright 1977, D. C. Heath and Company), pp. 102-3. See also ibid., p. 2; Edward K. Hamilton, "Productivity: The New York City Approach," Public Administration Review 32 (November-December 1972): 784; and John V. Lindsay, "Address at National Productivity Conference," in Holzer, Productivity in Public Organizations, p. 52.

82. Hayes, Productivity in Local Government, pp. 121-22.

83. Ibid., p. 231.

84. Poole, Cutting Back City Hall, p. 49.

85. Information on the Orange police incentive plan was obtained from John M. Greiner et al., Productivity and Motivation: A Review of State and Local Government Initiatives (Washington, D. C.: Urban Institute Press, 1981), pp. 90-92; Chester A. Newland, "Labor Relations," in Productivity Improvement Handbook, ed. Washnis, pp. 519-21; and Paul D. Staudohar, "An Experiment in Increasing Productivity of Police Service Employees," Public Administration Review 35 (September-October 1975): 518-21.

86. Dorothy Guyot, "What Productivity? What Bargain?" Public Administration Review 36 (May-June 1976): 340-41.

87. Hayes, Productivity in Local Government, pp. 125-40.

88. Ibid., p. 153.

89. Ibid., pp. 151-68; and James R. Stewart and Rackham S. Fukuhara, "Improving Efficiency: Work Planning and Control," ICMA Innovations Report No. 12 (November 1976), reprinted in Kellar, Managing with Less, pp. 89-99.

90. McClure, "Cost-Saving Ideas for Cities," pp. 76-77.

91. Rackham S. Fukuhara, "Improving Effectiveness: Responsive Public Services," ICMA Innovations Report No. 10 (June 1976), reprinted in Kellar, Managing with Less, pp. 100-7.

92. See Institute for Local Self-Government, Alternatives to Traditional Public Safety Delivery Systems: Civilians in Public Safety Services (Berkeley, Calif.: Institute for Local Self-Government, 1977), pp. 64-108; Fred S. Knight, "Fire Service Productivity: The Scottsdale Approach," ICMA Innovations Report No. 16 (March 1977), reprinted in Kellar, Managing with Less, pp. 108-15; and Poole, Cutting Back City Hall, p. 27.

93. David N. Ammons, "Taking the Best of a Private Fire Service and Making it Public," Municipal Management: A Journal 2 (Winter 1980): 103-9; and idem, "Oak Ridge: Doing More with Less," Fire Service Today 48 (October 1981): 16-20.

94. Reprinted by permission of the publisher from Productivity in Local Government by Frederick O'R. Hayes (Lexington, Mass.: Lexington Books, D. C. Heath and Company, copyright 1977, D. C. Heath and Company), pp. 200-4.

95. Ibid., p. 255.

96. See, for example, Cordtz, "City Hall Discovers Productivity," pp. 31-33; William A. Duynslager, "Water Supply," in Productivity Improvement Handbook, ed. Washnis, p. 866; GAO, State and Local Government Productivity Improvement, pp. 11-14; Greiner et al., Productivity and Motivation, p. 1; and Roger Lubin, "Technology and Capital Investment," in Productivity Improvement Handbook, ed. Washnis, p. 328.

97. See, for example, GAO, State and Local Government Productivity Improvement, pp. 11-14; Greiner et al., Productivity and Motivation, p. 1; and Raymond A. Katzell and Daniel Yankelovich, Work, Productivity, and Job Satisfaction: An Evaluation of Policy-Related Research (New York: Psychological Corporation, 1975), p. 18.

98. See, for example, Norman I. Fainstein and Susan S. Fainstein, "Innovation in Urban Bureaucracies," American Behavioral Scientist 15 (March-April 1972): 513-14; and Greiner et al., Productivity and Motivation, p. 1.

99. Katzell and Yankelovich, Work, Productivity, and Job Satisfaction, p. 18.

100. Greiner et al., Productivity and Motivation, p. 1.

101. Katzell and Yankelovich, Work, Productivity, and Job Satisfaction, pp. 18-20.

102. See, for example, William F. Fox, Size Economies in Local Government Services: A Review, Department of Agriculture Rural Development Research Report no. 22 (Washington, D. C.: U.S. Government Printing Office, 1980), p. 2; Werner Z. Hirsch, "The Supply of Urban Public Services," in Harvey S. Perloff and

Lowdon Wingo, Jr., eds., Issues in Urban Economics (Baltimore: Johns Hopkins University Press, 1968), pp. 504-8; and David R. Morgan, Managing Urban America: The Politics and Administration of America's Cities (North Scituate, Mass.: Duxbury Press, 1979), p. 27.

103. Morgan, Managing Urban America, pp. 25-26.

104. Greiner et al., Productivity and Motivation, p. 323.

105. John S. Thomas, "Parks and Recreation," in Productivity Improvement Handbook, ed. Washnis, p. 1427.

106. See, for example, Hayes, Productivity in Local Government, p. 12; and Poole, Cutting Back City Hall, p. 91.

107. "Final Report of the ICMA Committee on the Future Horizons of the Profession," excerpted in Kellar, Managing with Less, pp. 2-7.

108. George P. Barbour, Jr., "Law Enforcement," in Productivity Improvement Handbook, ed. Washnis, p. 936.

109. Harry P. Hatry, "Issues in Productivity Measurement for Local Governments," Public Administration Review 32 (November-December 1972): 776-77.

110. See, for example, Mushkin and Sandifer, Personnel Management and Productivity in City Government, p. 42; and Dennis R. Young, "Institutional Change and the Delivery of Urban Public Services," Policy Sciences 2 (1971): 425-38.

111. National Center for Productivity and Quality of Working Life, Total Performance Management: Some Pointers for Action (Washington, D.C.: U.S. Government Printing Office, 1978).

112. Nancy Hayward and George Kuper, "The National Economy and Productivity in Government," Public Administration Review 38 (January-February 1978): 4.

113. Price Waterhouse, Productivity Improvement Manual for Local Government Officials (New York: Price Waterhouse, 1977), p. 10.

114. See, for example, Charles H. Goldstein, "Proposition 13 and Local Government Labor Relations," in Kellar, Managing with Less, pp. 50-51.

115. See, for example, Carol W. Lewis and Anthony T. Logalbo, "Cutback Principles and Practices: A Checklist for Managers," Public Administration Review 40 (March-April 1980): 186; Patrick J. Lucey, "Wisconsin's Productivity Policy," Public Administration Review 32 (November-December 1972): 798-99; and idem, "Wisconsin's Progress with Productivity Improvements," Public Administration Review 38 (January-February 1978): 9-12.

116. See, for example, Selma J. Mushkin, ed., Public Prices for Public Products (Washington, D.C.: Urban Institute, 1972), p. 32; William M. Petrovic and Bruce L. Jaffee, "The Use of Con-

tracts and Alternative Financing Methods in the Collection of Household Refuse in Urban Areas," Public Productivity Review 3 (Summer-
Fall 1978): 48-60; and Poole, Cutting Back City Hall, pp. 3-34.

117. For comments on productivity bargaining see Greiner et al.,
Productivity and Motivation, p. 93; Herbert L. Haber, "The New York
City Approach to Improving Productivity in the Public Sector," in
Holzer, Productivity in Public Organizations, pp. 159-72; Hayes,
Productivity in Local Government, p. 235; and Raymond D. Horton,
"Productivity and Productivity Bargaining in Government: A Critical
Analysis," Public Administration Review 36 (July-August 1976):
407-14.

118. Greiner et al., Productivity and Motivation, pp. 128-29
lists six types of performance targets: work-load or level-of-effort
targets, project completion targets, project due-date targets, effectiveness targets, efficiency targets, and cost targets. The Joint
Federal Productivity Project, Guidelines for Evaluating Work Measurement Systems in the Federal Government (1972), reprinted in
Holzer, Productivity in Public Organizations, pp. 114-18, lists
seven means commonly utilized for establishment of performance
standards: time study, work sampling, predetermined time systems,
standard data, technical estimates, historical (statistical) standards,
and staffing patterns. See also Greiner et al., Productivity and
Motivation, pp. 119, 140-41, 171; GAO, State and Local Government
Productivity Improvement, pp. 11-14; Hayes, Productivity in Local
Government, p. 145; National Center for Productivity, Improving
Governmental Productivity, p. 43; and John S. Thomas, "Demand
Analysis: A Powerful Productivity-Improvement Technique," Public
Productivity Review 3 (Spring 1978): 32-43.

119. Cordtz, "City Hall Discovers Productivity," p. 128; Donald
Fisk, Herbert Kiesling, and Thomas Muller, Private Provision of
Public Services: An Overview (Washington, D.C.: Urban Institute,
1978); Morgan, Managing Urban America, pp. 26-27; Barbara J.
Nelson, "Purchase of Services," in Productivity Improvement Hand-
book, ed. Washnis, pp. 435-36; Ostrom, The Intellectual Crisis in
American Public Administration, pp. 72, 121; Poole, Cutting Back
City Hall, pp. 28, 39; and Thomas, "Parks and Recreation," p. 1440.

120. For comments regarding the importance of pay-for-per-
formance standards, see Greiner et al., Productivity and Motivation,
pp. 109-13; Selma J. Mushkin and Frank H. Sandifer, "Personnel
Management," in Productivity and Motivation, ed. Washnis, p. 541;
Chester A. Newland, "Personnel Concerns in Government Productivity Improvement," Public Administration Review 32 (November-
December 1972): 811; and Vough, Productivity, pp. 8-15.

121. See, for example, Balk, "Why Don't Public Administrators
Take Productivity More Seriously?" pp. 319-23; John M. Greiner,

"Incentives for Municipal Employees: An Update," The Municipal Year Book 1980, vol. 47 (Washington, D.C.: International City Management Association, 1980), pp. 192-209; Greiner et al., Productivity and Motivation, p. 1; National Commission on Productivity, Employee Incentives; and Vough, Productivity, pp. 8-11.

122. Katzell and Yankelovich, Work, Productivity, and Job Satisfaction, p. 101.

123. GAO, State and Local Government Productivity Improvement, pp. 11-14.

124. For comments, see Greiner et al., Productivity and Motivation, pp. 233-34, 308-9; Katzell and Yankelovich, Work, Productivity, and Job Satisfaction, p. 18; and Vough, Productivity, pp. 81-84.

125. Sam Zagoria, "Are City Workers Bored with Their Jobs?" American City 88 (August 1973): 51-52, 121.

126. Poole, Cutting Back City Hall, p. 54.

127. Ibid., p. 53.

128. Patricia Haynes, "Industrial Engineering Techniques," in Productivity Improvement Handbook, ed. Washnis, p. 208.

129. Thomas, "Parks and Recreation," pp. 1426-27.

130. Bruce B. Talley, "Intergovernmental Cooperation," in Productivity Improvement Handbook, ed. Washnis, p. 452.

131. Hayes, Productivy in Local Government, p. 12.

132. Wayne C. Turner and R. J. Craig, "Productivity-Improvement Programs in the Public Sector," Public Productivity Review 3 (Spring 1978): 4-5.

133. Katzell and Yankelovich, Work, Productivity, and Job Satisfaction, pp. 19-20.

134. Ibid., pp. 5, 12. Reprinted with permission.

135. Ibid., pp. 27-29, 182.

136. Rensis Likert, The Human Organization: Its Management and Value (New York: McGraw-Hill, 1967), pp. 78-79.

137. Ibid., pp. 46. Reprinted with permission.

138. Katzell and Yankelovich, Work, Productivity, and Job Satisfaction, p. 35. Reprinted with permission.

139. Ibid.

140. Greiner et al., Productivity and Motivation, pp. 340-42; and Greiner, "Incentives for Municipal Employees," p. 210.

141. Robert T. Golembiewski and Carl W. Proehl, Jr., "Public Sector Applications of Flexible Workhours: A Review of Available Experience," Public Administration Review 40 (January-February 1980): 72-85. For similar conclusions regarding recent research, see also Glenn W. Rainey, Jr., and Lawrence Wolf, "Flex-Time: Short-Term Benefits; Long-Term . . .?" Public Administration Review 41 (January-February 1981): 52-63.

142. Katzell and Yankelovich, Work, Productivity, and Job Satisfaction, p. 26. Reprinted with permission. For comments on the effectiveness of pay as a motivator for public sector employees, see Greiner et al., Productivity and Motivation, p. 18.

143. Katzell and Yankelovich, Work, Productivity, and Job Satisfaction, p. 36.

144. Ibid., p. 313. Reprinted with permission.

145. Ibid., pp. 316-20, 322-23, 334.

146. Greiner et al., Productivity and Motivation, pp. 148-51, 172-73.

147. National Commission on Productivity, Employee Incentives, p. 142.

148. Katzell and Yankelovich, Work, Productivity, and Job Satisfaction, pp. i(c), i(d).

149. Elinor Ostrom, "Multi-Mode Measures: From Potholes to Police," Public Productivity Review 1 (March 1976): 52.

150. Poole, Cutting Back City Hall, p. 86.

151. E. S. Savas and Barbara J. Stevens, "Solid-Waste Collection," in Productivity Improvement Handbook, ed. Washnis, pp. 618, 621.

152. Patricia S. Florestano and Stephen B. Gordon, "Public vs. Private: Small Government Contracting with the Private Sector," Public Administration Review 40 (January-February 1980): 33.

153. National Commission on Productivity and Work Quality, Improving Police Productivity: More for Your Law Enforcement Dollar (Washington, D.C.: U.S. Government Printing Office, 1975), p. 6. See also Vough, Productivity, for reported success of total responsibility in a private sector setting.

154. Peter W. Greenwood and Jean Petersilia, The Criminal Investigation Process, Volume I: Summary and Policy Implications, Report no. R-1776-DOJ (Santa Monica, Calif.: Rand Corporation, October 1975), p. vi.

155. Greiner et al., Productivity and Motivation, p. 333.

156. National Commission on Productivity, Employee Incentives, p. 102.

157. For a concise overview of the literature on these topics, see Richard D. Bingham, The Adoption of Innovation by Local Government (Lexington, Mass.: Lexington Books, 1976), pp. 9-12; George W. Downs, Jr., Bureaucracy, Innovation, and Public Policy (Lexington, Mass.: Lexington Books, 1976), pp. 48-49, 89-91, 97-99; Mushkin and Sandifer, Personnel Management and Productivity in City Government, pp. 104-5; and Yin, Heald, and Vogel, Tinkering with the System, p. 68.

158. Yin, Heald, and Vogel, Tinkering with the System, p. 80; Downs, Bureaucracy, Innovation, and Public Policy, pp. 115-16.

159. Downs, Bureaucracy, Innovation, and Public Policy, p. 21, based upon John Loy, "Social Psychological Characteristics of Inno-

vators," American Sociological Review 34 (1969): 73-82; and Everett Rogers and Floyd Shoemaker, Communication of Innovations: A Cross-cultural Approach (New York: Free Press, 1971).

160. See, for example, George P. Barbour, Jr., "Key Factors Influencing Productivity of State and Local Government Activities," Public Productivity Review 4 (September 1980): 274-75; Hayes, "Leadership and Politics of the Productivity Process," p. 19; Hayward, "The Productivity Challenge," p. 547; Frederick Herzberg, Work and the Nature of Man (Cleveland: World, 1966); and Katzell and Yankelovich, Work, Productivity, and Job Satisfaction, pp. 38-39.

161. Hayward, "The Productivity Challenge," p. 544.

3

QUALITY OF SERVICE:
ITS RELEVANCE TO
PRODUCTIVITY

Productivity should not be estimated in such a way as to ignore the "quality" of the product or service, particularly in relation to the effects or impacts on the citizens and the community.

Hatry and Fisk*

Adjustments for changes in output quality are necessary in order to appropriately measure the changes in resources used per unit of similar type good or service. If a reduction in labor requirements per unit of output results from a change in the dimensions of the output or in the quality of the service, then the resultant measure does not reflect productivity improvement.

Jerome Mark†

Improvements in unit costs or, conversely, output per unit of input, achieved at the expense of quality of service, can be said to represent an improvement in efficiency only by twisting the meaning of that term.

Hatry et al.‡

---

*Harry P. Hatry and Donald M. Fisk, Improving Productivity and Productivity Measurement in Local Governments (Washington, D. C.: Urban Institute, 1971), p. 3. Reprinted with permission.

†Jerome A. Mark, "Measuring Productivity in Government: Federal, State, and Local," Public Productivity Review 5 (March 1981):27.

‡Harry P. Hatry, et al., How Effective Are Your Community Services? Procedures for Monitoring the Effectiveness of Municipal Services (Washington, D. C.: Urban Institute, 1977), p. 4.

Municipal output, the numerator in the output-to-input ratio by which municipal productivity is appropriately measured, incorporates both quantity and quality aspects of municipal services. Productivity improvement may be achieved by actions that increase the output-to-input ratio in any of several ways, including input reduction while holding services constant, service improvement while holding inputs constant, or simultaneous adjustment of both factors as long as such adjustments produce a greater ratio. Input reductions achieved through equal or greater reductions in service quality do not constitute productivity improvement.

A hypothetical example will demonstrate the importance of service quality and quantity in the productivity ratio. Suppose a city's officials decide to cut operating expenses by reducing the hours of operation at the municipal swimming pool, reducing the number of lifeguards on duty, and changing residential garbage services from backdoor pickup to curbside collection. Output in the recreation and sanitation departments will have remained the same if measured only as number of municipal pools operated or number of tons of refuse collected. Inputs in each case would decline, providing, perhaps, an illusion of productivity improvement. A more precise measurement, however, would reveal a reduction in quality of services at the municipal pool, unless operation was suspended only at times when the pool was virtually vacant (rendering the reduction almost imperceptible) and the reduction in lifeguards was offset by the employment of better-trained, more capable lifeguards or by some mechanical means of surveillance or rescue. More precise measurement would also reflect a declining level of service in refuse collection in the output portion of the productivity ratio and a transferral of responsibility for a portion of the inputs from one source to another. While the municipality's inputs would decline, the residents' input (in terms of the labor required to transport their refuse to the designated curbside location at regular intervals) would be increased. Clearly, the question of quality of service is an integral element in municipal productivity considerations.

In this chapter, the dimensions of service quality are explored, followed by a discussion of the need for intercity productivity comparisons and the significance of quality-of-service considerations in such comparisons. The approach for dealing with the quality-of-service problem in this study will also be described.

DIMENSIONS OF QUALITY

It is important at the outset to determine both what quality is and what it is not. In the context of public sector productivity-improvement efforts, quality of service generally is considered to be an element of service effectiveness. Quality of service is thought to be an important element in an agency's ability to achieve its service objectives as well as a factor tending to work against municipal economy. Hence, service quality is typically linked to effectiveness in consideration of the dual performance objectives of efficiency and effectiveness. Brian Usilaner and Edwin Soniat, however, divide performance productivity not into efficiency and effectiveness, but into the three elements efficiency, service quality, and program effectiveness.[1] A useful description of quality of service is provided by their listing of service-quality elements: level of service, timeliness, convenience, accuracy, and responsiveness. Essentially quality of service is a measure of how well a service is provided along these dimensions.

The simplicity of a brief statement of what quality of service is belies the complexity inherent in the measurement of service quality. The measurement of outputs is a fundamental problem in public sector productivity analysis. Moreover, it is not even clear at a conceptual level just what it is that should be measured. Organizational outputs are the immediate products of organizational activities; outcomes, on the other hand, reflect the consequences of those outputs. Should municipal service quality be a measure strictly of output, since ultimate effects are influenced only partially by governmental services, or should it be measured by outcomes, since governmental activities are of value only to the extent that they produce desirable results? Given a choice, a municipal productivity analyst could present strong philosophical reasons for selection of either measure of quality. Given the reality of limited measures of municipal output, the prudent analyst is likely to worry less about whether immediate products or ultimate consequences are measured than about the validity and reliability of the measure at whichever level is available.

Whether based upon output in the narrow sense or output in a broader sense (to encompass both immediate products and outcomes), quality of service is a characteristic of output rather than input. Despite the elementary nature of this statement, a surprising number of public sector agencies and activities are judged on the basis of inputs. At the federal level, for example, national defense is assessed as frequently on the relative size of the Pentagon budget as on the capability of the weaponry and manpower devoted to national security. Analogous municipal examples abound: national statistics on police officers and firefighters per 10,000 population are used to support additional hiring based upon the premise that more such employees will enhance the quality of service; pupil-teacher ratios are perhaps the quintessential measure of quality of education; dollars expended for new book acquisitions is a commonly employed measure for quality of municipal libraries at budget time. Such measures are more a reflection of input than a direct indicator of quality of output.

THE NEED FOR PRODUCTIVITY COMPARISONS

Without the market pressures of the private sector or public pressure for greater accountability, the performance of municipalities is likely to improve only gradually. At present, few municipal officials have more than a subjective basis for judging one of the most basic of all performance characteristics—how well their organization is performing relative to some reasonable performance standard. Few can assess empirically their organization's performance against that of other municipalities or even against the performance of their own organization in previous years.

Conceivably intercity comparisons, well documented and highly publicized, could generate citizen interest and promote the municipal accountability necessary to propel productivity improvement. Harry Hatry describes the problems associated with and the need for intercity productivity comparisons.

Assuming commonality of data, a further question is: what jurisdictions are sufficiently similar to provide fair comparisons? Hundreds of characteristics differentiate the various cities and counties, with each jurisdiction as unique as is each human being. Yet categories can narrow the band of significant differences for certain purposes. The little data that is currently collected on local governments, such as fiscal data, is generally grouped by population category. Demographic, socioeconomic, organizational, and miscellaneous characteristics abound—climate; central city vs. suburban vs. rural area; form of government (e.g., manager-council vs. elected executive); racial composition; household income; class mix; and so forth.

There is surprisingly little theory or research on how such characteristics should be expected to affect efficiency, effectiveness, or productivity of specific local services. . . .

What seems clear, however, from existing data sources is that major city-to-city productivity differences often do exist. This is true even after allowing for variations in selected service and community variables. An examination of solid waste collection data from a special 1971 survey indicated that for once-a-week curbside or alley pickup the tons collected per man varied from 940 to 1,900. Tons collected per $1,000 expended varied from 41 to 90. Based on 1970 police data, the number of clearances of reported crimes per police employee ranged from 1 to 7 among cities of approximately 100,000 population.

While a portion of such wide ranges may result from different data collection practices, real productivity differences appear to exist after adjusting for these practices. What is not known is how much of the remaining differences are due to inherent local characteristics not found elsewhere and how much due to better practices by some of the jurisdictions.

Much closer examination is needed to determine why certain jurisdictions appear to be doing better. Once this is accomplished, the insights gained may be used to help improve the poorer-performing jurisdictions.[2]

Intracity comparisons among departments, where appropriate, and across years would enable a municipality to know whether its own performance is improving or declining. Much as an athlete records his best performance not in competition with his earlier best efforts but in competition with other contestants, however, the motivating power of intercity performance competition may be a key to much greater and more rapid productivity improvement.

QUALITY-OF-SERVICE CONSIDERATIONS IN PRODUCTIVITY COMPARISONS

Adjustments in the quality of services are likely to impact both the numerator and the denominator of the productivity equation ($P = O/I$, where P = productivity, O = output, and I = input). Although greater than average expenditure is no guarantee of higher than average quality of service (hence the inappropriateness of the use of input as a proxy for quality of service),[3] it is likely that an alteration in quality-of-service output will have a direct impact upon the magnitude of required resource input. In some cases, services can be improved while the cost of service is reduced or services can decline in quality while unit costs increase; but more commonly, decisions to change the quality of a given service anticipate associated changes in resource requirements with the direction of change in resource requirements corresponding to the direction of quality change.

Multiple problems thwart efforts to apply the productivity formula to municipal service comparisons. Problems are encountered in both the numerator and the denominator. The numerator, output (O), is extremely difficult to measure for public sector products. Even in productivity studies at the federal level, which are relatively advanced compared with municipal level analyses, output measurement has proved to be a serious difficulty, resulting frequently in the use of weak indicators of output.[4] According to John Ross and Jesse Burkhead,

The major deficiency with the studies of federal government productivity is the lack of attention to changes in the quality of outputs. None of the studies have incorporated quality changes into output estimates, implying that over the period of the particular study the quality of federal government services has not changed. Such a position is difficult to accept. Ignoring quality leaves the analyst (and the reader) in the rather awkward position of having no idea of exactly what is measured.[5]

At the municipal level, measurement of output causes similar problems. Ideally an output measure should remain constant only if there is no change in quantity or quality of the product. Unfortunately, the inadequacies of most municipal measurement systems make fine distinctions in the status of output quality, and sometimes even quantity, of secondary importance to concern over the validity and general reliability of the basic measure itself. For a given municipality, output measures may be simply the number of clients served, the number of units processed, a general community characteristic related in some sense to a municipal function (even when municipal output can be explicitly associated with the characteristic only to a modest degree), or achievement of a performance target by a given date.

The denominator of the equation, resource input (I), is somewhat more easily measured. Although measurement problems exist in terms of cost-accounting inadequacies and the proper allocation of capital expenditures for any given year, annual appropriations reflect a degree of input measurement precision that typically surpasses the precision of output measures. The magnitude of inputs so measured may be affected by a wide array of variables. A major factor, of course, is the scope of municipal services. A community's socioeconomic characteristics, its density, the availability of economies of scale in municipal service provision, municipal management style, and assorted political factors are but a few other variables that may also impact the level of resource input. An underlying variable that is affected by many of the other variables and may in turn affect expenditures is the quality of a given municipality's services. No simple linkage, however, exists between the quality-of-service variable and all others. An economically poor central city may be forced for financial reasons to provide substandard public services; conversely, another economically poor city, because of severe social problems, may perceive itself to be forced to provide social services of higher than average quality. An affluent suburban community may feature exceptional municipal services; conversely, because of the conservativeness of its residents, another affluent community may prefer only modest municipal services. In any case, quality of service may have an important bearing on municipal resource input.

Another hypothetical example further demonstrates the relevance of quality considerations in intercity productivity comparisons. In this example, the city manager of city A believes that a more participative style of management will enhance performance. That style is adopted and, through group processes, strategies are developed that emphasize quality-of-service enhancement rather than cost reductions. Unless output (O) includes measures of service quality, productivity (P) under such circumstances may appear not to have been improved even if participatory management has led to more efficient use of resources. Improved management may free resources that may either be saved as an input reduction or applied to improved quantity or quality of output. In the former instance, productivity (P) clearly would be increased since input (I) would be reduced while output (O) would remain constant; in the latter instance, if freed resources were applied to quality enhancement but output were measured strictly in terms of quantity of units produced, productivity (P) would remain constant since both output (O) and input (I) under such crude measurement would appear to be unchanged. In this example, a parks maintenance operation may apply freed resources to a higher quality of park care. If productivity is measured as the number of park acres maintained divided by the resources consumed, no productivity change will have been recorded. The same acreage will have been maintained for the same total expenditure.

In neighboring city B, the chief administrative officer (CAO) may prefer strict hierarchical control of decision making. If city B is experiencing financial difficulties, the CAO may decide to reduce the number of parks-maintenance employees in order to save funds. Upon the protests of the parks and recreation director that the reduced crews will not be able to keep up with their work, the CAO may authorize a reduced frequency of grass mowing in city parks. In the case of city B, the number of parks maintained will have remained constant and the input will have declined, producing an apparent improvement in productivity. But the quality of park care will have declined. Without consideration of service quality, it would appear that the strict hierarchical control exercised in city B is a superior management tool for improving productivity when compared with the participatory style of city A. In fact, the reverse may be true but may be apparent only if adjustments are made for quality-of-service differences.

INTERCITY COMPARISONS WITH QUALITY OF SERVICE HELD CONSTANT

Productivity measurements are relevant only as intertemporal or interspatial comparisons. The productivity of a particular department or municipality may be usefully compared with productivity performance of the same unit at an earlier point in time as long as adjustments are made for quality-of-service changes. Appropriate comparison of the productivity of two or more cities is in many respects more difficult since quality-of-service differences are likely to be greater for different cities than for one city over time. Particular varieties of service offered in one city may not even be available in another. Yet in many respects, intercity comparisons offer potentially more useful information than does analysis of intracity productivity change.

Detection of community, administrative, and political factors that have a significant impact as independent variables on the dependent-variable productivity would require extensive experimentation over a lengthy period of time if analysis were restricted to longitudinal studies of one or two cities. Cross-sectional analysis, on the other hand, offers the advantages of wide variation among multiple independent variables and a reduced time requirement for analysis of effects but is practical only if intercity measurement problems can be overcome.

The approach taken in this study is cross-sectional analysis of 14 cities matched for similar scope and quality of municipal services. Financial reports, budgets, census information, published municipal tabulations, and survey data have been utilized to explore potential explanations for productivity differences among cities with similar service output. All of the cities analyzed have been selected for the broad scope and high quality of their municipal services. By this means, the quality-of-service problem that has plagued so many earlier studies at the data-analysis stage has been addressed and neutralized prior to arrival at that stage. Quality-of-service differences among the cities being examined are believed to be minimal.

Coupled with the matching of cities providing a similar scope of services, elimination of the problem of intercity variation in service quality permits analytical concentration on potential explanatory variables for municipal productivity differences.

SUMMARY

Municipal service quality is an element of output in the productivity formula ($P = O/I$, where P = productivity, O = output, and I = input). Only when the output-to-input ratio is increased—including consideration of service quality—is productivity improved.

Quality-of-service dimensions include level of service, timeliness, convenience, accuracy, and responsiveness.[6] Rarely, however, is a city's performance along these dimensions measured for more than a few functions. More common is the inappropriate substitution of input measures as proxies for output quality (for example, police officers per 10,000 population, expenditures for library book acquisitions).

Productivity measures, including the service-quality element, provide a more useful basis for judging municipal performance. Intercity comparisons could generate healthy competition and provide relevant information for productivity improvement. By matching for scope and quality of services those cities to be examined in this study, quality-of-service variations are controlled and intercity productivity comparisons are made possible.

NOTES

1. Brian Usilaner and Edwin Soniat, "Productivity Measurement," in Productivity Improvement Handbook for State and Local Government, ed. George J. Washnis (New York: John Wiley & Sons, 1980), p. 93.

2. Harry P. Hatry, "Issues in Productivity Measurement for Local Governments," Public Administration Review 32 (November-December 1972): 781. Reprinted with permission from Public Administration Review, © 1972 by The American Society for Public Administration, 1225 Connecticut Avenue, N.W., Washington, D.C. C All rights reserved.

3. See, for example, Ira Sharkansky, "Government Expenditures and Public Services in the American States," American Political Science Review 61 (1967): 1066-71; and Robert C. Wood, 1400 Governments: The Political Economy of the New York Metropolitan Region (Cambridge, Mass.: Harvard University Press, 1961), pp. 57-59.

4. John P. Ross and Jesse Burkhead, Productivity in the Local Government Sector (Lexington, Mass.: Lexington Books, 1974), p. 80. The authors report, for instance, that the output measure for the Bureau of Indian Affairs program for direct education is simply the number of students enrolled.

5. Reprinted by permission of the publisher, from ibid. (Lexington, Mass.: Lexington Books, D. C. Heath and Company, copyright 1974, D. C. Heath and Company), p. 83.

6. Usilaner and Soniat, "Productivity Measurement," p. 93.

4

SELECTION OF CITIES WITH HIGH-QUALITY MUNICIPAL SERVICES

Municipal functions have developed even more rapidly than urban population during the last twenty years. Not only have
police corps, fire brigades, water supplies, and street paving
come to be provided in the newer cities, and to be greatly extended in older cities, but new standards of efficiency have
arisen which have required a development far beyond that accounted for by the growth of population.

In other departments, the advance from former standards
of municipal activity has been so great as to constitute prac-
tically new fields of action. Public education has been entirely
reorganized, and elementary schools have been supplemented
by tax-supported high schools and free public libraries. . . .
Extensive public parks are now general in all important cities,
while the larger places have in addition connecting boulevards
and many small parks in the congested districts. Street lighting by electricity, street cleaning, and garbage disposal are
important municipal functions almost unknown a quarter of a
century ago.

John A. Fairlie, 1901*

The development of local government services since the nineteenth century has been remarkable. The array of local services
about which Professor Fairlie marveled at the turn of the century is
taken for granted by the modern city dweller. Police and fire departments are expected to be well equipped and proficient in the conduct

---

*Quotation from John A. Fairlie, <u>Municipal Administration</u> (New
York: Macmillan, 1901), pp. 95-96.

of their activities. Public libraries are expected to be well stocked
in books, periodicals, and perhaps even records and circulating artwork. Streets are expected to be paved, clean, and relatively free
of potholes. Parks are thought inadequate if they are not attractive,
convenient, and properly equipped for athletic activities as well as
for picnics and more pastoral pursuits. Garbage-collection services
are expected to be thorough and regular.

Some city governments meet popular service-delivery expectations more fully than others. The range and quality of municipal services differ markedly from central cities to suburban and rural communities, from large cities to small villages, from one geographic
area to another, and from affluent to poor communities. Some are
full-service municipalities, while others perform only a few functions
in a crowded field of special districts. Some provide high-quality
services; some perform at minimal levels; most rank somewhere
in between.

The quality and scope of services provided by cities are relevant
to the study of municipal productivity. A city that provides services
of modest quality and array naturally can be expected to furnish its
total service offering at a lower aggregate per capita cost than can
a high-quality, full-service city. To be valid, productivity comparisons must match cities of approximately equivalent quality and scope
of services. Otherwise the cost ramifications of unequal services
would distort the findings. Equally efficient municipalities can be
expected to provide differing qualities of service at per capita costs
commensurate with those differences. Cost-of-service differences
based upon unequal service quality fail to reveal actual differences
in relative productivity of performance.

Differences in the range of services provided has an obvious
impact on intercity comparisons of per capita costs for aggregate
service offerings and a more subtle impact on such cost comparisons
for individual services. A simple hypothetical example demonstrates
the implications. City A is a full-service municipality, while in
city B the local library is operated by the county government, fire
services are provided by a special district, and garbage collection
is handled strictly through private enterprise. Those services provided by both cities are of comparable quality. Naturally, the total
per capita cost of aggregate services for city A exceeds that of the
more limited city B. Even for individual services, the costs may
not be comparable. For example, the cost of operating the equipment
shop of city A exceeds that of city B's garage, since the former
maintains expensive fire department and garbage vehicles while the
latter does not, because fire and garbage services are not municipal
functions in city B. The finance department similarly experiences
greater per capita costs, since it processes the payroll and accounts

of three more departments than does its counterpart in city B. On the other hand, a comparison of recreation department expenses on a cost-accounting basis may favor city A's recreation department, since those same payroll processing and accounting costs, now attributed to the recreation department on a pro rata basis, may be lower by virtue of economies of scale in city A's larger-scale finance department.

Any particular array of services and any quality stratum for those services could be selected for intercity-productivity-comparison. purposes. For this study, the elite of municipalities will be examined. The municipalities selected for analysis will be those that offer a full range of services and provide such services at a consistently high quality. This choice of cities not only meets the productivity-analysis needs of this study but also secures, as a by-product, the documentation of a set of realistic, high-quality service credentials toward which other cities may wish to aspire.

FULL-SERVICE MUNICIPALITIES

Without the existence of a recognized delineation of those factors that together mark a full-service city, freedom exists to formulate such a definition. Accordingly, cities shall be considered full-service municipalities for purposes of this study if they provide an array of services that includes the following: police protection, fire protection, refuse collection, street maintenance, library services, parks and recreation, and water and sewer services. This listing does not, of course, exhaust the full range of departments functioning in full-service cities. The office of the chief administrator; the tax office; the purchasing office; the city clerk's office; and other staff departments, such as finance and personnel, exist in virtually every instance. The activities of these operations may be handled in different fashions and in different organizational configurations, but their functions are almost certain to be performed in some manner. Such services are frequently of an internal organizational nature and normally are invisible to the majority of citizens. Therefore, emphasis in this study is upon selected basic service areas included among those enumerated. Other direct citizen services, such as the provision of natural gas and electricity, are city functions in some places but not so commonly as to be deemed requisite for full-service classification.

It is important to understand at the outset that the categorization of a city as a full-service municipality or the classification of its services as being of the highest quality is not an endorsement of the level of services or the manner of service provision. The intent is to identify comparable cities. Some of the services might be more effectively handled privately or by another public entity; the quality of service may exceed the general public's taste and, in fact, reflect the standards of local government bureaucrats rather than citizen desires. Refuse collection, for example, may be quite effectively handled in a particular community on a private basis with the only city involvement being the provision of a franchise. Fire, water, sewer, parks, and recreation services might be provided satisfactorily by special districts. County provision of library services may be found to be entirely adequate. To be sure, functional fragmentation has its drawbacks, but it may offer a preferable means of service provision in some instances. Unless all of the basic services are provided under the control of the city government, however, the city cannot be considered a full-service municipality.

Control of the multiple service functions is the essential factor for classification as a full-service municipality. It is not essential that all of the prescribed functions be performed by employees on the city payroll but simply that the governing body have ultimate responsibility for service provision in each instance. Many of the services may be contracted out to private companies or to other governmental entities. As long as the contracting city prescribes the service levels, has the flexibility to terminate funding, and maintains primary responsibility for all of the delineated functions, it remains a full-service municipality. Many cities contract with private firms for refuse-collection services; some, notably the city of Scottsdale, Arizona, have contracted for fire protection services. The Lakewood Plan, developed in the California city of that name, offers a prototype for virtually total municipal service provision through contractual arrangements. Even in such instances, the governing body of the city retains ultimate control over service provision.

The matter of control in public libraries offers a particularly perplexing problem in the determination of full-service-municipality status. If the city is only contributing financially to a library controlled by another entity, for example, a county library or a regional library, the city should not be considered a full-service municipality. If, on the other hand, the library is operated by the city, it should be considered a municipal function, even if it benefits from extensive county and state funding. The real question once again is control. Does the city control the library? When the library is a city department, the answer is yes. When the library is governed by a special board, the answer is not quite so clear.

In many instances, a library board is established with members appointed by several entities. A few might be appointed by the mayor, some by the county or counties involved, and perhaps, some by an association of citizens with a special interest in the local library.

Funding from the city might represent a large or a very small percentage of total library funding. Because of the importance of control, a library governed by a special board will not be considered a municipal library unless a majority of board members are appointed by the mayor or city council. Furthermore, a library governed by a special board, the majority of whose members are city appointed, will be considered a municipal library only if more than half of its funding is derived through municipal appropriation and is not tied to a statutory formula but rather is subject to annual deliberation and appropriation by the city council. The degree of control exercised by the city council over libraries failing to meet these criteria is too limited for them to be considered comparable to a library that is a department of the municipal government.

QUALITY-OF-SERVICE STANDARDS

The importance of comparing cities with roughly equivalent service responsibilities is matched only by the importance of comparing cities with equal quality of service in those functional areas. A city that provides only minimal fire-protection services, for example, can probably do so much less expensively than a city that provides fire services at a higher level.

The overall level of municipal services offered in U.S. cities has risen dramatically since the adoption in 1686 of the charter for Albany, New York, the country's oldest incorporated city.[1] Most of the dramatic changes in municipal services have occurred since the mid-nineteenth century, a period that marked the organization in New York City of the first disciplined police force in the United States and a paid fire brigade (1845); major water works developments in Boston, Chicago, and Baltimore; and major public park dedications in New York, Philadelphia, and Baltimore.[2] Since that time, municipally provided services have expanded, improved in quality, and come to be taken for granted in most U.S. communities. Standardized systems for measuring the quality of municipal services, however, are virtually nonexistent.

Many popularly utilized performance measures of municipal services are clearly inappropriate. Per capita expenditure, for example, constitutes an extremely crude quality-of-service measure. Yet in such service areas as education and libraries, per capita expenditure has been used as a proxy for output.[3] Contrary to the interests of efficiency in government, expenditures in such instances are perceived as an operational element to be maximized. Not only does such a measure have little validity—since greater expenditure levels do not guarantee a higher quality of service—but the use of such a measure may be extremely dysfunctional insofar as a government's economy and efficiency aims are concerned. The identification of inadequate quality-of-service measures, however, is much easier than the securing of adequate measures.

Quality-of-service measures may fall into either of two categories. They may pertain to how well a particular activity is performed—an assessment of the process and its direct outputs; or they may deal with the results of the governmental activity—an assessment of what difference the activity made, of its consequences. In the realm of local government productivity studies, the debate over the preferability of measures of direct outputs versus measures of consequences has failed to produce a clear winner. [4] The hard reality of the matter is that few measures of either type are readily available for performance-comparison purposes. An Urban Institute survey of 30 local governments revealed that routine work-load data were collected by about three-fourths, activity-cost data by only about one-half, cost-per-unit work-load information by less than one-fourth; and effectiveness or impact data by only 13 percent of the jurisdictions. [5] The realities of the state of performance measurement in local governments compel the prudent researcher to be more concerned with securing the best available or the most readily collectable and acceptable performance measure—be it a measure of direct outputs or consequences—than with the debate over relative desirability. In that spirit, quality-of-service standards are proposed in seven functional areas for purposes of selecting the high performers among full-service U.S. municipalities. Some are measures of direct output and others are measures of consequences.

Police

Modern U.S. police forces trace their development in this country from the night watch system of colonial days. Under that system, each adult male citizen had an obligation to serve night watch when his turn came or to hire a substitute. Unfortunately, the night watch frequently was manned by the loafers, drunkards, and ruffians who made themselves available and were hired as substitutes, severely reducing the effectiveness of the system and even rendering it counterproductive in many cases. [6] In the mid-nineteenth century, day watches were established and movement began in the direction of organized police departments. By 1865, however, organized police forces could be found only in the nation's seven largest cities. [7] The most rapid development of police activities and techniques still lay ahead, following the turn of the century.

The development of modern means of transportation and communication as well as sophisticated techniques for criminal investigation have produced remarkable changes in the manner in which the police conduct their activities. Undoubtedly some police departments utilize technology, personnel, and other available resources more effectively than others. Despite popular interest in crime prevention and apprehension, however, only the widely quoted Federal Bureau of Investigation (FBI) crime statistics provide any basis for intercity comparisons. Universally accepted measures by which more precise differentiation in police performance might be made have not been adopted.

Several police performance measures have been proposed, but most suffer from shortcomings in validity, reliability, or ease of collection. Some of the better suggested performance measures include the percentage of arrests surviving initial judicial screening; the same measure per patrol man-year; the percentage of arrests leading to conviction; victimization rates; and the effectiveness of specially targeted efforts as measured by changes in crime statistics.[8] Another frequently recommended measure is response time,[9] although the value of rapid response for many offenses is increasingly being called into question.[10] Even the most desirable of such measures, however, are generally unavailable for multicity comparisons. They simply are not collected on a large-scale, uniform basis.

As a result, multicity comparisons generally must be based upon data from the FBI Uniform Crime Report. The use of such statistics as measures of police performance has been criticized for several reasons, including the significance of criminal-justice-system actors other than police to the rate of crime; the likelihood of under-reporting of crime; the possibility of falsification; and the fact that crime statistics ignore the quality of arrests.[11] While it is true that the crime rate of a given community is affected by many factors and agencies other than the police department, including unemployment and other socioeconomic factors, the performance of prosecutors and judges, the education system, recreation departments, and even health departments (in the treatment of narcotic addicts), the appre- hension of criminals and reduction of crime remains the ultimate purpose of police departments.[12] As noted by Clarence Ridley and Herbert Simon,

> The police cannot entirely avoid responsibility for an unsatis- factorily high rate of crime. In the first place, efficiency in the detection and apprehension of criminals should be an effec- tive deterrent. In the second place, modern police administra- tion does not narrowly limit itself to traditional techniques for dealing with crime, but attempts to attack the problem at its very origins. The police should be an active force in pointing out and remedying situations in the city which are responsible

for crime. The amount of crime in the community is the only
index which measures the extent to which this has been done.[13]

Even if uniform crime statistics are the best available measure
of crime deterrence and police performance among cities, potentially
serious problems remain in the use of those statistics if substantial
vagaries exist in reporting. Wesley Skogan examined the nature and
extent of this problem and reported national surveys indicating that
official statistics underreport the incidence of some offenses by one-
fifth to one-half the actual rate.[14] He found, however, that some
categories of crime are more fully reported than others. Victimization surveys indicate, for instance, that auto theft, representative
of crimes of profit, is very accurately reported. For a ten-city
sample, the Pearson product-moment correlation between survey
and official rates of auto theft was found to be .94.[15] Because of
the tendency for auto theft to be accurately reported and since it is
likely to be more preventable by police activity than are crimes of
passion, the rate of auto theft is perhaps the most reliable interjurisdictional measure of police performance. Even so, the inability of
the police to control various community social and economic factors
that may influence rates of crime cannot be ignored; therefore it is
advisable that the standard for assessing police performance be somewhat loose.

The measure used for distinguishing the performance of police
departments will be the motor-vehicle theft rate for 1979. In that
year, the national average rate of motor vehicle thefts was 498.5
per 100,000 population.[16] Cities with a rate higher than the national
average in that year will not be considered among the high-quality
performers in crime prevention. The police departments in such
cities may make magnificent efforts toward reducing the rate of crime,
but it would seem to be impossible to vouch for the effectiveness of
their performance based upon a greater-than-average theft rate.
Some cities with motor-vehicle theft rates below the national average
may benefit from favorable socioeconomic conditions or other community characteristics associated with low rates of crime more than
from effective police work. Police departments in such cities may inappropriately receive credit for high-quality service by virtue of a
favorable crime rate primarily attributable to factors other than their
own positive actions; but given the unavailability of more rigorous
measures, they cannot be denied high-quality categorization. This
measure serves more effectively to screen out poor performers than
to identify excellent performers, but even such limited differentiation
is of use, particularly when employed in concert with performance
measures for other municipal functions in an overall rating exercise.

Fire

Like the police service, organized fire fighting in the United States had a rather rudimentary beginning in colonial America. Early fire protection ordinances prohibited wooden chimneys and required colonial households to keep leather buckets filled with water on hand, as well as ladders in some instances. Persons were required to rush with their equipment to the scene of any fire and to participate in bucket brigades to limit fire damage. Gradually, ad hoc bucket brigades gave way to more organized volunteer fire companies that often competed with one another for social prestige as well as for recognition of superiority in fire-fighting skills. Fire-fighting techniques and equipment lacked sophistication, with the state-of-the-art practice consisting of volunteers rushing hand pumps to the scene of a fire and throwing themselves into the exhausting work of pumping water onto the fire. Frequently the effectiveness of this early approach to fire fighting was limited by inadequate water supplies—a shortcoming gradually reduced with the introduction of crude water mains and the first wooden fire plugs. [17]

With the initiation of the use of horses to pull fire engines in the 1820s; the introduction of the first U.S.-built, steam-powered fire engine in 1840;[18] the introduction of high-pressure water systems in downtown areas in the 1860s; and the development of mechanically operated aerial ladders and automatic sprinkler systems in the 1870s, fire-fighting effectiveness improved substantially. Volunteer companies had yielded to smaller but better-organized professional brigades in all of the nation's large cities by 1865, when New York City replaced its 3,500 volunteers with a 583-member professional department. [19]

Although it is clear that over a wide span of history fire-fighting effectiveness as a whole has improved dramatically, the quality of fire services differs from one community to another. For more than a few communities, fire fighting remains the function of volunteers, equipment is rudimentary, and water systems are inadequate for the demands of fire suppression. Many cities, on the other hand, are in a relatively sound position in terms of personnel, equipment, and water supply to combat most fires in their jurisdictions. An adequate performance measure should provide an approximate gauge of the ability of a fire department to provide fire services to its community.

A measure frequently suggested for assessing fire-service performance is fire loss (or a variant thereof, such as fire loss per $1,000 valuation). As Ridley and Simon point out, however, fire loss may be a relatively poor measure for intercity comparisons, since differences in a fire-loss measure may be as likely to reflect "differences in the physical conditions of the cities as they would their relative administrative efficiencies."[20] Perhaps even more significant, fire loss may fluctuate wildly, especially in a small community, from year to year if one or two major fires occur.[21] The incidence of one devastating fire may be as much a matter of chance occurrence, occupant neglect, or even arson as a reflection of anything over which the fire department or the city has direct control.

The best available measure of fire-service quality is one that is currently computed for private purposes. Insurance companies providing fire insurance for a particular structure are interested not only in the characteristics of that structure and its built-in fire protection features but also in the fire-suppression capabilities of the local fire service. The Insurance Services Office (ISO) serves more than 1,200 affiliated insurance companies and establishes public protection classifications for all of the communities in most of the nation's 50 states. Classifications range from 1 to 9 (with 1 being excellent) based upon such factors as fire-alarm adequacy; fire-department equipment, personnel, training, and distribution of companies; and adequacy of water supply and hydrants.[22] For purposes of this study, public protection classifications of 1, 2, 3, and 4 are considered to be a reflection of high-quality fire services. In those states without an ISO public protection classification rating, a comparable criterion based upon the insurance rating schedule employed by insurers in those states is used.

Refuse Collection

The state of refuse collection has advanced considerably since the eighteenth and early nineteenth centuries, when "the job of garbage collection was left to unreliable contractors, scavengers, and the pigs."[23] As in other service areas, however, remarkable diversity exists among cities in the provision of refuse-collection services. For most, such services are considered to be a municipal responsibility; yet in some, residents and businesses are responsible for disposing of their refuse either on their own or through a private contractor perhaps franchised by the city. Even among the cities that assume responsibility for refuse collection, the mode of operation and level of service differ substantially. Some function through a city sanitation department using city employees, while others specify the level of service and contract privately for its provision. Cities that are not responsible for residential refuse collection either through city crews or contract have not been included among the full-service cities.

Level of service varies among cities, with primary service-level factors being frequency and location of collection. Frequency of collection appears to be split along regional lines, with a 1975 survey revealing that 75 percent of the cities in the north central region of the United States have once-a-week collection, while a similar percentage in the south have twice-a-week collection.[24] Point of collection varies among curbside, alley, and backdoor collection from community to community.

Because variations in frequency of collection and point of collection may influence rather substantially the cost of service provision[25] and because these factors have a clear impact on the manual effort required of citizens and the expenditure they must make for garbage receptacles, the distinction made in this service area will exclude all except the providers of the highest quality of refuse service. High-quality refuse-collection service will be defined as twice-a-week backdoor collection.

Streets

The development of modern city streets has coincided with the evolution of popular means of travel from horseback and pedestrian movement of colonial times to the mass transit and automobile traffic of today. The early American streets that were paved—and many of them were not—were typically cobblestone. Granite blocks, wood, and a variety of other paving materials were tried as alternatives to cobblestone before the eventual popularization of asphalt. Wooden pavement was used fairly extensively in Washington, D.C., and in Chicago, but proved to be "a source of danger, for in October, 1871, a great conflagration in Chicago took place, and a few blocks of street pavement were burned."[26] Asphalt replaced the other surfaces as the most acceptable paving material and gained increasing utilization.

Today, well-paved streets with curbs and gutters are no longer uncommon in U.S. communities. Ideally a measure of street quality would include not only the percentage of streets paved and having curbs but also would include quality criteria, such as street dimensions, roughness, thickness, and the adequacy of subsurface construction for a given locale. Such detailed information, however, is not readily available; therefore the measures to be used in this study are the percentage of the total miles of city streets that are paved and the percentage of residential streets that have curbs. The first element is considered to be the more important of the two, so its weight is doubled in the development of a street-quality index. The index simply doubles the percentage of streets that are paved, adds the percentage of residential streets with curbs, and divides the total by three. High-quality street systems are those with an index of 80 or greater.

Library

Public library services are provided in a variety of ways. In many communities, the local library is governed by a special library board or by the county government. Although municipal libraries are not uncommon, municipal responsibility for library services is much less typical than for the other functions examined. For the sake of comparability, city governments that do not control the local library— or at least influence it significantly through board appointment and appropriation—are excluded from consideration as full-service municipalities.

Once again, some practical means of assessing relative differences in the quality of services is needed. A few measures of library quality are generally available but are inadequate for a variety of reasons. For example, the number of volumes in the library collection is frequently cited as a quality measure. A large number of volumes, however, may simply indicate a poor weeding process and a high percentage of outdated materials in the collection.[27] Another performance measure might be the volume of reference activity. A simple tabulation of the number of reference questions answered, however, may say something about level of activity, but it says little about the quality of responses provided.[28]

The best indicator of quality of service among those measures that are readily available is one that allows patron activity to serve as a gauge of the quality of service—that is, if citizen utilization of the library is high, it may be assumed that general library services are considered to be of high quality by the users of those services. The measure that provides such an indication is per capita circulation. If citizens use the library extensively, that level of utilization reflects favorably upon library administration in the selection of materials, patron assistance, efficient handling of materials for recirculation, and perhaps even the pleasant atmosphere of library facilities.

Survey information indicates a wide range of circulation-per-capita figures among U.S. libraries. In a limited survey of prominent urban and suburban libraries conducted for a major annual compilation of library statistics, the reported 1981 per capita circulations of the 36 responding libraries ranged from a high of 12.8 at the Baltimore County Public Library to a low of 1.4 at the Detroit Public Library.[29] Different editions of that survey indicated median per capita circulation figures for responding libraries of 4.3 in 1978 (N = 47), 4.0 in 1979 (N = 31), 4.6 in 1980 (N = 36), and 4.75 in 1981 (N = 36).[30] Municipal libraries with a circulation of at least 4.6 items per capita are considered for purposes of this study to be providing high-quality library services.

Parks and Recreation

There were very few municipal parks or recreational areas in U.S. communities of the early nineteenth century. In fact, a large sandpile located in front of a Boston children's home in 1885 was reputedly the nation's first playground.[31] The acquisition of park land, primarily for aesthetic rather than recreational purposes, had begun only a little earlier. Central Park was acquired by New York City, for instance, in 1853.[32]

Great diversity exists in the provision of publicly owned park acreage and recreational facilities. Some cities, such as Phoenix, Arizona, have purchased enormous quantities of park acreage, only a portion of which may be intended for actual park development of any kind, with most remaining in a natural state for aesthetic purposes. On the other hand, many suburban communities created since World War II have acquired virtually no park acreage at all.[33]

Park acreage is a relatively poor measure of parks-and-recreation activity and service quality. Some cities have acquired considerable park acreage but have developed for recreational purposes only small portions of it, while others have acquired lesser amounts of acreage but have undertaken more extensive recreational development. Total acreage may reveal little about the emphasis placed upon recreation in a community or the level of recreation services. Recreational-facility development may be a better indicator.

A fairly common facility among public recreational programs is the tennis court. The National Recreation and Park Association recommended in 1971 a ratio of one tennis court per 2,000 population as one of several standards for adequate recreational offerings.[34] Although this standard appears to be reasonable, it has been altered somewhat prior to being used as a proxy for quality of parks and recreation services in this study. Tennis courts are constructed and maintained at a variety of quality levels. Courts that are lighted for nighttime use, however, not only reflect a higher quality of service in the expansion of hours available for use but probably also tend to be better tennis courts, assuming some correlation between a municipality's willingness to purchase lighting and its desire for good nets and playing surfaces. Therefore, parks and recreation services have been considered to be of high quality if at least one lighted tennis court is available per 5,000 population.

Financial Administration

Each of the six previously described functional areas involves a service provided directly to the public. In reviewing service quality, it is also important to consider staff functions that have a bearing on the quality of other service offerings. One such area of particular importance is financial administration. The proficient handling of funds and reporting of financial data not only reassure citizens regarding the integrity of the governmental unit but also maximize resource availability within the constraints of a particular tax levy.

The Municipal Finance Officers' Association (MFOA) established a Certificate of Conformance in Financial Reporting program in 1945 through which local governments may have their financial reports judged. According to the MFOA,

> To earn a Certificate of Conformance, a [comprehensive annual financial report] must tell its financial story clearly, thoroughly, and understandably. Certificate of Conformance reports are efficiently organized, employ certain standardized terminology and formatting conventions, minimize ambiguities and potentials for misleading inference, enhance understanding of current [generally accepted accounting principles] theory, and generally demonstrate a constructive "spirit of full disclosure."[35]

Receipt of a Certificate of Conformance is considered to be evidence of a high-quality level of financial administration.

SELECTION PROCESS

There are more than 35,000 municipalities and townships in the United States.[36] Of that number, 3,072 are municipalities or townships of more than 10,000 population—a population threshold used in this study for reasons described in the paragraphs that follow.[37] Comparative quality-of-service data in major functional areas for all of these entities are simply not available in published form. Rather than attempting the mammoth task of securing such measures for all cities and towns as a means of identifying full-service municipalities with high-quality services, the more practical approach is to utilize an iterative screening process. In that manner, those measures that are more readily available may be used to eliminate some local governments from further consideration and thereby minimize the number of cities and towns for which additional quality-of-service measures must be secured. Such an iterative selection procedure was followed to determine which cities and towns met the specified quality-of-service standards.

It would be unreasonable, perhaps, to expect a city to provide the highest service quality in all functional areas. Once-a-week or curbside garbage collection, for example, may be perfectly satisfac-

TABLE 4.1

High-Quality Municipal Service Standards

Function	Standard
Police	Less than national average rate of motor vehicle thefts (1979: 498.5 thefts per 100,000 population)
Fire	Public Protection Classification of 4 or better (ISO class or equivalent)
Refuse collection	Twice-a-week backdoor residential collection
Streets	Pavement and curb index of 80 percent or greater (Index $= \dfrac{2A + B}{3}$ where A = percentage of streets that are paved and B = percentage of residential streets with curbs)
Library	Per capita circulation of 4.5 or greater
Parks and recreation	At least one lighted municipal tennis court per 5,000 population
Financial administration	Recipient of Municipal Finance Officers Association (MFOA) Certificate of Conformance for Financial Reporting

Source: Compiled by the author.

tory to the citizenry in a given community and may not detract, in their minds, from an otherwise exceptional service array. Another city may have an excellent financial report and manage its financial affairs quite well but for some reason choose not to submit its report for MFOA Certificate of Conformance review. If all other service activities are clearly of exceptional quality, it would be difficult to exclude such municipalities from the high-quality service list. For this reason, cities and towns that complied with at least six of the seven criteria, as restated in Table 4.1, were considered to be high-quality service organizations. Variation in one service area is considered to have minimal impact on overall cost comparisons among the cities. Any city that failed to exercise control over a service area, however, was excluded from further consideration.

Since a town or city could fail to meet any single criterion and remain eligible for consideration, the first narrowing of the total list occurred with the application of the first two screening criteria, fire insurance rating and possession of an MFOA Certificate of Conformance. Any city or town complying with neither of the first two criteria had two misses and could not possibly comply with six of the seven standards. Those communities were excluded from further consideration.

Communities in all but five states were rated by the Insurance Services Office for public-protection classification purposes as of the summer of 1981, when all fire rating information was compiled. Two of the five excluded states utilized a system similar to that of the ISO but maintained their own rating bureaus. For these states, Idaho and Washington, no adjustments were necessary for rating-system compatibility. For the other three states, Louisiana, Mississippi, and Texas, adjustments were necessary. In those states, special bureaus or associations maintained public-protection classifications to serve the same purpose as the ISO schedule in the ISO-rated states. For purposes of this study, Louisiana, Mississippi, and Texas towns and cities were simply ranked according to the fire-protection rating assigned to them by their state's rating bureau, and, for the sake of comparability to an ISO classification of 4 or better, a cutoff point was established in conformance with the percentage of cities in ISO-rated bordering states with public-protection classifications of 4 or better. For example, Mississippi borders on three ISO-rated states: Alabama, Arkansas, and Tennessee. In those states, 27 of the 343 cities and towns over 2,500 population (or 7.9 percent) have a public-protection classification of 4 or better.[38] Applying the same percentage to the 82 cities and towns in Mississippi indicates that the top-rated six or seven communities should be selected as being likely to have fire-service capabilities comparable to their neighbor state counterparts with ISO ratings of 4 or better. The Mississippi rating system utilizes protection classes from 1 to 10. Only five towns and cities qualified for ratings of 4 or better under that rating system in the summer of 1981. Eight more cities had a classification of 5, making the total 13 cities with ratings of 5 or better. The cutoff, therefore, was established at class 4, with five Mississippi towns and cities considered to be among the highest-quality fire-service organizations.

For Louisiana the ISO border-state-classification ratio indicated that the four top-rated cities should be included in the national listing; however, the Louisiana protection classes listed one city at class 1, no cities at class 2, and eight cities at class 3. It was decided, therefore, to make the cutoff point for Louisiana class 3 and to include nine Louisiana cities.

The ISO border-state ratio indicated that the 21 top-rated cities in Texas should be included in the national listing. In Texas a key rate, ranging from one cent to one dollar, is established for each community by the State Board of Insurance. A low key rate indicates a favorable fire-protection situation. Eighteen Texas towns and cities had a key rate of 16 cents or less in the summer of 1981; 24 had a key rate of 17 cents or less. A cutoff point of 17 cents was selected, and 24 Texas cities were added to the national list.

In addition to the public-protection classification information, which reflected classifications as of the summer of 1981, a roster of MFOA Certificate of Conformance recipients as of July 1, 1981, was used as part of the first stage of the screening process. Any city or town that both failed to have an ISO public-protection classification of 4 or better (or an equivalent non-ISO rating) and did not possess a Certificate of Conformance was eliminated from further consideration. Compliance with either measure, or both, allowed a city to remain in the running. Although this screen reduced the number of cities dramatically, still 1,065 communities complied with the fire-service criterion, the financial administration criterion, or both.

The third screening device used was the motor-vehicle theft rate, indicating in some measure the quality of police services. The FBI's crime statistics are most readily available for cities and towns of 10,000 population and greater;[39] therefore, the use of this measure had the practical effect of restricting this study to an analysis of cities of at least 10,000 population. This data limitation is not considered to be a particular handicap for two reasons: first, few cities of less than 10,000 population can realistically be expected to provide consistently high-quality services across all functional areas and second, sufficient differences in community characteristics and administrative or political practices may exist between towns of less than 10,000 population and larger cities to warrant separate treatment. Although use of the national average motor-vehicle theft rate is not a particularly rigorous screen, some indication of police performance is an important element in determining which are the highest-quality-service cities. A total of 438 cities of 10,000 population or greater survived the combined screens for the first three functional areas, complying with two or more of the criteria for fire services, financial administration, and police services.

The existence of a municipal library and the circulation of that library in fiscal 1979 were explored for each of the cities emerging from the previous screen.[40] Of the 438 cities surviving the previous screen, a total of 342 cities met at least three of the four criteria to this point: favorable fire-service rating, MFOA Certificate of Conformance, a motor-vehicle theft rate less than the national average, and per capita municipal library circulation of 4.5 or greater.

Each of the cities passing through the previous screens was surveyed individually for frequency and point of collection for residential refuse-collection services. Responses were obtained for all 342 communities. Those that failed to respond by mail were contacted by telephone. Only 20 of the cities provided twice-a-week, backdoor refuse collection as of the summer of 1981. However, failure to comply with the refuse-collection criterion was the first miss for several cities, allowing 37 municipalities to remain among the high-quality contenders and to be considered on the sixth service standard.

Responses were secured for all 37 communities being examined in the sixth service area, parks and recreation. The total number of lighted municipal tennis courts was obtained for each city as of the summer of 1981 and was divided by the Bureau of the Census population estimate for that city as of July 1, 1979.[41] Eighteen cities either failed to meet the criterion of one lighted tennis court per 5,000 population or were found to be served by a special recreation district rather than a municipal parks and recreation department. Only two cities failing to meet the tennis court standard survived this screen by virtue of its being their first miss. Only 21 cities of 10,000 population or greater met at least five of the first six service standards and were therefore examined in the final selection round.

Each of the 21 remaining cities was surveyed to obtain an estimate of the percentage of total miles of city streets that were paved and the percentage of total miles of residential streets that had curbs as of the summer of 1980. Fourteen cities had a score of 80 or greater for a weighted index obtained by doubling the percentage of paved streets, adding the percentage of residential streets with curbs, and dividing by three. Failure of the other seven cities to meet this standard was the second miss for each and eliminated all seven from the final list. Only 14 full-service municipalities serving populations of 10,000 or greater throughout the entire United States complied with at least six of the seven quality-of-service standards. Only one city met all seven standards.

FOURTEEN CITIES

The 14 high-quality, full-service municipalities of 10,000 population or greater are as follows:

Sunnyvale, California	Greensboro, North Carolina
Fort Walton Beach, Florida	Upper Arlington, Ohio
Gainesville, Florida	Oak Ridge, Tennessee
Saint Petersburg, Florida	Austin, Texas
Lake Forest, Illinois	Richardson, Texas
Owensboro, Kentucky	Newport News, Virginia
Chapel Hill, North Carolina	Roanoke, Virginia

FIGURE 4.1

The 14 Full-Service Municipalities That Meet or Exceed at Least Six of the Seven High-Quality-Service Standards

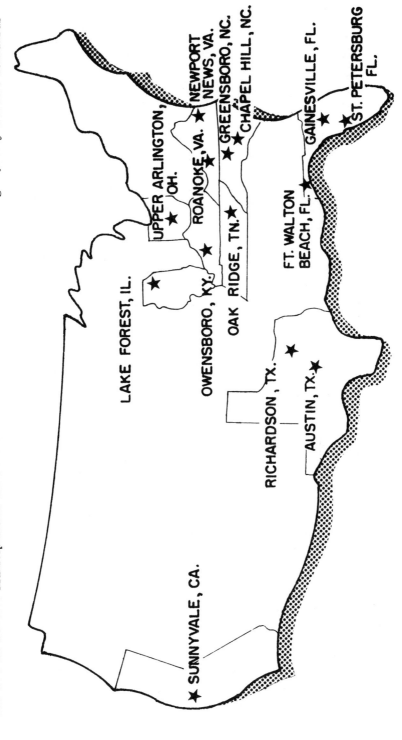

TABLE 4.2

Performance Measures for the 14 Full-Service Cities over 10,000 Population That Meet or Exceed at Least Six of the Seven High-Quality Municipal Service Standards

	Police Less than 498.5 motor-vehicle thefts per 100,000 population[a]	Fire Public-protection classification of 4 or less[b]	Refuse Collection Twice-a-week backdoor[c]	Streets Index of 80 or greater[d]	Library Per capita circulation of 4.5 or greater[e]	Parks and Recreation At least one lighted tennis court per 5,000 population[f]	Financial Administration MFOA Certificate of Conformance[g]
Sunnyvale, California	434.1	3	Once-a-week curbside*	100% paved; 98% residential curbed; I = 99	6.5	1.6	Yes
Fort Walton Beach, Florida	292.6	4	Twice-a-week backdoor	96% paved; 80% residential curbed; I = 91	5.1	4.3	No*
Gainesville, Florida	362.5	3	Twice-a-week curbside*	95% paved; 65% residential curbed; I = 85	8.4	1.3	Yes
Saint Petersburg, Florida	195.4	4	Twice-a-week alley and curbside*	97.5% paved; 75% residential curbed; I = 90	4.9	1.2	Yes
Lake Forest, Illinois	92.0	4	Twice-a-week backdoor	99% paved; 50% residential curbed; I = 83	10.9	0.0*	Yes
Owensboro, Kentucky	276.5	3	Once-a-week curbside*	100% paved; 87% residential curbed; I = 96	5.9	2.9	Yes
Chapel Hill, North Carolina	235.4	4	Twice-a-week backdoor	90% paved; 65% residential curbed; I = 82	11.0	3.3	No*
Greensboro, North Carolina	297.1	2	Twice-a-week curbside*	98.5% paved; 80% residential curbed; I = 92	6.9	2.4	Yes

Upper Arlington, Ohio	94.4	4	Twice-a-week backdoor	98% paved; 80% residential curbed; I = 92	18.7	1.6	No*
Oak Ridge, Tennessee	315.0	3	Twice-a-week backdoor	99% paved; 90% residential curbed; I = 96	7.3	4.7	Yes
Austin, Texas	469.6	4	Twice-a-week alley and curbside*	98% paved; 80% residential curbed; I = 92	6.5	1.3	Yes
Richardson, Texas	256.6	4	Twice-a-week alley and curbside*	100% paved; 93% residential curbed; I = 98	8.1	1.6	Yes
Newport News, Virginia	314.3	3	Twice-a-week backdoor	100% paved; 88% residential curbed; I = 96	5.2	0.8*	Yes
Roanoke, Virginia	492.7	3	Once-a-week backdoor*	100% paved; 40% residential curbed; I = 80	4.8	1.6	Yes

*Does not meet specified standard.

aBased upon 1979 national average motor-vehicle theft rate. Rates for individual cities obtained from U.S., Department of Justice, Crime in the United States: 1979 (Washington, D.C.: U.S. Government Printing Office, 1980).

bPublic-protection classifications reported for individual cities are Insurance Services Office (ISO) ratings or equivalent as of summer 1981. Includes copyrighted material of ISO Commercial Risk Services, Inc., with its permission. Copyright, ISO Commercial Risk Services, Inc., 1981.

cResidential refuse-collection frequency and point-of-collection information for individual cities obtained by survey, summer 1981.

dStreet index I = paved (2 × percentage of total miles of streets that are paved) + (percentage of residential streets with curbs)

Information for individual cities obtained by survey of municipal street and engineering departments, summer 1981. Percentages reported are estimates.

ePer capita circulation figures for individual libraries are based upon circulations reported in American Library Directory: 33rd Edition—1980 (New York: R. R. Bowker, 1980), or obtained directly from the library itself. Circulation figures are for fiscal year 1979. Population figures used to calculate per capita circulation are estimates of the Bureau of the Census as of July 1, 1979, as reported in U.S., Department of Justice, Crime in the United States: 1979.

fNumber of lighted tennis courts was obtained by survey of recreation departments, summer 1981. Population figures used to calculate number of lighted tennis courts per 5,000 population are estimates of the Bureau of the Census as of July 1, 1979.

gAs reported in Municipal Finance Officers' Association, "Certificate of Conformance," Supplement to MFOA Newsletter, July 1, 1981.

Source: Compiled by the author.

3

Figure 4.1 indicates the geographic location of the cities; Table 4.2, their performance on each of the quality-of-service measures. Only the city of Oak Ridge, Tennessee, met all seven quality-of-service standards.

The quality-of-service roster would list different cities if a different set of standards were utilized. A relaxation of some standards and tightening of others would remove some of these cities from the roster and add others now omitted. The use of a different set of measures would likely have a similar effect. Almost certainly, the roster would have a different appearance if the criteria used were the more popular (but less valid) "measures of effectiveness" that are commonly cited in support of budget requests, such as number of fire fighters or police officers per 1,000 population, library volumes or expenditures per capita, acres of parkland, and health or welfare caseload or expenditures. With the possible exceptions of library and recreation services, the services examined in the selection of the 14 cities for this study are among the traditional, perhaps even fundamental, services of local government—even library and recreation services have relatively long histories in some communities when compared with health and welfare functions, which have often developed more recently or have previously been handled exclusively by other levels of government. In some respects, one could contend that under the criteria used in this study, high-quality service cities is simply a euphemism for cities that perform well according to middle-class values. Relatively affluent communities do indeed tend to value the services being examined. Perhaps they value these services more than they do certain health and welfare functions, but the existence of a service dichotomy in which one set of services is valued greatly by one economic class and not at all by another is highly unlikely. Most of the service areas examined are valued, at least in some aspect, by low-income citizens, too. Yet it is likely that many of the 14 cities identified would be regarded as "amenities" communities, with their local governments directed toward greater amenities rather than toward serving as instruments of community growth, caretakers, or arbiters of conflicting interests in the Williams typology.[42]

The list might be challenged if it were presented simply as the best of cities. Conditions apart from municipal service provision could prevent a city that performs well on the measures examined from being a particularly desirable community in which to reside. Certainly many livable communities with high-quality public services are excluded from the roster simply by virtue of the fact that those services are provided by some entity other than the city government. Littleton, Colorado, for example, survived the iterative selection process until the next to the last stage, when it was discovered that recreation services in Littleton were provided by a special district for that purpose. As other examples, the cities of Ames, Iowa, and Rochester, Minnesota, are not responsible for the collection of refuse and were not, therefore, considered to be full-service cities, but they met all six of the other service standards. Many excellent communities were eliminated because the local library was controlled by the county or a special district. Niles, Illinois, for instance, met six of the seven quality-of-service standards but was eliminated from the list because parks and library services in Niles are provided by special districts. Similarly, Kirkwood, Missouri, met six of the seven quality-of-service standards but was eliminated because library services are provided by a special district.

Value judgments cannot be dismissed easily if the goal is an ideal mix of local services. Ideal to some persons means few services and low taxes. To an economically disadvantaged person, it probably means expanded welfare services, even if that requires eliminating the library or allowing the quality of local streets to decline. To a northern community with year-round cool temperatures, twice-a-week garbage collection might have little marginal value, while a municipal ice rink might be considered the ideal recreational facility.

But the purpose of this procedure has not been to select every city that meets every possible conception of the perfect community. The purpose has been to identify a group of full-service cities that perform at a high-quality level in traditional municipal functions that are likely to be of importance to the citizens and governing bodies in those communities. For the sake of comparison in the analysis that follows, it is important that all of the cities are high achievers in a comparable array of services. These 14 cities meet that criterion. All disclaimers aside, they provide an excellent level of services to their citizens. Their service quality and array are impressive when compared with their contemporaries and, especially, when compared with their counterparts of only a century ago.

SUMMARY

The scope and quality of municipal services are important factors in productivity assessment. Both are aspects of municipal output and both may be expected to influence input requirements.

In this study the impact of intercity scope and quality differences in municipal services will be controlled by making productivity comparisons involving only cities matched for their full range of municipal services and the consistently high quality of their services. To achieve that end, service-quality standards for seven municipal functions were developed (see Table 4.1) against which U.S. cities were measured. Fourteen cities have been classified as high-quality, full-service municipalities by virtue of their scope of services and their meeting at least six of the seven service-quality standards. They are

Sunnyvale, California	Greensboro, North Carolina
Fort Walton Beach, Florida	Upper Arlington, Ohio
Gainesville, Florida	Oak Ridge, Tennessee
Saint Petersburg, Florida	Austin, Texas
Lake Forest, Illinois	Richardson, Texas
Owensboro, Kentucky	Newport News, Virginia
Chapel Hill, North Carolina	Roanoke, Virginia

NOTES

1. Alfred R. Conkling, City Government in the United States (New York: D. Appleton, 1894), p. xii.

2. John A. Fairlie, Municipal Administration (New York: Macmillan, 1901), p. 86.

3. Harry P. Hatry et al., How Effective Are Your Community Services? Procedures for Monitoring the Effectiveness of Municipal Services (Washington, D.C.: Urban Institute, 1977), p. 234.

4. John P. Ross and Jesse Burkhead, Productivity in the Local Government Sector (Lexington, Mass: D. C. Heath, Lexington Books, 1974), pp. 83-89.

5. Harry P. Hatry and Donald M. Fisk, Improving Productivity and Productivity Measurement in Local Governments, prepared for the National Commission on Productivity (Washington, D.C.: Urban Institute, 1971), pp. 24-25.

6. See, for example, Henry G. Hodges, City Management: Theory and Practice of Municipal Administration (New York: F. S. Crofts, 1939). pp. 416-17; and Lent D. Upson, Practice of Municipal Administration (New York: Century, 1926), pp. 320-22.

7. Douglas Yates, The Ungovernable City: The Politics of Urban Problems and Policy Making (Cambridge, Mass.: MIT Press, 1977), p. 70.

8. National Commission on Productivity and Work Quality, Improving Police Productivity: More for Your Law Enforcement Dollar (Washington, D.C.: U.S. Government Printing Office, 1975), p. 9.

9. Paul D. Staudohar, "An Experiment in Increasing Productivity of Police Service Employees," Public Administration Review 35 (September-October 1975): 519.

10. John M. Stevens, Thomas C. Webster, and Brian Stipak, "Response Time: Role in Assessing Police Performance," Public Productivity Review 4 (September 1980): 229-30.

11. George P. Barbour, Jr., "Measuring Local Government Productivity," The Municipal Year Book 1973, vol. 40 (Washington, D.C.: International City Management Association, 1973), p. 42.

12. Ibid., p. 39.

13. Clarence E. Ridley and Herbert A. Simon, Measuring Municipal Activities: A Survey of Suggested Criteria for Appraising Administration (Chicago: International City Managers' Association, 1943), p. 17.

14. Wesley G. Skogan, "The Validity of Official Crime Statistics: An Empirical Investigation," Social Science Quarterly 55 (June 1974): 26.

15. Ibid., pp. 30-31.

16. U.S., Department of Justice, Crime in the United States: 1979 (Washington, D.C.: Government Printing Office, 1980), p. 40.

17. See, for example, Ruben C. Bellan, The Evolving City (New York: Pitman, 1971), pp. 271-77; Upson, Practice of Municipal Administration, pp. 226-27; and Yates, The Ungovernable City, p. 70.

18. Bellan, The Evolving City, p. 275. It is interesting to note the resistance of volunteer fire fighters to the introduction of steam-powered engines. According to Bellan, "No doubt fearful that the new apparatus would undermine their role, many volunteer companies refused to accept steam-engines, contending that they were awkward, heavy, complicated, slow at getting up steam, and prone to blow up. Manually operated engines continued to be manufactured and used for many years after the first steam fire-engine was built. New York finally ordered two of the new engines in 1856, and during the 1860s a good many cities bought them to replace their hand-operated machines."

19. Ibid.

20. Ridley and Simon, Measuring Municipal Activities, p. 14.

21. Edward Vickery et al., "Operational Productivity Measures for Fire Service Delivery," The Municipal Year Book 1976, vol. 43 (Washington, D.C.: International City Management Association, 1976), p. 175.

22. Jerry A. Foster, "ISO's New Rating Schedule," Fire Chief 25 (January 1981): 42-43.

23. Yates, The Ungovernable City, p. 70.

24. E. S. Savas, "Service Levels for Residential Refuse Collection," in The Organization and Efficiency of Solid Waste Collection (Lexington, Mass.: Lexington, 1977), p. 68.

25. See, for example, Act Systems, Report Summary, Residential Collection Systems, vol. 1: (Washington, D.C.: U.S. Environmental Protection Agency, 1974), p. 7.

26. Conkling, City Government in the United States, p. 139.

27. Vernon E. Palmour, Donald W. King, and R. Boyd Ladd, "Public Library Services," in Productivity Improvement Handbook for State and Local Government, ed. George J. Washnis (New York: John Wiley & Sons, 1980), pp. 1460-61; and Barbara M. Robinson, "Municipal Library Services," The Municipal Year Book 1979, vol. 46 (Washington, D.C.: International City Management Association, 1979): 63-70.

28. Palmour, King, and Ladd, "Public Library Services," p. 1461.

29. Joseph Green, "Urban-Suburban Public Library Statistics," in The Bowker Annual of Library and Book Trade Information: 1982, ed. Joanne O'Hare and Betty Sun (New York: R. R. Bowker, 1982), p. 328.

30. Ibid.; and idem, "Urban-Suburban Public Library Statistics," in The Bowker Annual of Library and Book Trade Information: 1980, ed. Filomena Simora (New York: R. R. Bowker, 1980), pp. 387-91.

31. John C. Bollens and Henry J. Schmandt, The Metropolis: Its People, Politics, and Economic Life (New York: Harper & Row, 1970), p. 192.

32. Ibid.

33. Ibid.

34. Robert D. Buechner, ed., National Park, Recreation, and Open Space Standards (Washington, D.C.: National Recreation and Park Association, 1971), p. 13.

35. Municipal Finance Officers Association, "Certificate of Conformance," MFOA Newsletter, Supplement (July 1, 1981), p. 1.

36. U.S., Department of Commerce, Governmental Organization: 1977 Census of Governments 1, no. 1 (Washington, D.C.: U.S. Government Printing Office, 1978): 1.

37. Richard P. Nathan and Mary M. Nathan, America's Governments (New York: John Wiley & Sons, 1979), pp. 18-20.

38. The authoritative source used for determining the total number of cities and towns of the specified population in the states was The Municipal Year Book: 1980, vol. 47 (Washington, D.C.: International City Management Association, 1980): 241-349.

39. U.S., Department of Justice, Crime in the United States: 1979, pp. 87-136.

40. Circulation data were secured from Linda Burns, ed., American Library Directory: 1980, 33rd ed. (New York: R. R. Bowker, 1980).

41. Census Bureau population estimates were reported in U.S., Department of Justice, Crime in the United States: 1979, pp. 3, 87-136.

42. Oliver Williams, "A Typology for Comparative Local Government," Midwest Journal of Political Science, May 1961, pp. 150-64.

5

DIFFERENCES IN PRODUCTIVITY AMONG HIGH-QUALITY-SERVICE CITIES

Unless you are keeping score, it is difficult to know whether you are winning or losing. This applies to ball games, card games, and no less to government productivity. . . . Productivity measurements permit governments to identify problem areas and, as corrective actions are taken, to detect the extent to which improvements have occurred.

Harry P. Hatry*

To use Hatry's analogy, relatively few cities have advanced very far beyond the stage of comparing gate receipts with the cost of fielding a team. They know how current revenues and expenditures compare with those of the previous year and the year before that, and they can project what their needs will be next season; but they know very little about players' batting averages or fielding percentages. Most managers probably believe that their team's performance has improved from year to year and that they are better than most teams in the league, but such opinions typically are arrived at subjectively, with little scorekeeping, no actual competition, and a tendency to make comparisons with teams that actually belong in a different league.

Scorekeeping is not impossible. The principles of performance measurement for local government are reasonably well articulated. In practice, however, the rigors of performance measurement and the reality of substantial difficulties in the quantification of output (and even input) combine to reduce the priority assigned to performance

*Quotation from Harry P. Hatry, "The Status of Productivity Measurement in the Public Sector," Public Administration Review 38 (January-February 1978): 28.

measurement and, consequently, the value of the measurement systems of most local governments that choose to bother with them at all.

PERFORMANCE MEASUREMENT IN THEORY

Performance measurement has long been advocated as a means of assessing systematically the efficiency and effectiveness of municipal services. [1] The types of measures compiled by various local governments in this pursuit, however, are of unequal quality and usefulness. Some are of no performance-measurement value at all. Hatry has identified the following 11 types of performance measures, each of which will be reviewed briefly:

- Cost measures
- Work-load-accomplished measures
- Effectiveness/quality measures
- Efficiency/productivity measures
- Actual unit-cost to work-load standard ratios
- Efficiency measures and effectiveness quality
- Resource-utilization measures
- Productivity indexes
- Pseudomeasures
- Cost-benefit ratios
- Comprehensive performance measurement[2]

The simple reporting of program or service costs is sometimes presented as a performance measure, but such a label is actually inappropriate. A reporting of costs reflects neither efficiency nor effectiveness unless accompanied by actual measures of performance.

Work-load measures indicate the quantity of work done over a specified period of time. Measures such as tonnage of garbage collected or number of applications processed are typical work-load measures.

Effectiveness or quality-of-service measures deal not with the number of units of work accomplished or the costs involved but, instead, with the quality of the service, how much it contributed to the achievement of program objectives, or how well it satisfied the clientele. Effectiveness measures may also address the degree to which service equity between geographic areas and subpopulations is achieved and, when citizen surveying is used, may serve in lieu of private market mechanisms as a means of demand articulation regarding desired levels of service. [3]

Efficiency/productivity measures reflect the relationship between output and input of the organization, program, or work unit being measured. When presented as the ratio of input to output, unit cost is reflected and the result is sometimes distinguished as an efficiency measure as opposed to an output-to-input-ratio productivity measure.[4] The distinction, however, is artificial, applying only to interpretation, since both measure the same characteristic using the same mathematical function and merely present the result in a different format. Like its industrial counterpart, local government productivity's input component may in some usages include only the labor involved, normally in man-hours or man-years, or may include all other required resources as well, such as the costs of supplies, equipment, and energy.

Ratios of actual unit costs to work-load standards comprise another form of performance measure. With this measure, the amount of time or expense actually required to complete a task is compared with the amount theoretically required as the basis for assessing a work unit's performance.

Combinations of efficiency and effectiveness measures have been designed in an effort to avoid loss of effectiveness in the pursuit of greater efficiency. Such measures adjust the output component of efficiency or productivity ratios for unsatisfactory products. The result may appear, for example, as the amount of park acreage maintained satisfactorily per dollar or the number of clients rating service as satisfactory per dollar.

Resource-utilization measures pertain to the amount of downtime for equipment or personnel in the unit being examined. Although valid performance measures, they indicate less about the overall efficiency of an operation than about the opportunity for improving efficiency through greater utilization of resources.

Productivity indexes constitute another form of performance measurement that, in the private sector, can be used to gauge relative performance among industries as well as performance improvement or decline for a single industry or group of industries over time. In the public sector, interorganizational measurement problems have generally limited the use of productivity indexes to the comparison of productivity in a single organization over time.

Several commonly reported ratios, such as municipal service expenditures per capita, municipal service expenditures per dollar of assessed value of property, number of library books per capita, and municipal employees per capita or police officers per capita, have been appropriately labeled pseudomeasures, unworthy of being considered actual performance measures.[5] In the absence of companion measures of work load or effectiveness, such ratios represent nothing more than resource input. Nothing can be concluded from such pseudomeasures regarding efficiency or effectiveness.

Cost-benefit ratios constitute yet another form of performance measure. Although frequent references are made to the cost-benefit of a given program in the public sector, valid municipal applications of this form of measurement are relatively rare. A major problem involves the difficulty of specifying the dollar value of most municipal services. Public sector services with direct private sector counterparts are amenable to shadow pricing (the estimating of program or service value in the absence of actual market prices); however, those without private sector counterparts and those involving social values present a considerably more difficult problem. [6]

Finally, some performance-measurement systems have been designed that combine various types of measures. Employee attitude data, for example, has reportedly been found to be managerially useful when combined with efficiency and effectiveness measures. This particular combination has been labeled Total Performance Management (TPM). [7]

Various types of performance measures differ in form, in meaningfulness, and in the difficulty involved in their compilation and maintenance. Work-load measures are relatively simple to compile but convey nothing regarding the quality, effectiveness, or efficiency of a service. Productivity measures reveal a great deal more about the performance of an organization or a work unit but involve the difficult matter of identifying outputs and inputs in fairly precise terms. This difficulty has resulted in an unimpressive record of development of productivity measurement in the public sector.

Productivity measurement in the private sector was well under way as early as the 1930s, with the work of the National Bureau of Economic Research and the Bureau of Labor Statistics Division of Productivity and Technological Developments. Productivity-measurement efforts for public sector activities have been modest in comparison, with only sporadic flurries of activity involving a limited number of federal agencies constituting the principal public sector attempts.

Advocates of greater use of performance measurement in local government recommend the establishment of a set of performance measures for each function or service. The use of multiple measures for a given service enhances performance evaluation and helps to minimize the likelihood of perverse behavior unintentionally induced by performance measurement (for example, the potential for a rash of police-harassment charges attributable to an overzealous effort to improve arrest ratios may be minimized by a companion measure of the quality of arrests, such as the percent leading to conviction or surviving initial court review). The development and maintenance of performance-measurement systems, however, is not a simple task. The complexity involved is suggested by the following list, compiled by Hatry, of relevant considerations when developing a set of performance measures:

- Validity/accuracy
- Understandability
- Timeliness
- Potential for encouraging perverse behavior
- Uniqueness
- Data collection costs
- Controllability
- Comprehensiveness[8]

Operationalizing Hatry's considerations (with the possible exception of data collection costs) in the development of multiple measures for police performance might produce the following set, suggested by George Barbour:

- Reported crime rate
- Clearance rates
- Arrests per police department employee and per $1,000 of expenditure
- Clearances per police employee and per $1,000 of expenditure
- Population served per police employee and per dollar of expenditure
- Crime rates including estimates of unreported crimes based on victimization survey data
- Clearance rates based on victimization survey data
- Percentage of arrests that lead to convictions
- Percentage of arrests that survive court of limited jurisdiction
- Average response time for calls for service
- Percentage of crimes cleared within X days
- Percentage of population expressing lack of feeling of security
- Percentage of population expressing satisfaction with police services[9]

Unfortunately, few actual measurement systems even begin to approach the comprehensiveness of Barbour's recommended set.

PERFORMANCE MEASUREMENT IN PRACTICE

Joel Ross notes that "the art of management has been defined as the making of irrevocable decisions based on incomplete, inaccurate, and obsolete information."[10] The state of information upon which management decisions are made in the public sector converts that observation from one of humor and admiration for the skills of effective managers to an indictment of managerial inaction in the crucial area of productivity measurement. As Frederick Hayes observes, "Long traditions of intuitive and sloppy management styles" in municipal government contrast sharply with the "analytical and statistical mode of operation" needed for substantial improvements in local government management. [11] The presence of productivity measurement does not guarantee an advanced management system, but no such system can exist in the absence of performance measurement of some type.

The extent of performance measurement in the public sector varies widely between levels of government, between governments on the same level, and between services. All governments record expenditures; many collect work-load data; a few compute unit costs; and a few attempt to measure program effectiveness. [12] In 1971, 55 percent of the cities responding to a survey by the International City Management Association (ICMA) reported the use of effectiveness measures in the review of operating budgets and 52 percent reported the use of efficiency measures in the same context. In another ICMA survey five years later, 86 percent of the responding cities reported the use of work-load measures, 65 percent reported the use of efficiency measures, and 70 percent claimed the use of effectiveness measures. [13] In many instances, however, local government officials have tended to overstate the existence of desirable characteristics or techniques thought to be progressive and may have done so in the ICMA surveys. [14] Perhaps more accurate assessments of the state of performance measurement in local government have been obtained through the actual examination of municipal budget documents.

In a limited examination of budgets and other financial documents of 30 local governments reported by the Urban Institute in 1971 and noted in Chapter 4, 77 percent were found to present work-load data in such documents, 23 percent presented unit-cost information (that is, the input-to-output ratio, which is the reciprocal of the productivity ratio), and only 13 percent presented effectiveness data. [15] In 1976 the Urban Institute examined the budget documents of 247 cities and counties and found at least one effectiveness measure displayed in only 25 percent and at least one efficiency measure in only 10 percent. [16] In a more recent review of budget documents and budget preparation manuals from 123 cities primarily over 100,000 population, 59 percent of the cities were found to require work-load measures with budget requests, 43 percent required effectiveness measures, 31 percent required efficiency measures, and 8 percent required measures of equity. No measures at all were required in 34 percent of the cities examined, and only work-load measures were required in 19 percent. [17] Based upon surveys that permit analysis of various characteristics of state and local governments and their use of efficiency measures, such measures appear more likely to be used in large cities, for services with tangible outputs, and for services that are subsidized or regulated by the federal government. [18]

Why is the state of performance measurement in local government so underdeveloped? Why cannot more cities see the value of performance measures? The answer is probably that productivity measurement is difficult, time-consuming, imperfect, and vulnerable to criticism. Productivity measures are subject to misinterpretation and manipulation and may induce perverse behavior if not developed carefully. Furthermore, performance as reflected in such measures may be strongly influenced by environmental factors beyond the control of the organization, making reporting very undesirable when such factors impact performance measures adversely.

Productivity measurement in the public sector faces several difficulties that are less common or nonexistent in the private sector. These include the nonexclusionary nature of public goods and services (making it difficult to determine the number of service units provided or, often, the demand for services), the absence of a pricing mechanism, the intangible nature of many benefits, the uncertain relationship between some work-load measures and productivity (for example, police patrols), the uncertain causal relationship between productivity and some result measures (for example, crime rates), and the possibility of manipulation and misrepresentation of performance measures.[19] Given these difficulties and the absence of any real stigma for laxity in performance measurement, productivity measurement tends to be given a low priority in competition with other tasks—typically, other budgetary activities in the common placement of the measurement function in budget offices.[20]

Some ideal effectiveness measures are virtually impossible to obtain. The number of undesirable events prevented by the police, fire, or public health department fits into this category. In the absence of these measures, local governments are forced to compile measures of the reverse: undesirable events (for example, crimes, fires, diseases) not prevented.[21] Typically, such measures are simply the tabulation of reported events or easily collected work-load data. Much less common are performance measures using trained-observer ratings, citizen surveys, and client surveys.[22] Rather than basing performance assessments on measures obtained by these means, local governments often base their assessments on subjective administrative opinions or the "grateful testimonials" of carefully selected clients or, not uncommonly, on recipients of special services who hope to forestall impending program curtailment.[23]

Not only is performance measurement difficult, the recording of such measures does not guarantee simple decision making. Even when developed well, performance measurement often fails to provide a clear distinction between the desirability of two modes of operation. The valuation of marginal benefits may remain a problem, as when hypothetical organizational arrangement A requires a per capita expenditure of $12 for police patrol and provides a response time of five minutes while organizational arrangement B costs $25 per capita and provides a three-minute response time.[24] The choice between the two options rests on the rather subjective value given to a two-minute variation in response time.

Furthermore, advocates of public sector performance measurement are vulnerable to anecdotal criticism when unorthodox attempts are made to deal with difficult measurement problems or when imaginative output proxies are developed (for example, the development of the hernia equivalent by the National Bureau of Economic Research as a means of measuring the performance of surgeons has received such criticism).[25] Productivity measurement has also been criticized as a factor contributing to an alleged overemphasis on efficiency—even a ruthless pursuit of efficiency[26]—at the expense of more important goals for government, such as justice and equity.[27]

Unless a productivity measurement system is developed and maintained properly, perverse bureaucratic actions may result. For example, an organization that attempts to assess performance on the basis of a single measure rather than on multiple indicators or that fails to consider all of the consequences of pursuit of a particular objective may inadvertently promote unintended performance. Fire fighters or police officers who are judged strictly on response times may resort to excessive speed and develop a poor record of vehicle safety. Police officers judged solely on their number of arrests may neglect to consider the quality of their arrests and engage in behavior that appears to the public to be harassment.[28] Performance measures may also be misused or misinterpreted by supervisory personnel, city management, or city councils. Mandated improvements in performance measures without the means of achieving such gains are unreasonable, as are instances of blind reactions to performance numbers without thought given to their meaning—as in the reported case of a fire department called to task because the number of calls to which it had responded had fallen 20 percent below expectations.[29]

Environmental factors beyond the control of service officials may influence measures of program results. Crime statistics, for example, may be favorably influenced by a changing population profile that includes fewer teenage males or may be adversely impacted by increases in local unemployment.[30] The specter of judgment based upon performance measures not fully controllable by organizational efforts is an influential dissuader of the use of such measures.

Enthusiasm for performance measurement varies from service to service and from department head to department head. Managers of departments with a tangible, relatively easily measured output may be more receptive to performance measurement, assuming they believe their performance to be satisfactory, than their counterparts in softer services, where performance ratings may be perceived to be subject to the whims of the public, as reflected in, for instance, a citizen survey. It is not uncommon for department managers to express disdain for efficiency measures and to contend from some subjective basis that the citizens demand a higher quality of service requiring greater resource input. It is unusual, however, for service officials to request measurement of that demand. All too often, estimates of demand are subjective and performance assessments are made by service officials and clientele on the basis of resource input. In such cases a function is judged not on its output or the results it produces but upon input factors such as staff credentials, whether it ranks first in expenditures among its counterparts in the region, or whether, for example, it has the most "favorable" police officer-to-citizen or teacher-to-pupil ratio.[31]

For performance measurement to be developed and utilized effectively, high-level managerial commitment is required. Impetus for improved measurement per se is unlikely to come from the local legislative body and must, therefore, come in most instances from administrators. City councils generally have been found to play at most an indirect role in promoting performance measurement through requests for a program budget or more budgetary information or, in some cases, a negative role critical of the costs of the work unit responsible for compiling and analyzing performance measures.[32]

The state of local government performance measurement in general is unimpressive. The state of local government productivity measurement, one of the more demanding types of performance measurement, has been described by Marc Holzer as "uneven," by analysts in the Bureau of Labor Statistics as being in need of "more developmental work," and by Hatry as "disappointing."[33] Holzer, however, sounds a note of optimism. "Some measures," he writes, "are relatively sophisticated, others crude. But in the common absence of any yardstick of productivity, even crude information is of value. At least it is a means of introducing systematic quantitative analysis into the decision-making process. Once that precedence is established, incremental refinements will undoubtedly lead to more sophisticated measures."[34]

VALUE OF PRODUCTIVITY MEASUREMENT

Quoting a former deputy mayor of New York City,

For too long, the citizen has been forced to rely for his productivity judgments on the whims, the impressions, and the often uninformed opinion of public spokesmen innocent of any real knowledge of the workings of government. . . .

. . . Urban dwellers everywhere have a right to a more solid measure of the efficiency of their government. They have a right to know where we are succeeding, where we are falling short of potential, and why. [35]

There has been little basis upon which citizens or even public officials could judge in an objective sense the strengths and weaknesses of local municipal services. Subjective impressions based on a few isolated incidents often are all citizens and administrators have available to them upon which to assess performance or to base expectations. In a 1972 publication prepared for the National Commission on Productivity by the Urban Institute and the ICMA, the following six reasons for productivity measurement were identified:

To encourage the kinds of comparisons and public scrutiny that lead to better value for citizens from their local governments;

To provide an index of progress—or lack of progress—to individual local governments;

To develop standards of performance, based on aggregate data for similar communities;

To dramatize diversity and thus generate effort to determine the reasons for success and whether these reasons can be applied more widely to treat the causes of poor showing;

To serve as a basis for performance incentives that can be used by government management and labor in wage and working-condition establishment;

To guide the federal government in allocating resources to raise the level of performance throughout the nation. [36]

Productivity measurement alone cannot prescribe solutions for poor performance, but it can help to identify those activities that warrant closer scrutiny. It could cause management to question operational practices and, more important, could instill a productivity-mindedness and perhaps a newfound competitiveness within local governments. [37]

A sense of competitiveness may be fostered by the use of a variety of performance comparisons. Hatry suggests the following types:

- Compare actual performance against performance standards
- Compare current performance measurements to performance in previous time periods
- Compare the performance for different units where a service is being delivered by more than one unit doing essentially the same activities

- Compare outcomes for various client groups within the jurisdiction
- Compare performance to that of other jurisdictions
- Compare performance to that of the private sector
- Compare performance against preset and planned targets[38]

Writers frequently warn of the pitfalls in performance comparisons, especially comparisons of productivity indexes of different organizations.[39] Even in prescribing performance comparisons between jurisdictions, Hatry notes several problems.

> Officials often want to be able to compare their own performance
> with those of other, similar, jurisdictions. A major problem
> here is the lack of similar performance measurement by local
> governments. Another problem lies in the hidden assumptions
> that are made when saying that two jurisdictions are similar.
> Population and density similarities do not necessarily mean
> that the type and difficulty of incoming workloads as well as
> other factors that affect measurement are the same. Also, data
> collection procedures are likely to differ, and special factors
> unique to individual jurisdictions abound. However, when local
> governments are using approximately the same procedures such
> comparisons can be made. Even now some comparisons and
> possible on crime and clearance rates, and citizen ratings of
> certain services can be made among a few governments that
> have been using similar questionnaires.[40]

The potential benefits to be obtained from overcoming the difficulties in interorganizational productivity comparisons are substantial. Through the cross-section analysis of different organizations with different structures, philosophies, managerial styles, and productivity levels, researchers would have the opportunity to explore the causal relationships between a vast array of potential explanatory variables and local government productivity. A systematic inquiry following the precepts of Herbert Simon's call for the scientific examination of the "production functions of administrative activities" would involve three steps: (1) definition of values or objectives in order to permit observation and measurement, (2) enumeration of variables that determine the degree of attainment of objectives, and (3) empirical examination of the impact of changes in administrative and extra-administrative variables.[41] The potential benefits of such an inquiry warrant the challenging of intergovernmental comparison pitfalls. Despite these pitfalls, in many ways intergovernmental comparison may be more pragmatic than its alternatives. Reliance upon longitudinal analysis or upon case studies to determine the impact of changes in relevant variables on local government productivity belies the im-

patience of researchers and the impracticality of experimental manipulation and control in local government.

Despite the many complexities and imperfections involved, the
cross-section analysis of an array of administrative and extraadministrative variables and their effect on local government productivity
is highly desirable. Unfortunately, most interorganizational comparisons to date have dealt primarily with extraadministrative factors
and their impact on total expenditures or, if intended to reflect performance differences between municipal organizations, have been
ill conceived and have produced inadequate results. Typically, comparisons of the latter type have been per capita expenditure comparisons with little if any adjustment for differences in quality of service,
scope of services, economies of scale, or factor prices.

OVERCOMING THE DIFFICULTIES IN
INTERORGANIZATIONAL PRODUCTIVITY COMPARISONS

The difficulties in interorganizational productivity comparisons
are problems of comparability and measurement. Jurisdictions providing different mixes of services or different levels or quality of
service provide little basis for productivity comparisons. They simply are not comparable organizations. Jurisdictions providing identical mixes of services and similar levels or quality of service but
failing to record the same types of performance measures or recording them at different degrees of rigor are not amenable to comparison
on the basis of those measures. In most cases, performance measurement is highly irregular between even the best-matched cities,
making the assembly of a set of suitable comparison cities difficult—
and for valid interorganizational comparisons, several comparable
cities would be required.

Ideally, local government performance data collected at the national level should hold the key to comparisons among organizations.
In reality, however, several problems exist with national data, as
noted by Harry Hatry and Donald Fisk.

> In summary there are several troublesome problems with these
> nationally collected data. First, several local government
> areas of operation are largely ignored. There is much data
> on education and crime, but little on solid waste collection and
> fire. Second, most of the reports are voluntary and some ju-
> risdictions do not respond. The FBI has worked long and hard
> for many years to get local police departments to provide crime
> statistics but not always successfully. Third, output data are
> generally not related to input data. Fourth, the accuracy and

comparability of the data may be poor. A wide variety of different data definitions and collection procedures are used by local governments. Fifth, many of the reports are aggregated so that the identity of individual local governments is buried. And sixth, some data are not available until years after the event. [42]

The expansion and standardization of performance measurement and the collection of such information at the national level would still leave researchers with the problem of reconciling differences in service mix and quality of service, unless effectiveness measurements were included. Such a national compilation does not appear imminent. Similarly, there appears to be no move afoot for the widespread adoption by local governments or by the federal government of an approach similar to that used for measuring industrial productivity. The termination of the National Center on Productivity and Quality of Working Life; reduced funding for and deemphasis of special efforts directed toward public sector productivity by the National Science Foundation, the Department of Housing and Urban Development, and the Office of Personnel Management; and the resulting decline in interest among researchers are probable precursors of a general reduction in federal support for local government productivity efforts. [43] The National Productivity Council has concluded that

> the costs and relative benefits of a federal effort in this area compared to other forms of federal support do not warrant a major federal investment at this time. More analysis of the conceptual problems and approaches should be made. In the meantime, federal agencies should be encouraged to continue their individual efforts to support state and local government productivity measurement and, where possible within their own budget priorities, expand such efforts. [44]

In the absence of local pressure or major coordination or funding by national organizations or the federal government, uniform reporting is unlikely and the adoption of improved performance measures will remain sporadic.

One final problem with interorganizational comparisons, owing to the incompatibility and inadequacy of municipal performance measures and the difficulty of comparing financial documents, is the possibility that estimates and assumptions made in the course of assembling comparison cities and extracting data for analysis may inadvertently introduce errors into the process. Interorganizational comparisons relying on cross-section analysis may be expected to lack the precision possible in a carefully structured longitudinal study involv-

ing a single organization with a single system of performance measurement and greater opportunity for complete familiarity by the researcher. Differences in municipal services and performance measures pose a difficult but not insurmountable problem that, in an effort to achieve compatibility, will require assumptions and generaliza-
tions that may adversely impact precision. Some loss of precision,
however, may not seriously impair the analysis, depending upon the
nature of the inquiry. For example, a high degree of precision may
be necessary for detailed wage-and-price analysis, but when the objective is the determination of general relationships between selected
variables and relative productivity levels, some imprecision in productivity measures or indexes is tolerable. [45]

Per Capita Expenditures

Per-capita-expenditure comparisons are common in local government. Many municipal administrators make such comparisons on
a limited and often highly selective basis to defend budget proposals.

In per-capita-expenditure comparisons, the problems associated
with output measurement are usually ignored altogether. The fact
that tabulations often include cities of dramatically different service
mixes and service quality often goes unmentioned in their presenta-
tion. It is unreasonable, however, to assume that such differences
are irrelevant to performance comparison.

Per-capita-expenditure comparisons are also vulnerable to
input-measurement problems. Such problems involve, in general,
the need for reconciliation of expenditure-reporting documents from
different cities in order to achieve consistency in including for analysis purposes (or consistently excluding where data limitations require
it) employee-benefit costs, capital costs, costs of support and supervisory personnel, and costs of service departments (for example,
purchasing, warehousing, and maintenance activities for equipment
and facilities). Also required is the sometimes difficult allocation
of costs among subactivities when comparisons are limited to particular services, or the consolidation of costs for major activities that
draw resources from numerous budget units. [46] It is common to exclude some of the costs, especially capital costs, owing to data limitations; but such exclusions must be made consistently to retain the
validity of comparisons. Even when consistently applied, exclusions
may affect results (for example, the exclusion of capital costs may
overstate the relative efficiency of a capital-intensive service).

In this study the selection process described in Chapter 4 minimizes problems of comparability for the selected services of the
cities involved. All 14 cities are full-service municipalities with a

consistently high quality of service in the identified functional areas. Expenditure information, permitting per-capita-expenditure comparisons, was requested from each city in the form of budgets or financial statements that display actual expenditures by service functions for fiscal year 1979 and fiscal year 1980. The requested financial documents were obtained from all 14 cities.

Actual expenditures were tabulated for each of the two fiscal years for five selected functions: library, parks and recreation, public safety, refuse collection and disposal, and a group of common administrative activities referred to as general government. The activities included within each function are identified in Appendix A. The adjustment of capital expenditures to annualized amounts was found to be impracticable, so major capital expenditures were excluded for the sake of comparability. Similarly, debt service was omitted from the tabulation. Although street-maintenance performance was used in the identification of high-quality-service cities, street expenditures were excluded owing to major intercity differences in reporting practices for direct and overhead expenses and the likelihood that differences in development activity would seriously distort expenditure comparisons. The two expenditure tabulations for each city (one for fiscal year 1979 and one for fiscal year 1980) were sent to the respective city managers while still in preliminary form with a request for feedback regarding the accuracy of the tables. Responses confirming the accuracy of the financial information or indicating that corrections were needed were received from the city manager or a financial or budgetary official in all 14 cities. Confirmed or corrected expenditure tabulations were used in all subsequent analyses.

In order to minimize distortions owing to any one-year expenditure anomalies, a two-year average expenditure was computed for each expenditure category in each of the 14 cities and for the aggregate of all five service categories. These average expenditures were then divided by the 1980 population figures shown in Table 5.1 to arrive at the per capita expenditures shown in Table 5.2. Per capita expenditures were found to vary from a low of $118.60 for aggregate expenditures for general government, library, parks and recreation, public safety, and refuse collection and disposal in Richardson, Texas, to a high of $260.19 in Lake Forest, Illinois. The percentage of variation was considerably greater within individual functional areas.

Per-capita-expenditure comparisons for cities with the same mix and quality of services allows distinctions to be drawn between expenditure patterns from one place to another, but nothing more. If the objective is to determine the relative efficiency of local governments or to judge managerial performance in one organization against that of others, a simple comparison of per capita expenditures, even among cities carefully matched for service mix and quality, is woe-

TABLE 5.1

1980 Population of the 14 Cities that Meet at Least Six of Seven
Quality-of-Service Standards

City	Population (1980)
Sunnyvale, Calif.	106,618
Fort Walton Beach, Fla.	20,829
Gainesville, Fla.	81,371
Saint Petersburg, Fla.	236,893
Lake Forest, Ill.	15,245
Owensboro, Ky.	54,450
Chapel Hill, N.C.	32,421
Greensboro, N.C.	155,642
Upper Arlington, Ohio	35,648
Oak Ridge, Tenn.	27,662
Austin, Tex.	345,496
Richardson, Tex.	72,496
Newport News, Va.	144,903
Roanoke, Va.	100,427

Source: U.S., Department of Commerce, Bureau of the Census, 1980 Census of Population and Housing: Advance Reports (Washington, D.C.: Government Printing Office, 1981).

fully inadequate. Population differences in per capita comparisons are treated as a simple linear relationship; factor-price differences, or the difference from one location to another in the cost of basic process inputs including labor, are ignored entirely. Under such a restricted comparison, local officials would be unjustly judged as if they had at their control the power to merge with other jurisdictions or to deannex as needed to achieve economies of size as well as the power to adjust the local cost of living. Such assumptions, of course, are absurd and seriously limit the usefulness of per-capita-expenditure comparisons, even among cities matched for service mix and quality.

Ross-Burkhead Approach to Intraorganizational
Productivity Measurement

Considerable research has been directed toward exploring the socioeconomic and political determinants of municipal expenditures,

TABLE 5.2

Ranking of Cities by Average Annual per-Capita-Service Expenditures in Fiscal Years 1979 and 1980 for Selected Municipal Functions

(in dollars)

City	General Government		Library		Parks and Recreation		Public Safety		Refuse Collection and Disposal		Aggregate[a]	
	Rank	Per Capita Expenditure	Rank	Per Capita Expenditure	Rank	Per Capita Expenditure	Rank	Per Capita Expenditure	Rank	Per Capita Expenditure	Rank	Per Capita Expenditure
Richardson, Tex.	1	10.38	5	7.56	6	18.10	1	61.56	6	21.00	1	118.60
Newport News, Va.	9	19.31	2	5.98	4	14.73	2	63.98	5	19.99	2	123.99
Chapel Hill, N.C.	8	19.24	7	9.21	3	14.29	3	65.09	3	18.36	3	126.19
Owensboro, Ky.	2	14.82	4	7.46	7	18.73	4	72.28	13	32.32	4	145.61
Oak Ridge, Tenn.	6	18.36	10	11.35	10	24.73	5	72.50	10	25.44	5	152.38
Gainesville, Fla.	7	18.43	8	9.94	2	11.89	13	101.62	7	22.13	6	164.00
Roanoke, Va.	13	37.92	6	8.27	1	11.34	9	88.99	4	18.65	7	165.16
Austin, Tex.	11	29.81	12	11.96	12	27.11	7	84.71	1	11.81	8	165.39
Fort Walton Beach, Fla.	12	35.93	3	6.16	11	25.10	6	74.33	11	28.78	9	170.29
Greensboro, N.C.	10	21.33	11	11.47	9	24.45	12	95.61	2	17.91	10	170.77
Upper Arlington, Ohio	3	17.45	14	27.77	5	17.55	10	92.46	8	22.70	11	177.93
Saint Petersburg, Fla.	5	17.79	1	4.94	8	21.16	11	95.09	14	39.45	12	178.42
Sunnyvale, Calif.	4	17.51	9	10.22	13	33.31	8	88.85	12	29.99	13	179.88
Lake Forest, Ill.	14	40.07	13	20.63	14	51.59	14	123.93	9	23.96	14	260.19

[a]Some aggregate figures differ slightly from the sum of the per capita expenditures for individual services owing to rounding.

Source: Compiled by the author.

albeit with little attention to differences in service mix and quality.
A more limited amount of research, generally of a longitudinal rather
than cross-sectional nature, has been directed toward methods of ad-
dressing or avoiding the problems of factor-price differences, quality-
of-service differences, and inadequate output measures in the analysis of municipal performance. The work of John Ross and Jesse Burkhead in measuring productivity changes over time belongs in the latter
category. Noting the deficiencies of cross-section analysis in dealing
with differences in the scope and quality of services, Ross and Burkhead developed an approach for explaining changes in expenditure by
accounting for changes in work load, cost, quality of service, and
productivity. [47] Their approach is based upon the following formula:[48]

$$\frac{\text{Expenditure in time}_2}{\text{Expenditure in time}_1} = \frac{\text{Work load in time}_2}{\text{Work load in time}_1} \times \frac{\text{Cost in time}_2}{\text{Cost in time}_1}$$

$$\times \frac{\text{Quality and productivity in time}_2}{\text{Quality and productivity in time}_1}$$

The basis for the Ross-Burkhead approach is fairly straight-
forward. Some of the change in expenditures for a local government
from one time to another may be explained by changes in work load.
Increasing or decreasing work load may be expected to affect expenditures in the same direction as the work-load change. Other changes
in expenditures may be explained in part by changes in costs: the
changing amount a local government has to pay for labor, equipment,
supplies, and other items necessary for operation. Expenditure
changes not attributable to work-load or cost changes are assumed to
be the result of changes in a third factor, essentially a residual element representing productivity changes, quality changes, and an error term reflecting any inaccuracies in cost and work-load measurement.

The work-load factor is defined as population served. Costs are
defined in terms of a cost index based upon the entry-level salary of
primary workers (for example, teachers in the case of education, case
workers in welfare, and police officers and fire fighters in public safety), representing "the cost of a basic, relatively homogeneous input
that has a high positive linear correlation with cost trends."[49] Increases or decreases in the residual factor reflect expenditures in
time$_2$ different than what could have been anticipated owing solely to
changes in work load and costs. An increase in the residual is assumed to reflect an increase in the quality of services, a decline in
productivity, or a combination of the two. Conversely, a decline in
the residual is assumed to reflect declining service quality, increased

productivity, or a combination of the two. Ross and Burkhead suggest three ways for distinguishing quality-of-service changes from productivity changes in the residual but concede that "there are no completely satisfactory ways to separate the quality-productivity component."[50] Through the use of proxies, however, they attempt to estimate that portion of expenditure change that is attributable to quality-of-service change as opposed to productivity change.

The Ross-Burkhead approach to measuring productivity change is useful and relatively simple. It reduces the need for massive data collection and relies instead upon a few relevant, relatively accessible variables for gauging productivity change. A few weaknesses, however, are evident—some of relatively minor importance, but two of major significance.

As acknowledged by Ross and Burkhead, some difficulties are involved in the selection of appropriate work-load and cost measures. Work load is assumed, for example, to be the number of students in education, the number of persons on the rolls in welfare, and the total population in police services, each of which is subject to debate as a precise measure of work load. The use of entry-level salaries as a cost index is useful as a gauge of cost changes and is reasonable given the high proportion of municipal expenditures devoted to payroll,[51] but changes in selected salaries may be construed only as cost-change indicators and not as precise measures. Furthermore, the productivity-change model assumes that cost, work load, and the residual are independent, but Ross and Burkhead acknowledge that "in the operational world of local government they are most certainly not independent."[52] Increasing costs, for example, may lead program administrators to restrict clientele or reduce the quality of service. None of these weaknesses, however, would appear to seriously undermine the usefulness of the Ross-Burkhead approach.

Two further weaknesses, on the other hand, are more substantial. The Ross-Burkhead approach is restricted to measuring productivity change in a single organization or an aggregate of organizations over time. It is impossible for citizens or city officials using this approach to determine whether their local government performs better or worse than other local governments. They may only gauge the status of the organization against itself at an earlier time. Such a restriction does little to obviate the opportunity losses owing to the gradual, incremental change characteristic of local government.

A second major weakness is the problem of separating quality changes from productivity changes in the residual. Normally, from one year to the next the impact of quality changes will not be as great as over several years. When multiyear analysis is attempted, the problem of assessing quality change and distinguishing it from productivity change grows to fairly major proportions.

A Revised Approach to Interorganizational
Productivity Comparisons

By converting the Ross–Burkhead approach from an algebraic
to a regression equation, interorganizational comparisons become
possible. By controlling for quality of service through the selection
of comparison cities matched for service mix and quality, the problem
of separating quality-of-service differences from productivity differences can be minimized in interorganizational comparisons.

Stated simply, the technique of regression provides a means of
defining by formula the relationship between two or more variables.
The product of the regression process is an equation that identifies
the line that most closely approximates the pattern of empirical observations along the dimensions of the respective variables or that
allows the projection of a dependent variable based upon the knowledge
of explanatory variables. In simple linear form, the regression equation for interorganizational productivity comparisons based upon expenditures, work load, and costs would be

$$E = a + b_1 W + b_2 C$$

where E is the projected expenditure, a is a constant, W is work
load, C is cost, and b_1 and b_2 are weights.

Expenditures may be represented either by expenditures for a
particular functional area or by expenditures for several functions in
aggregate form. Work load may be represented by total population.
Cost may be represented by an index based upon entry-level salaries
for selected municipal occupations.

Once a collection of cities is matched for service mix and quality, the actual observations for the expenditure, work-load, and cost
variables for each may be introduced into the regression computation.
The resulting computation identifies a line from which many, if not
all, of the actual expenditure observations will vary to some degree
or another. The direction of variation, or the sign of the residual,
identifies the positive or negative nature of the relative productivity
of a particular observation. The magnitude of the residual compared
with the fitted estimate, or formula-based expenditure projection,
indicates the magnitude of the positive or negative relative productivity
value.

A positive residual indicates that actual expenditures for a given
local government exceed the formula-based expectations. Since quality of service is assumed to be constant among the comparison cities,
this finding would reflect relatively low productivity. A negative
residual, on the other hand, would indicate an expenditure less than
the formula-based projection and greater than average productivity.

The ratio of the residual to the formula-based projection establishes the relative magnitude of the deviation from the projection. Reversing the sign of the residual and computing the relative magnitude ratio produces a Relative Productivity Index, as defined by the following formula:

$$P_i = -1 \, (R_i/F_i)$$

where P_i is the Relative Productivity Index score for a particular city, R_i is the residual for that city, and F_i is its fitted, or formula-based, projection of expenditure.

This discussion has been based upon an assumption of a simple linear relationship between the variables of expenditure, work load or population, and costs. Substantial research, however, has indicated that economies of scale exist in the provision of some municipal services, suggesting the inadequacy of a simple linear model. Reviewing recent literature on economies of scale, William Fox, for example, found reported size economies in fire protection for towns up to 10,000 population and in refuse collection for cities up to 20,000 residents. [53] Barbara Stevens reports economies of scale for refuse collection for cities up to 50,000 population. [54] It seems plausible, moreover, that at some organizational size, bureaucratic inefficiencies could introduce diseconomies of scale.

The regression equation may be adjusted to accommodate a curvilinear relationship between expenditure and population by taking the following form:

$$E = a + b_1 W + b_2 W^2 + b_3 W^3 + b_4 C$$

where E is the projected expenditure, a is a constant, W is work load or population, C is the cost index, and b_1, b_2, b_3, and b_4 are weights.

Regression-Based Productivity Comparison of the
14 High-Quality-Service Cities

The curvilinear multiple-regression approach to interorganizational productivity comparisons was applied to the 14 high-quality-service cities. In order to minimize distortions owing to any single-year anomalies, averages of expenditures for fiscal year 1979 and fiscal year 1980 were used. Although individual regression analysis was undertaken for each of the selected functions of general government, library, parks and recreation, public safety, and refuse collection and disposal, the overall assessment of relative productivity levels among the cities was based upon the regression analysis per-

TABLE 5.3

Starting Salaries for Selected Positions: Average Cost Index for the 1979/80 Period for the 14 High-Quality-Service Cities (in dollars)

City	Entry-Level Starting Salary, January 1, 1979			Cost Index 1979[a]	Entry-Level Starting Salary, January 1, 1980			Cost Index 1980[b]	Average Cost Index 1979/80[c]
	Police Officer	Fire Fighter	Clerk-Typist		Police Officer	Fire Fighter	Clerk-Typist		
Sunnyvale, Calif.	15,676[d]	15,676[d]	11,328	14,227	17,009[d]	17,009[d]	13,248	15,755	14,991
Fort Walton Beach, Fla.	8,863	8,039	6,781	7,894	10,025	9,089	7,467	8,860	8,377
Gainesville, Fla.	11,612	10,742	6,983	9,779	11,825	11,440	7,437	10,234	10,007
Saint Petersburg, Fla.	11,660	10,900	6,780	9,780	12,476	11,772	7,218	10,489	10,134
Lake Forest, Ill.	15,108	14,736	8,532	12,792	16,212	16,464	9,300	13,992	13,392
Owensboro, Ky.	9,971	9,971	7,277	9,073	10,868	10,868	7,932	9,889	9,481
Chapel Hill, N.C.	9,308	9,308	7,657	8,758	9,773	9,773	8,040	9,195	8,977
Greensboro, N.C.	10,896	9,876	7,740	9,504	12,240	10,566	8,280	10,362	9,933
Upper Arlington, Ohio	10,483	10,483	7,550	9,505	10,483	10,483	8,195	9,720	9,613
Oak Ridge, Tenn.	9,173	9,173	6,510	8,285	10,795	10,795	7,467	9,686	8,986
Austin, Tex.	12,264	12,264	7,717	10,748	13,008	13,008	8,112	11,376	11,062
Richardson, Tex.	12,684	12,744	7,260	10,896	14,901	14,772	7,992	12,555	11,726
Newport News, Va.	9,991	9,991	6,134	8,705	10,491	10,491	6,441	9,141	8,923
Roanoke, Va.	10,224	10,224	7,397	9,282	10,673	10,673	7,917	9,754	9,518

[a]The cost index for 1979 is the average of the starting salaries for the three selected positions for that year.
[b]The cost index for 1980 is the average of the starting salaries for the three selected positions for that year.
[c]The average cost index for 1979/80 is the average of the cost indexes for 1979 and 1980.
[d]Public safety officer.

Sources: Most police officer and fire fighter salary information was obtained from "Police, Fire, and Refuse Collection and Disposal Departments: Manpower, Compensation, and Expenditures," The Municipal Year Book 1980 (Washington, D. C.: International City Management Association, 1980), pp. 119-71; and Mary A. Schellinger, "Police, Fire, and Refuse Collection and Disposal Departments: Manpower, Compensation, and Expenditures," The Municipal Year Book 1981 (Washington, D. C.: International City Management Association, 1981), pp. 93-146. Adapted by permission. Some police officer and fire fighter salary information and all clerk-typist salary information was obtained from the personnel departments of the individual cities.

TABLE 5.4

Ranking of Cities by Percentage Deviation of Average Annual Expenditures in Fiscal Years 1979 and 1980 from Expected Expenditures Based upon Regression Equations, by Selected Municipal Functions

(in percent)

City	General Government[a]		Library[b]		Parks and Recreation[c]		Public Safety[d]		Refuse Collection and Disposal[e]		Aggregate[f]	
	Rank	Expenditure Deviation	Rank	Expenditure Deviation	Rank	Expenditure Deviation	Rank	Expenditure Deviation	Rank	Expenditure Deviation	Rank	Expenditure Deviation
Richardson, Tex.	1	-52.6	3	-35.8	4	-19.8	2	-23.4	11	26.3	1	-22.6
Newport News, Va.	9	-3.2	6	-14.6	5	-13.4	1	-25.0	3	-25.6	2	-20.6
Lake Forest, Ill.	14	2,069.2[g]	12	23.0	1	-37.3	4	-10.7	1	-73.7	3	-20.4
Chapel Hill, N.C.	5	-23.1	4	-24.9	9	8.6	3	-11.9	7	2.9	4	-11.3
Austin, Tex.	10	0.8	11	1.2	7	0.5	8	-0.4	5	-5.8	5	-0.3
Saint Petersburg, Fla.	7	-8.8	5	-20.8	6	-5.5	10	2.6	10	18.0	6 (tie)	2.4
Oak Ridge, Tenn.	4	-24.0	9	-5.6	13	83.8	5	-4.7	8	10.2	6 (tie)	2.4
Sunnyvale, Calif.	8	-4.1	10	-0.4	10	17.6	9	0.1	9	17.4	8	5.1
Greensboro, N.C.	11	11.5	13	68.2	12	28.6	11	9.1	2	-38.8	9	5.5
Owensboro, Ky.	2	-40.4	2	-38.0	11	21.8	7	-2.0	14	172.5	10	5.6
Fort Walton Beach, Fla.	12	52.1	1	-40.0	14	235.5	6	-3.9	4	-14.3	11	11.8
Roanoke, Va.	13	71.7	7	-10.6	3	-30.3	12	11.9	6	-0.1	12	13.3
Gainesville, Fla.	6	-19.7	8	-5.9	2	-30.5	14	30.9	13	43.0	13	14.1
Upper Arlington, Ohio	3	-27.9	14	117.1	8	2.1	13	21.8	12	30.4	14	20.6

(continued)

TABLE 5.4 (continued)

[a]Based upon the following equation:

General Government Expenditure $= \$287,440 + 40.567W - (1.9957W^2 \cdot 10^{-4}) + (4.9634W^3 \cdot 10^{-10}) - 66.628C$

where W (workload) = 1980 population and C (cost) = salary index average for fiscal years 1979 and 1980 ($R^2 = .950$).

[b]Based upon the following equation:

Library Expenditure $= -\$391,000 + 20.99W - (1.3512W^2 \cdot 10^{-4}) + (3.1651W^3 \cdot 10^{-10}) + 26.654C$

where W = 1980 population and C = salary index ($R^2 = .916$).

[c]Based upon the following equation:

Parks and Recreation Expenditure $= -\$1,974,400 + 8.1724W + (6.2202W^2 \cdot 10^{-5}) - (3.6536W^3 \cdot 10^{-11}) + 230.79C$

where W = 1980 population and C = salary index ($R^2 = .973$).

[d]Based upon the following equation:

Public Safety Expenditure $= -\$741,660 + 40.491W + (3.887W^2 \cdot 10^{-4}) - (7.7718W^3 \cdot 10^{-10}) + 160.78C$

where W = 1980 population and C = salary index ($R^2 = .980$).

[e]Based upon the following equation:

Refuse Collection and Disposal Expenditure $= \$512,200 - 47.521W + (6.4774W^2 \cdot 10^{-4}) - (1.4132W^3 \cdot 10^{-9}) + 108.52C$

where W = 1980 population and C = salary index ($R^2 = .868$).

[f]Based upon the following equation:

Aggregate Expenditure $= -\$2,307,500 + 62.699W + (7.6395W^2 \cdot 10^{-4}) - (1.414W^3 \cdot 10^{-9}) + 460.12C$

where W = 1980 population and C = salary index ($R^2 = .988$).

[g]When applied to the general government regression equation, Lake Forest's small population and high salaries relative to the other cities yielded a negative projected expenditure, producing a percentage deviation of unusual magnitude. No other projected expenditure for any of the services in any of the cities was negative.

Source: Compiled by the author.

taining to the aggregate expenditures for all five of the selected functions. Not only does this approach allow an overall assessment of relative productivity, it also reduces the likelihood of overlooking the organizationwide impact of factors that may on their face appear to affect only an individual service. Factors influencing a particular function in one direction of expenditure may affect other functions in the same or the opposite direction (for example, collective bargaining may result in a redistribution of outputs, as when sanitation workers' gains come at the expense of new book acquisitions for the library). [55] Therefore, the impact of collective bargaining and perhaps other factors should be examined on a broader basis than a single service function.

The regression equation for aggregate expenditures in the five selected functions for the 14 high-quality, full-service cities is as follows:

$$E = -\$2,307,500 + 62.699W + (7.6395W^2 \cdot 10^{-4})$$
$$- (1.414W^3 \cdot 10^{-9}) + 460.12C$$

where E is the projected average expenditure for fiscal years 1979 and 1980; W is work load, represented by the 1980 population; and C is cost, represented by a salary index for each city.

The 1980 population for each city was used as the work-load factor. For the cost factor, an index was constructed using the entry-level salaries in 1979 and 1980 for the positions of police officer, fire fighter, and clerk-typist. The average starting salary for the three positions in 1979 and the average for 1980 were combined in a two-year average to serve as the overall cost index used in the equation. Individual starting salaries and the cost index for each of the 14 cities are shown in Table 5.3.

The regression of aggregate expenditures on work load and cost for the 14 cities has an R^2 value of .988, indicating that 98.8 percent of the variation in aggregate expenditures for the five selected functions is explained by the variables in the equation. Aggregate expenditure deviation from the formula-based projections ranged from 22.6 percent below the projection in the case of Richardson, Texas, to 20.6 percent above the projection for Upper Arlington, Ohio. Aggregate and individual function expenditure deviations are shown in Table 5.4.

Choice of Regression Approach over
Per-Capita-Expenditure Approach

The curvilinear regression approach to interorganizational productivity comparisons is superior to the per-capita-expenditure approach for several reasons. Primarily, the regression approach is less prone to confound matters of circumstance with matters of management.

Service work load is an important determinant of employment levels[56] and expenditures, but it is unreasonable to assume a precise linear relationship between population and expenditures, with no allowances for economies or diseconomies of scale. Managers, however, are unlikely to exercise much control over community population as it affects economies or diseconomies of scale or over the differences in the cost of labor in their city relative to the cost in other cities. Per-capita-expenditure comparisons fail to adjust for economies of scale or factor-price differences. The regression approach, on the other hand, provides adjustments for both. If the purpose of analysis is the assessment of organizational performance in terms of relatively controllable variables, as is the case in this study, then a ranking of cities by per-capita-expenditure levels—with those levels heavily influenced by economies or diseconomies of scale and labor-cost differentials—is of little value. What is of value is a mechanism for determining relative productivity in the use of resources, given a community's population level and its local factor prices, or costs.

Per-capita-expenditure comparisons provide information on the relative cost of services to citizens. Regression-based comparisons can provide information on relative managerial proficiency in the efficient delivery of services, given a community's population level and local factor prices. Under the regression approach, local officials being evaluated for managerial proficiency are neither given an advantage nor penalized for serving a community of a particular size.

As indicated, per-capita-expenditure comparisons also fail to make adjustments for factor-price differentials. Once again, if the purpose of analysis is simply a determination of relative costs to the citizenry, this omission presents no problem at all. If the purpose is an assessment of organizational performance, omitting differences in the cost of basic commodities and labor from one location to another is a serious deficiency. Empirical evidence indicates that public sector wages, a major component of local government costs with a high linear correlation with cost trends,[57] are responsive to external influence (for example, labor-market conditions) or wage roll-out.[58] Surveys have revealed that by 1960 prevailing wage rates were serving at least as a guide to managerial judgment in the setting of wages in most local governments.[59] To the extent that local officials are somewhat limited in their discretion regarding major labor or commodity costs, it would seem unreasonable to make performance judgments without adjusting for this factor. The regression approach provides a means for making such an adjustment.

Two basic comparisons between the regression approach and the per-capita-expenditure approach are relevant to the choice of the former over the latter. The percentage of variation in aggregate expenditures explained by the three population factors (W, W^2, and W^3) and the cost factor in the regression approach (R^2 = .988) is 98.8 percent for the 14 cities. The percentage of variation in expenditures explained by population (W) alone (R^2 = .981), as implied in a simple per-capita-expenditure comparison, is a slightly lower 98.1 percent.* Although the R^2 for each approach is very high, more than one-third of the variation left unexplained by an assumed simple linear relationship is explained by the curvilinear regression approach.

A second useful comparison regarding the relative adequacy of the two approaches involves the degree of deviation from the norm prescribed by the respective models. As indicated in Table 5.4, deviation ranged from 22.6 percent less than the projected expenditure in one case to 20.6 percent more than the projection in another for the regression approach. The total range represented by these two extremes is 43.2 percentage points. In contrast, the average per capita expenditure (that model's expected value) from Table 5.2 is $164.20. The percentage deviation from that figure ranged from 27.8 percent less than the average to 58.5 percent more than the average, or a range of 86.3 percentage points. The fit for observations in the per-capita-expenditure approach was not nearly as good as for the regression approach.

Table 5.5 shows a modest positive relationship between rankings according to per capita expenditure and those according to the regression equation (Spearman's rank correlation coefficient = .313).[60] It is noteworthy that one city, Lake Forest, Illinois, with a small population and relatively high salaries, experienced an 11-step improvement in ranking going from the per-capita-expenditure approach to the regression approach, which made adjustments for both factors. One city experienced a seven-step adjustment, two experienced six-step adjustments, and two experienced five-step adjustments in going to the regression-based approach.

Tables 5.6 and 5.7 help to demonstrate the impact of choosing the regression-based percentage deviation ranking over the per-capita-expenditure ranking. In Table 5.6 the 14 cities are listed according to 1980 population, with the impact of going to the percentage deviation ranking shown for each in terms of steps improved or steps of decline. The smallest city enjoyed a substantial improvement.

---

*The reported R^2 of .981 pertains to the regression of expenditures on population—not to per capita expenditures per se. Both of these approaches, however, assume a simple linear relationship between the two variables rather than a curvilinear relationship as reflected in the alternate approach.

TABLE 5.5

Comparison of City Ranking by Average Annual per-Capita-
Expenditures in Fiscal Years 1979 and 1980 with Ranking by
Percentage of Deviation from Expected Expenditures Based upon
Regression Equation

City	Rank according to per Capita Expenditures[a]	Rank according to Percentage Deviation from Regression-Based Expected Expenditures[b]
Richardson, Tex.	1	1
Newport News, Va.	2	2
Lake Forest, Ill.	14	3
Chapel Hill, N.C.	3	4
Austin, Tex.	8	5
Saint Petersburg, Fla.	12	6 (tie)
Oak Ridge, Tenn.	5	6 (tie)
Sunnyvale, Calif.	13	8
Greensboro, N.C.	10	9
Owensboro, Ky.	4	10
Fort Walton Beach, Fla.	9	11
Roanoke, Va.	7	12
Gainesville, Fla.	6	13
Upper Arlington, Ohio	11	14

$r_s = .313$

[a]Ranked from lowest per capita expenditure for a collection of
selected functions to highest. See Table 5.2.

[b]Ranked from greatest negative percentage deviation to greatest
positive percentage deviation from the regression-based expected
expenditure for a collection of selected functions. See Table 5.4.

Source: Compiled by the author.

Ranking improvements were also registered for four of the five largest cities. With only one exception (no change in ranking for Richardson, Texas), all of the cities between 20,000 and 101,000 population
experienced a decline in ranking in going from a per-capita-expenditure comparison to a regression-based comparison. This pattern
suggests a curvilinear relationship between expenditures and population and demonstrates a rather systematic inadequacy of the per-capita-

expenditure approach as a means of assessing managerial proficiency.

In Table 5.7 the 14 cities are ranked according to salary index, with steps of improvement or decline again noted for each city. The division in the pattern of improvement or decline is as striking as was the case for population rankings. With only one exception, all of the cities experiencing improvement in going to the percentage deviation ranking are clustered at the high end of the salary index. When an adjustment is made for the fact that these cities experience higher labor costs, their rating relative to other cities is improved.

TABLE 5.6

Impact of Choice of Regression-Based Percentage Deviation Ranking over per-Capita-Expenditure Ranking, by City Population

City	Population (1980)	Impact
Lake Forest, Ill.	15,245	11-step improvement
Fort Walton Beach, Fla.	20,829	2-step decline
Oak Ridge, Tenn.	27,662	1-step decline
Chapel Hill, N.C.	32,421	1-step decline
Upper Arlington, Ohio	35,648	3-step decline
Owensboro, Ky.	54,450	6-step decline
Richardson, Tex.	72,496	0 (no change)
Gainesville, Fla.	81,371	7-step decline
Roanoke, Va.	100,427	5-step decline
Sunnyvale, Calif.	106,618	5-step improvement
Newport News, Va.	144,903	0 (no change)
Greensboro, N.C.	155,642	1-step improvement
Saint Petersburg, Fla.	236,893	6-step improvement
Austin, Tex.	345,496	3-step improvement

Source: Compiled by the author.

Relative Productivity Index

The 14 high-quality, full-service cities are listed once again in Table 5.8 in order of the percentage of deviation of two-year average aggregate expenditures from regression-based expenditure projections. Also shown are the rankings for fiscal year 1979 and fiscal year 1980 individually.

TABLE 5.7

Impact of Choice of Regression-Based Percentage Deviation Ranking
over per-Capita-Expenditure Ranking, by Salary Index
(in dollars)

City	Salary Index	Impact
Fort Walton Beach, Fla.	8,377.33	2-step decline
Newport News, Va.	8,923.17	0 (no change)
Chapel Hill, N.C.	8,976.50	1-step decline
Oak Ridge, Tenn.	8,985.50	1-step decline
Owensboro, Ky.	9,481.17	6-step decline
Roanoke, Va.	9,518.00	5-step decline
Upper Arlington, Ohio	9,612.83	3-step decline
Greensboro, N.C.	9,933.00	1-step improvement
Gainesville, Fla.	10,006.50	7-step decline
Saint Petersburg, Fla.	10,134.33	6-step improvement
Austin, Tex.	11,062.17	3-step improvement
Richardson, Tex.	11,725.50	0 (no change)
Lake Forest, Ill.	13,392.00	11-step improvement
Sunnyvale, Calif.	14,991.00	5-step improvement

Source: Compiled by the author.

As noted previously, the Relative Productivity Index is defined
as follows:

$$P_i = -1 \; (R_i/F_i)$$

where P_i is the Relative Productivity Index score for a particular
city, R_i is the residual for that city, and F_i is its fitted, or formula-
based, projection of expenditure. The ranking of cities by Relative
Productivity Index is shown in Table 5.9. This ranking serves as
an indicator of the relative efficiency with which these cities deliver
comparable high-quality services given the realities of their population size and labor costs.

The Relative Productivity Index has not been developed to replace the more operationally revealing performance measures described earlier in this chapter. Precise measures of unit cost and
effectiveness are needed in order to gauge progress in service improvements. In fact, the uniform collection and compilation of rigorous performance measures on a national basis would render the

TABLE 5.8

Ranking of Cities by Percentage of Deviation of Actual Expenditures from Expected Expenditures Based upon Regression Equation, for Fiscal Years 1979 and 1980, and Two-Year Average Expenditure

(in percent)

City	Fiscal Year 1979		Fiscal Year 1980		Average	
	Rank	Expenditure Deviation	Rank	Expenditure Deviation	Rank	Expenditure Deviation
Richardson, Tex.	1	-25.2	2	-20.3	1	-22.6
Newport News, Va.	3	-19.2	1	-21.8	2	-20.6
Lake Forest, Ill.	2	-23.0	3	-18.0	3	-20.4
Chapel Hill, N.C.	4	-13.7	4	-9.2	4	-11.3
Austin, Tex.	5	-0.3	6	-0.3	5	-0.3
Saint Petersburg, Fla.	6	2.1	7	2.6	6(tie)	2.4
Oak Ridge, Tenn.	10	7.9	5	-1.8	6(tie)	2.4
Sunnyvale, Calif.	8	5.7	9	4.6	8	5.1
Greensboro, N.C.	7	5.6	10	5.4	9	5.5
Owensboro, Ky.	9	7.7	8	3.8	10	5.6
Fort Walton Beach, Fla.	13	14.7	11	9.5	11	11.8
Roanoke, Va.	11	11.3	13	15.0	12	13.3
Gainesville, Fla.	12	14.0	12	14.2	13	14.1
Upper Arlington, Ohio	14	21.5	14	19.6	14	20.6

Note: Includes expenditures for general government, library, parks and recreation, public safety, and refuse collection and disposal. See Appendix A.

Source: Compiled by the author.

TABLE 5.9

Ranking of Cities by Relative Productivity Index

City	Rank	Relative Productivity Index
Richardson, Tex.	1	.226
Newport News, Va.	2	.206
Lake Forest, Ill.	3	.204
Chapel Hill, N. C.	4	.113
Austin, Tex.	5	.003
Saint Petersburg, Fla.	6 (tie)	-.024
Oak Ridge, Tenn.	6 (tie)	-.024
Sunnyvale, Calif.	8	-.051
Greensboro, N. C.	9	-.055
Owensboro, Ky.	10	-.056
Fort Walton Beach, Fla.	11	-.118
Roanoke, Va.	12	-.133
Gainesville, Fla.	13	-.141
Upper Arlington, Ohio	14	-.206

Note: The Relative Productivity Index was obtained by reversing the sign of the average expenditure deviation for fiscal years 1979 and 1980 from Table 5.8. Cities with actual expenditures that were less than those projected from the regression equation had an expenditure deviation with a negative sign. The sign has been reversed to reflect a positive Relative Productivity Index score in this table. Cities with actual expenditures greater than those projected by the regression equation have negative Relative Productivity Index scores.

Relative Productivity Index imprecise in comparison and would replace it as a preferred means of intercity comparisons. In the absence of uniformity and rigor in performance measurement, however, the Relative Productivity Index may serve as a diagnostic tool and as a dependent variable that permits the examination of the relationship between administrative and extraadministrative factors and municipal productivity. It may serve a diagnostic role in focusing managerial attention on services that rank poorly and a prescriptive role in identifying municipal counterparts where hints or even blueprints for improvement may be found. It provides a means of assessing factors that may contribute to or detract from municipal productivity by establishing the relative productivity of various cities that possess such factors to differing degrees, thereby allowing subsequent statistical analysis of their relevance.

Relative differences in the productivity-index scores from city to city may be explained by two broad categories of conditions: the degree to which pressures resistant to productivity improvement, or productivity barriers, exist in a given organization and the presence or absence of factors—managerial, legislative, or environmental—that are conducive to favorable productivity. Before substantial progress can be made in removing or reducing barriers and enhancing conditions conducive to productivity improvement, local officials must develop a keen awareness of the nature of such factors and their impact on municipal performance. The remaining chapters of this volume will be directed toward exploring administrative and extraadministrative factors potentially relevant to municipal productivity.

SUMMARY

Measures of productivity constitute only one category of the many types of performance measures available to municipal government. More complex than many of the other types of performance measures, productivity measures are compiled and maintained by relatively few cities, despite their usefulness as a gauge of municipal performance; as a means of developing performance standards; and if adopted on a wide-scale, uniform basis, as a potential means of instilling a healthy sense of competition among municipal service providers.

The difficulties in interorganizational productivity comparisons are problems of comparability and measurement. Per-capita-expenditure comparisons are often offered as measures of intercity productivity differences, but they typically ignore output differences and input reporting inconsistencies. Furthermore, as a tool for assessing municipal performance, per-capita-expenditure comparisons fail to recognize the impact of economies of scale and factor-price differences on relative performance.

A regression-based method of comparing the productivity of cities matched for municipal-service scope and quality is used in this study to avoid the inadequacies of per-capita-expenditure comparisons. By making adjustments for population size and labor-cost differences, the method employed provides a means of assessing relative productivity in the use of resources, given a community's population level and its local factor prices. The resultant Relative Productivity Index indicates a number 1 ranking for Richardson, Texas, among high-quality, full-service cities.

Differences in relative productivity among the cities may be explained by differences in the degree to which factors conducive or resistant to productivity exist in each setting, the focus of the remaining chapters of this volume. Substantial progress in productivity improvement depends upon an improved understanding of such factors and their relevance.

NOTES

1. See, for example, Clarence E. Ridley and Herbert A. Simon, Measuring Municipal Activities: A Survey of Suggested Criteria for Appraising Administration (Chicago: International City Managers' Association, 1943), p. iii.

2. Harry P. Hatry, "Performance Measurement Principles and Techniques: An Overview for Local Government," Public Productivity Review 4 (December 1980): 315-23. Reprinted with permission. Much of the discussion in this section is based on this work.

3. Public Technology, Improving Productivity and Decision-Making through the Use of Effectiveness Measures: Literature and Practice Review (Washington, D.C.: U.S. Department of Housing and Urban Development, 1979), pp. 3-4.

4. Hatry, "Performance Measurement Principles and Techniques," p. 317.

5. Ibid., pp. 321-22.

6. Robert D. Lee, Jr., and Ronald W. Johnson, Public Budgeting Systems (Baltimore: University Park Press, 1978), p. 163.

7. See, for example, National Center for Productivity and Quality of Working Life, Total Performance Management: Some Pointers for Action (Washington, D.C.: U.S. Government Printing Office, 1978).

8. Hatry, "Performance Measurement Principles and Techniques," pp. 313-14. Reprinted with permission.

9. George P. Barbour, Jr., "Measuring Local Government Productivity," The Municipal Year Book 1973, vol. 40 (Washington, D.C.: International City Management Association, 1973), pp. 41-44. Reprinted with permission.

10. Joel E. Ross, Modern Management and Information Systems (Reston, Va.: Reston, 1976), p. 133.

11. Reprinted by permission of the publisher from Productivity in Local Government by Frederick O'R. Hayes (Lexington, Mass.: Lexington Books, D. C. Heath and Company, copyright 1977, D.C. Heath and Company), p. 239.

12. Harry P. Hatry and Donald M. Fisk, Improving Productivity and Productivity Measurement in Local Governments (Washington, D.C.: Urban Institute, 1971), p. 32.

13. Rackham S. Fukuhara, "Productivity Improvement in Cities," The Municipal Year Book 1977, vol. 44 (Washington, D.C.: International City Management Association, (1977), pp. 193-200.

14. See, for example, John M. Greiner et al., Productivity and Motivation: A Review of State and Local Government Initiatives (Washington, D.C.: Urban Institute, 1981), pp. 241, 294; and John M. Greiner, "Incentives for Municipal Employees: An Update," The Municipal Year Book 1980, vol. 47 (Washington, D.C.: International City Management Association, 1980), p. 194.

15. Hatry and Fisk, Improving Productivity and Productivity Measurement, p. 25.

16. Hatry, "The Status of Productivity Measurement in the Public Sector," p. 29.

17. Charles L. Usher and Gary C. Cornia, "Goal Setting and Performance Assessment in Municipal Budgeting," Public Administration Review 41 (March–April 1981): 229-35.

18. Jerome A. Mark, "Measuring Productivity in Government: Federal, State, and Local," Public Productivity Review 5 (March 1981): 39.

19. Alan Walter Steiss and Gregory A. Daneke, Performance Administration: Improved Responsiveness and Effectiveness in Public Service (Lexington, Mass.: Lexington Books, 1980), p. 205.

20. John R. Hall, Jr., Factors Related to Local Government Use of Performance Measurement (Washington, D.C.: Urban Institute, 1978), p. 11.

21. Harry P. Hatry et al., How Effective Are Your Community Services? Procedures for Monitoring the Effectiveness of Municipal Services (Washington, D.C.: Urban Institute, 1977), pp. 235-36.

22. Ibid., p. 7.

23. Donald T. Campbell, "Reforms as Experiments," Urban Affairs Quarterly 7 (December 1971): 164.

24. Elinor Ostrom et al., "Evaluating Police Organization," Public Productivity Review 3 (Winter 1979): 22-24.

25. Frederick C. Thayer, "Productivity: Taylorism Revisited (Round Three)," Public Administration Review 32 (November–December 1972): 837.

26. For a discussion of criticisms of efficiency as a criterion of administrative decision, see Herbert A. Simon, Administrative Behavior (New York: Free Press, 1957), pp. 182-86.

27. Patrick J. Lucey, "Wisconsin's Productivity Policy," Public Administration Review 32 (November–December 1972): 796.

28. For other examples of perverse behavior in response to performance measurement, see Marc Holzer, Constance Zalk, and Jerome Pasichow, "Corrections," in Productivity Improvement Handbook for State and Local Government, ed. George J. Washnis (New

York: John Wiley & Sons, 1980), p. 1013; and Michael Lipsky, Street-Level Bureaucracy (New York: Russell Sage Foundation, 1980), pp. 166-67.

29. Hall, Factors Related to Local Government Use of Performance Measurement, p. 10.

30. For an example of the impact of unemployment on crime in an evaluation of a crime-prevention program in York, Pennsylvania, see Theodore H. Poister, James C. McDavid, and Anne Hoagland Magoun, Applied Program Evaluation in Local Government (Lexington, Mass.: D. C. Heath, Lexington Books, 1979), pp. 147-49.

31. Ibid. , p. 21.

32. Hall, Factors Related to Local Government Use of Performance Measurement, pp. 22-23.

33. Marc Holzer, ed. , Productivity in Public Organizations (Port Washington, N. Y.: Kennikat Press, 1976), p. 19; Charles Ardolini and Jeffrey Hohenstein, "Measuring Productivity in the Federal Government," Monthly Labor Review 97 (November 1974): 20; and Harry P. Hatry, "Issues in Productivity Measurement for Local Governments," Public Administration Review 32 (November-December 1972): 783.

34. Holzer, Productivity in Public Organizations, p. 19.

35. Edward K. Hamilton, "Productivity: The New York City Approach," Public Administration Review 32 (November-December 1972): 785. Reprinted with permission from Public Administration Review, © 1972 by The American Society for Public Administration, 1225 Connecticut Avenue, N. W. , Washington, D. C. All rights reserved.

36. The Urban Institute and the International City Management Association, Improving Productivity Measurements in Local Government, reprinted in Holzer, Productivity in Public Organizations, pp. 120-21.

37. John W. Kendrick, "Exploring Productivity Measurement in Government," Public Administration Review 23 (June 1963): 64-65.

38. Hatry, "Performance Measurement Principles and Techniques," pp. 336-37. Reprinted with permission.

39. See, for example, Thomas D. Morris, William H. Corbett, and Brian L. Usilaner, "Productivity Measures in the Federal Government," Public Administration Review 32 (November-December 1972): 762-63.

40. Hatry, "Performance Measurement Principles and Techniques," pp. 336-37. Reprinted with permission.

41. Simon, Administrative Behavior, pp. 188-90.

42. Hatry and Fisk, Improving Productivity and Productivity Measurement, p. 37. Reprinted with permission.

43. Mark, "Measuring Productivity in Government," p. 41.

44. National Productivity Council, Federal Actions to Support State and Local Government Productivity Improvement (Washington, D. C. : National Productivity Council, 1979), p. vii.

45. For comments regarding the varying need for precision in different types of analysis, see Jerome A. Mark, "Meanings and Measures of Productivity," Public Administration Review 32 (November-December 1972): 752-53.

46. For a review of input measurement problems, see Hatry et al. , How Effective Are Your Community Services?, pp. 238-39.

47. Ross and Burkhead credit several researchers for earlier work in a vein similar to their approach, including Werner Z. Hirsch, Analysis of the Rising Costs of Public Education (Washington, D. C. : Joint Economic Committee, U. S. Government Printing Office, 1959); Dick Netzer, "State-Local Finance in the Next Decade," in Revenue Sharing and Its Alternatives: What Future for Fiscal Federalism?, vol. 3, prepared for the Joint Economic Committee (Washington, D. C. : U.S. Government Printing Office, 1967), p. 1344; Lawrence R. Kegan and George P. Ronniger, "The Outlook for State and Local Finance," Fiscal Issues on the Future of Federalism, Committee for Economic Development Supplementary Paper no. 23 (New York: CED, 1968), pp. 231-83; Selma J. Mushkin and Gabrielle C. Lupo, "Project '70: Projecting the State-Local Sector," Review of Economics and Statistics 49 (May 1967): 234-45; "State and Local Finances Projections: Another Dimension?" Southern Economic Journal 33 (January 1967): 426-29; "Is There a Conservative Bias in State-Local Sector Expenditure Projections?," National Tax Journal 20 (September 1967): 282-91; William H. Robertson, "Financing State and Local Governments: The Outlook for 1975," New York Chapter of the American Statistical Association, April 24, 1969 (unpublished); Robert D. Reischauer in Charles L. Schultze et al. , eds. , Setting National Priorities: The 1972 Budget (Washington, D. C. : Brookings Institution, 1971), pp. 134-57; "The State and Local Fiscal Crisis in Perspective" (Washington, D. C. : Brookings Institution, 1971), pp. 1-41; and Andrew F. Brimmer, "Inflation, Private Spending, and the Provision of Public Services," 171st Commencement Exercises of Middlebury College, Middlebury, Vt. , May 30, 1971, pp. 1-20.

48. Reprinted by permission of the publisher from Productivity in the Local Government Sector by John P. Ross and Jesse Burkhead (Lexington, Mass.: Lexington Books, D. C. Heath and Company, copyright 1974, D. C. Heath and Company), chaps. 5 and 6.

49. Ibid. , p. 101.

50. Ibid. , p. 113.

51. According to Mushkin and Sandifer, approximately 40 percent of city government general funds in the mid-1970s was going toward payroll, exclusive of city contributions for retirement, health

insurance, and other fringe benefits. With these benefits included, the figure approached 50 percent. Selma J. Mushkin and Frank H. Sandifer, Personnel Management and Productivity in City Government (Lexington, Mass.: D. C. Heath, Lexington Books, 1979), p. 1.

52. Reprinted by permission from Ross and Burkhead, Productivity in the Local Government Sector, p. 107 (see note 48 above).

53. William F. Fox, Size Economies in Local Government Services: A Review, Department of Agriculture Rural Development Research Report no. 22 (Washington, D.C.: U.S. Government Printing Office, 1980), p. ii.

54. Barbara J. Stevens, "Scale, Market Structure, and the Cost of Refuse Collection," Review of Economics and Statistics 60 (August 1978): 438-48.

55. David T. Methé and James L. Perry, "The Impacts of Collective Bargaining on Local Government Services: A Review of Research," Public Administration Review 40 (July-August 1980): 368-69.

56. Richard D. Gustely, Municipal Public Employment and Public Expenditure (Lexington, Mass.: Lexington Books, 1974), p. 10.

57. Ross and Burkhead, Productivity in the Local Government Sector, p. 101.

58. Gustely, Municipal Public Employment and Public Expenditure, pp. 10, 13-14, 44, 76.

59. David Lewin, "The Prevailing-Wage Principle and Public Wage Decisions," Public Personnel Management 3 (November-December 1974): 473-85.

60. For a description of Spearman's rank correlation coefficient, see Hubert M. Blalock, Jr., Social Statistics (New York: McGraw-Hill, 1972), pp. 416-18, or another basic textbook in statistics for the social sciences.

6

COMMON BARRIERS TO
PRODUCTIVITY
IMPROVEMENT

Let every public servant know, whether his post is high or low, that a man's rank and reputation in this administration will be determined by the size of the job he does, and not by the size of his staff, his office, or his budget.

President John F. Kennedy*

The criticism of the managerial rewards system to which President Kennedy alluded is neither unfamiliar nor appropriately leveled only against the bureaucracy of the national government. Department heads in local government, like their counterparts in federal agencies, often find their personal and professional rewards to be directly related to the size of their budget and the number of persons under their supervision. An anathema to productivity improvement, such a rewards system discourages leanness in staffing and operational efficiencies in general. But perverted systems for managerial recognition and remuneration represent only a single impediment among a relatively large number of common barriers to productivity improvement.

DESCRIPTION OF PRODUCTIVITY BARRIERS

Many of the most serious and most common obstacles that threaten the success of productivity-improvement efforts are described in this chapter. Several tend to have features that overlap one another, but their sometimes subtle distinctions make each worthy of separate mention.

---

*From "State of the Union Address," January 1961.

Insufficient Analytical Skills or Analytic Staffing

The research and analysis necessary for serious, sustained productivity improvement is far from simple. Even the design of basic performance measures is often a complex task that requires a special sensitivity to the analytical needs they are intended to address. Research and analysis identify performance strengths and weaknesses, suggest explanations for each, separate the operational alternatives that are likely to work from those that are not, and ultimately lead to a recommended course of action for productivity improvement. Analytical capabilities, preferably including some statistical skills, are necessary components of such an approach.

In their 1943 work, Clarence Ridley and Herbert Simon noted the importance of statistical skills for efficient management and lamented their typical absence from city staffs. "Perhaps some day the need will be recognized of having at least one person with broad statistical training in the city hall of every city of substantial size: a person who could encourage the use of measurement techniques by departmental officers and assist them with the statistical problems involved."[1]

Decades later, proponents of greater productivity efforts still identify the shortage of adequate analytical talent as an imposing barrier to improvement.[2] Charles Levine suggests that the deficiency is not simply a matter of organizational failure to recognize the value of and to secure a particular variety of administrative skill but is much more complex. In what he terms a management science paradox, Levine describes a pattern of organizational action that defies the possibility of both having and using analytic capacity.

When organizations have slack resources, they often develop elaborate management information systems, policy analysis capabilities, and hardware and software systems. But, when resources abound, this capacity is rarely used because public agencies usually prefer to spend slack resources building and maintaining political constituencies. In a decline situation, on the other hand, maintaining and using this analytic capacity often becomes impossible for a number of reasons. The scenario goes something like this: First, the most capable analysts are lured away by better opportunities; then, freezes cripple the agency's ability to hire replacements; and finally, the remaining staff is cut in order to avoid making cuts in personnel with direct service responsibility. All the while, organizational decisions on where to take cuts will be made on political grounds with important constituencies fully mobilized to protect their favorite programs. Therefore, in brief, the management science paradox means that when you have analytic capacity you do not need it; when you need it, you do not have it and cannot use it anyway. [3]

Without sufficient analytic capability, a local government risks the possibility that such improvement efforts as develop may be misdirected and perhaps even ill advised. The more likely consequence of inadequate analytic staffing is that significant productivity efforts will rarely be attempted.

Political Factors that Influence Decision Making

Public sector agencies respond to many stimuli other than the hard facts that support one alternative over another as an efficient operational decision. The realities of local politics may supersede the facts of a given case and have a substantial impact on administrative choices, flexibility, priorities, and even mode of operation. The decision to use a private consultant in the pursuit of solutions to city problems, for instance, can be an unemotional decision based upon a cool assessment of administrative needs, or it may become a matter embroiled in political controversy. An example of the latter occurred in New York City in the summer of 1970 when even the reputable Rand Institute felt the fallout from political infighting following a series of newspaper articles that revealed the unproductive use of other consultants by the city. [4] In such instances, even the most serious and expert of consultants may have less freedom than desired to concentrate exclusively upon the analysis of the problems they were hired to address. Political considerations may affect both their efforts to conduct analysis and the likelihood of acceptance and implementation of any recommended courses of action. But the plight of consultants is only a single case in point. Any administrative decision, even when supported by the best hardheaded business logic, may be torpedoed for purely political reasons.

A particular course of action may be pursued or dropped depending upon how it will appear to subordinates or constituents—how, for example, it will play in the press. Such political decisions in turn may have symbolic effects that could impact the likelihood of organizational success in implementing efficiency measures. City councils may grant generous pay increases to lower-level employees because of the employee support and favorable press that can be generated by pay hikes for policemen, firemen, and trash collectors; but they may find pay raises for higher-paid department heads to be a political liability. [5] A politically based decision to grant suitable pay increases only to lower-level employees, however, may have organizationally damaging consequences. In cases where managerial personnel are underpaid and the best of such employees are consequently lured away from city administration, the impact of failure to provide adequate compensation may cripple efforts to improve organizational performance. Similarly, the politically inspired hiring of unqualified candidates for city jobs may symbolize to employees a shallow top-level commitment to productivity improvement and demoralize lower-level employees upon whom success depends.[6] Politically inspired decisions that are seemingly contrary to the thrust for greater economy are not likely to escape the attention of employees.

Inadequate Research, Development,
and Experimentation

Considering the magnitude of annual expenditures by state and local governments, the amount of resources committed to research, development, and experimentation designed to alleviate state and local government problems is quite small. The disjointed nature of individual governmental units has been blamed for the absence of a cohesive research-and-development program. The apparent lack of a strong and certain market for technological developments has similarly been blamed for the low level of interest by private entrepreneurs in research and development aimed at solving the problems of the cities.

Some observers recommend a coordinated research-and-development effort funded by the federal government;[7] others suggest that the base of the problem lies not simply in inadequate research-and-development funding but more fundamentally with administrators who shun an experimental approach to problem solving and refuse to learn from feedback.[8] In either case, the need for increased research and development to enhance public sector performance is clear.

Requirement of Large Initial Investment
for Productivity Efforts

Ambitious productivity-improvement efforts are almost invariably expensive—and appear especially costly at the outset, when benefits are primarily speculative. Many involve the securing of special staff members to direct the effort. Often, some of the first savings identified require the acquisition of expensive, new capital equipment or facilities. First-year savings may not offset the cost of new staff and equipment, since many productivity-improvement decisions are based upon long-term costs and savings, with the projected breakeven point a few (or even more) years following initiation.

Where pressing financial problems threaten to overwhelm a city government, the prospect of spending more this year in hopes of saving more in the years to come may be a difficult proposition to sell. The annual pressure to hold the line on budget increases typically focuses extensively upon capital items[9] and new programs, the stuff of which organizational productivity improvement is often made.

Inadequate Information Dissemination and Reluctance to Use What Is Known

Numerous calls for improved productivity information dissemination—and frequently for federal funds to support such efforts[10]—are based upon the assumption that a major barrier to productivity improvement is inadequate information. Armed with better information, the reasoning goes, local administrators will be better prepared to improve local performance.

Without question, inadequate information increases the doubts associated with operational change and reduces the likelihood that a city will be willing to take the risks involved. As Frederick Hayes notes, the "peculiar isolation" of local governments restricts the flow of information regarding best practices.

> Most of the actors in local policy determination—employees, unions, senior bureaucrats, citizens, most elected officials, and the media—are conditioned almost entirely by local experience. A worker's sense of a fair day's work and a sensible work method reflects, primarily, actual work performance. Citizen notions of reasonable city service expectations are based almost entirely on the level and character of the services they are actually receiving. What is being done is legitimized by experience; what is proposed is speculative. It is scarcely surprising that so much of local government seems governed by a kind of law of the presumptive perpetuation of established practice. [11]

Although knowledge of the successful implementation elsewhere of a change being contemplated locally may relieve some apprehension and reduce opposition, Hayes points out that "knowing, or more commonly, suspecting the truth creates no mandate to use it, gives it no protective political authority or credibility, and provides no help in implementing it through an administrative cadre that may be hostile or inept."[12] The information barrier, however, may be as much internal in local officials as external in the system in which they function. To the extent that administrators simply choose not to avail themselves of the productivity literature, little can be expected from increased dissemination. [13] To the extent, on the other hand, that the information barrier is attributable to inadequate dissemination, its removal may simply expose more clearly an even more formidable obstacle to change—reluctance to use what is known when it represents a serious challenge to the status quo.

Inadequate Information on Intracity and Intercity Performance

Related to the presumed inadequacies in the dissemination of information regarding techniques for performance improvement is the paucity of information on intracity and intercity performance. Few cities have adequate performance measurement upon which to base relevent comparisons between departments, much less between city governments. Few administrators, in fact, have more than a subjective basis for assessing their city's performance relative to others. Without comparative performance information, problem areas go unnoticed and opportunities for improvement remain unexplored.

Antiproductivity Effect of Federal Grant Provisions

Federal grant programs, designed to enhance the ability of local governments to provide public services, often include provisions that have the unintended effect of restricting productivity improvement in the services they support. Red tape and delays owing to cumbersome procedures, for example, often increase the cost of federally supported projects dramatically. Few grant programs include reward or penalty mechanisms that reward the productive or penalize the unproductive use of federal funds. Many programs restrict local administrative flexibility, prescribing procedures based upon standard practices and thereby virtually eliminating the possibility of devising improved means of service delivery. Many include maintenance-of-effort provisions, which require local governments to maintain their prior levels of effort in order to receive federal funds, thereby ensuring that federal dollars are supplementary; however, such requirements destroy much of the local incentive for development of cost-cutting techniques. Some formula-based grants actually reward local governments for increasing expenditures in a given program area. Such program features, coupled with a tendency on the part of some local officials to spend federal dollars more freely than locally raised funds, undermine the incentive for productivity improvement in affected areas. [14]

Public Perceptions regarding Changes and Benefits

Even highly successful productivity-improvement programs rarely identify singular opportunities for savings that, in their first year of implementation, produce a sizable percentage reduction in the annual municipal budget. Over the years, the savings for multiple projects can be substantial in their cumulative effect; but as individual projects and on a single-year basis, most program changes appear to produce rather trivial savings in relation to the total budget. Consequently, there is typically little public appreciation for productivity-improvement efforts. The savings simply appear to be too small to generate popular enthusiasm.

While the immediate savings from a program change may be too small to produce vocal public support, employees and clients directly affected by such a change often can mobilize substantial opposition to program modification. The opposition is frequently emotional in nature and often quite effective. [15] Depicted by opponents as an alteration that will seriously erode the quantity or quality of service and produce savings of only a few pennies on the tax rate, even the most solidly based recommendations for change may face serious challenge in a political setting. A lack of public appreciation for productivity benefits and the relative ease with which the public can be mobilized against change are factors that tend to complement one another in the unbalanced appeal that often emerges in opposition to cost-controlling program modifications.

Lack of Political Appeal

Typically, more political mileage can be gained from a successful record in securing federal funds for local needs than from the seemingly more mundane task of seeing that maximum value is obtained from the expenditure of those and other funds. [16] Productivity-improvement efforts are commonly more tedious, expensive, and time consuming, as well as less glamorous, than perhaps is anticipated in campaign rhetoric aimed at reducing the bureaucracy and cutting red tape.

Lack of Accountability

Few local government managers, particularly at the lower levels of supervision, are held accountable for operational productivity. [17]

This lack of accountability reduces the extent to which they find it necessary or even desirable to experiment with operational changes for the sake of improvement.

Lack of accountability, however, is not confined to a single level in the administrative hierarchy. Lower-level supervisors take their cues from upper management. Any lack of accountability at lower levels exists simply because higher-level managers are not held responsible, or accountable, for demanding it.

Union Resistance

Few discussions of the barriers to organizational change exclude mention of resistance by employees and, more particularly, by unions. Numerous managerially desirable practices meet stiff opposition from unions. To a large degree, the opposition reflects contrary objectives held by managers and employee groups. Whereas management tends to value merit principles and practices designed to enhance organizational efficiency, unions are interested in improving pay and working conditions—and in increasing union membership and influence. Merit principles regarding recruitment and selection of employees, promotions, classification of positions, pay, and the handling of grievances typically are considered by unions to be inequitable or inappropriate in principle or in practice. [18] Seniority, work quotas, specific job definitions, merit standards only for measurement of minimum acceptable performance levels rather than levels of excellence, and automatic pay increases without consideration of merit tend to be highly valued by unions. [19] Differential treatment based upon productivity is normally opposed. [20] Even when handled strictly through attrition and reassignment, organizational changes leading to employment reductions have been opposed by unions fearing loss of membership and dues income, reduction of employer dependence on affected work groups and corresponding loss of union power, and the possibility of further changes following the opening wedge. [21]

Union apprehension that productivity changes lead inevitably to speedups, reduced morale, and loss of jobs is perhaps symptomatic of an overall feeling of mistrust and animosity that often pervades management-labor interactions. Despite frequent expressions of bilateral willingness to cooperate, [22] management often persists in its unilateral decision making and unions continue to press their demands with a single-minded fervor and little apparent interest in public impact. [23] Management blames the unions for resultant problems, and the unions return the criticism. [24]

The effectiveness of public sector unions in pressing their demands is owing to a peculiar source of power. As noted by David Stanley,

In both public and private sectors, organized employees use power to affect the distribution of resources and the management of men and materials. In the private sector they do this primarily as employees. In the public sector they exert influence as employees, as pressure groups, and as voting citizens. "Management" officials in government, who are responsible directly or indirectly to the voters, are in this sense in a weaker position than are corporation managers in dealing with the demands of the organized employees. This three-dimensioned structure of public employee power greatly complicates the employment transaction in government and elevates it to a major problem in public administration, public law, and public finance. [25]

Employee organizations are often singled out as the primary hindrance in efforts to improve the efficiency of public operations. Is this criticism justified or are unions simply a convenient scapegoat? The answer is not readily apparent. There are numerous examples of fierce union opposition to proposed changes designed to enhance efficiency, but examples can also be found of management-labor cooperation. Furthermore, serious questions can be raised regarding whether, given a strong managerial commitment to change, union opposition is actually as formidable a barrier as popular accounts would lead one to believe. Labor's ability to present an obstacle to change is readily apparent; less apparent is the relative magnitude of that barrier.

Unions have cooperated with management in productivity-improvement efforts in several instances. [26] Confrontations, however, would appear to have been more numerous. They have normally been fierce opponents, for example, of employment reductions, civilianization of desk jobs in police departments, and the contracting out of public functions. [27] The New York City police union successfully opposed the introduction of one-person patrol cars[28] and in numerous other cities, police and fire unions have strongly opposed the implementation of the public safety officer (PSO) concept, which utilizes cross-trained police and fire personnel for both functions. The PSO programs, in fact, have been a popular battleground for union-management conflict in recent years. In some instances, implementation of the PSO program has occurred over union objections; in others, unions have mounted sufficient opposition to prevent introduction. In one Wisconsin town, fire fighters sought, but were denied, a court injunction to block the establishment of a PSO program. [29]

Researchers have found that formation of a union local tends to be associated both with increases in wages and reduction in the length of the workweek. [30] Inflexible union agreements also tend to impede the adoption of innovations.[31] In a review of 20 studies of the impact of collective bargaining, David Methé and James Perry found that collective bargaining has driven municipal expenditures upward.[32] The positive impact of unionization on pay levels, however, has been offset somewhat in large cities by its negative impact on employment, according to one of the studies that Methé and Perry reviewed.

Work rules established through union pressure often restrict management's ability to alter procedures and operational structures for the sake of efficiency. Perhaps the most excessive and restrictive set of such work rules was achieved by the Social Service Employees Union (SSEU) in a contract between the New York City Department of Social Services and the SSEU in 1967.

> The union's contract contains unusually detailed provisions on working time and free time, including: travel time to get paychecks; grace periods for handicapped employees at the beginning and end of shifts; grace periods for delays due to inadequate elevator service; dismissal at 3 p.m. if the temperature reaches 92 degrees F.; dismissal at noon if the temperature falls below 50 degrees outside and 68 degrees inside; or if it falls below those levels after 12 noon, dismissal within an hour.[33]

Still, there is reason to believe that the popular impression of union power as an impediment to public sector efficiency is overstated. Hayes notes that highly publicized public sector union-management conflicts have occurred in relatively few cities and suggests that productivity improvements are probably viewed with "equanimity, if not indifference by most municipal employees."[34] He concedes, however, that most productivity-improvement efforts have been concentrated in areas where unions are least powerful and that union problems have tended to occur where management has taken on the more militant refuse-collection and fire unions.[35] Stanley suggests that the impact of unions on local government productivity has been mixed, with various factors offsetting one another. While union-accelerated cost increases and inflexible work rules severely limit program-level options and may impair efficiency, Stanley contends that union demands for adequate staffing, equal services for all clients, and safety programs have improved program effectiveness. He further contends that unionization has perhaps improved employee performance through the psychological security gained from the existence of satisfactory grievance procedures and fringe benefits but has probably restricted personal productivity through insistance on the principle of seniority.[36]

David Morgan provides further evidence that the obstructionist power of public sector unions and their adverse impact on productivity may be overstated. He notes that the economic gains of organized public sector employees relative to those not organized have been slight and that "the percentage gains for organized public employees apparently have not exceeded the monetary benefits attained by union members in private firms."[37] He suggests, however, that the major threat of unionization may be the impact of collective bargaining on bureaucratic autonomy. "There does seem to be a real threat that stronger unions may make public employees even less responsive than ever to the voice of citizens."[38]

Fragmentation of Local Government

Local government is fragmented both functionally and geographically. Relatively small geographic areas may be subdivided into numerous municipalities that are further overlapped by multiple special districts for schools, fire protection, water and sewer services, and other specific functions. Such fragmentation is frequently criticized for the difficulties it presents to areawide planning, the confusion it generates among citizens regarding service providers and the consequent loss of accountability, the interjurisdictional fiscal disparities it perpetuates, and the inability of multiple small entities to take advantage of economies of scale. Proponents of a centralized approach to management view fragmentation of governmental units and functions as an impediment to productivity improvement.

Civil Service Restrictions

Civil service rules and regulations become barriers to productivity improvement when restrictions designed to prevent the hiring and promotional abuses of the past limit the ability of modern managers to attain maximum benefit for each tax dollar spent. Rules designed to prevent undue preferential treatment by supervisors thwart productivity gains when they prevent differential treatment and rewards for varying levels of employee performance.

As noted by Selma Mushkin and Frank Sandifer, the civil service ideal of merit employment is subject to distortion that impedes productivity advances.

Without doubt, many of the traditional systems, practices, and procedures that have grown up around the concept of merit employment pose significant barriers to improving the productivity of governments. They especially do not provide adequate incentives to managers to manage well or to employees to perform

well—in short, performance does not appear to be the central
theme of many established systems of personnel management.
This does not mean that the concepts or principles of merit employment in government should be challenged. On the contrary,
it is meant to challenge the shrouding of incompetence, inflexi-
bility, invalidity, inaccuracy, and unreasonableness in the cloak
of merit. Merit is what is needed; it frequently is not what
exists. In effect, in terms of hiring, merit should mean the
capability to perform and the likelihood of good performance;
and in other personnel management decisions, it should mean
job performance as the basis of personnel actions taken.[39]

Perverse Rewards System

As noted by President Kennedy in his 1961 statement cited at
the beginning of this chapter, a managerial rewards system based
upon budget and staff size can have a perverse impact upon productivity. Unfortunately, such a system is seemingly the norm rather than
the exception in public sector operations. All too often the public
manager who reduces staff or otherwise cuts costs receives little
personal or professional gain and can expect the savings attained to
be redirected to offset the deficit of a less efficient manager and for
his or her own budget to be reduced accordingly in subsequent years.

This perversity in the managerial rewards system, which encourages large expenditures and big staffs, has harmful effects not
only on the tax-paying public but also on underutilized employees.
Walter Balk suggests that misemployed and subemployed individuals
join efficient managers as victims of the current rewards system.

> It should be possible to have employees themselves join in an
> effort to be assigned to meaningful work. But, contrary to com-
> mon opinion, no one deals kindly with workers who complain
> about working at useless tasks or having to fake out doing a job.
> Those who speak up are often branded as trouble-makers; so
> promotions, or even retaining jobs, could be at stake. Their
> managers fear being seen as incompetent. Most supervisors
> hate to see the size of their organizations reduced as a result
> of productivity improvement because they will suffer a budget
> and responsibility penalty, rather than recognition. The pity
> of such situations is not merely economic; it strikes at the very
> core of a person's self-worth. For there are uncounted num-
> bers of employees not realizing their potential, living lives of
> quiet desperation because of a hostile agency environment and
> a lack of joint management and union initiative.[40]

Legal Restrictions

Specific legal restrictions in addition to civil service laws and union contracts have been known to block some types of motivational programs designed to enhance productivity. Working-hour variations, modified performance-appraisal techniques, shared-savings plans, and other employee incentive programs, for example, have been prohibited in some instances by federal wage and hour laws, Equal Employment Opportunity Commission (EEOC) requirements, and requirements governing the use of state and federal grant funds.[41]

Ambiguous Objectives and Lack of Performance Measurement

The operationalization of overall goals—that is, the establishment of specific, measurable performance objectives—is often quite difficult in the public sector. Objectives are often presented in ambiguous terms, expressing a vague intention to improve the quality of life as it is affected by a specific service. Without clear objectives, adequate performance measurement is impossible. Much of what passes for performance measurement in local government is strictly a tabulation of work load—the number of applications processed, the number of fires fought, the number of offenders apprehended.

The absence of clear objectives and adequate performance measurement impairs not only the ability to effect productivity improvement but also the likelihood of program success. According to Peter Drucker, the establishment of lofty objectives can be very damaging.

> The first thing to do to make sure that a program will not have results is to have a lofty objective—"health care," for instance, or "to aid the disadvantaged." Such sentiments belong in the preamble. They explain why a specific program or agency is being initiated rather than what the program or agency is meant to accomplish. To use such statements as "objectives" thus makes sure that no effective work will be done. For work is always specific, always mundane, always focused. Yet without work there is non-performance.
>
> To have a chance at performance, a program needs clear targets, the attainment of which can be measured, appraised, or at least judged.[42]

Performance Myths

Several popularly held, deep-seated beliefs regarding public employment in general and specific functional operations in particular seriously constrain the ability of public sector managers to address productivity problems. While bemoaning the unsatisfactory level of public sector performance, many persons, for example, persist in believing that public sector jobs are less demanding, can be filled with less-skilled individuals, and should command lower levels of pay than similar jobs in the private sector. Edward Hamilton defines as myth the belief "that public service should not be an equal competitor with private business for the time and talent of the best people our society produces," and he notes that adherence to that belief has begun to erode only recently.[43] With inadequate personnel resources, public sector productivity advances are likely to be modest.

Another myth may be the conviction that turnover in an organization is bad. Saul Gellerman suggests that an organization may benefit both from an accommodating attitude toward outward mobility and from turnover itself. Openness in dealing with career plans may yield increased employee respect and more orderly transition. Financial advantages to the organization from turnover accrue through minimization of the number of employees at advanced steps in their pay ranges.

> In jobs where individual productivity does not increase significantly beyond a certain experience level, pay increases beyond that point (regardless of what they are called) are merely rewards for not having quit. On the other hand, with turnover holding average experience levels down, pay is more closely tied to accomplishments; and whatever motivational effect derives from the prospect of several future pay increases operates with maximum effect on a large number of employees.[44]

Among the many popularly held beliefs that are increasingly being challenged as myths are several pertaining to the proper provision of public services, especially police services. Robert Poole cites studies by respected research organizations that challenge the value of routine preventive patrol, rapid response for most offenses, detective work beyond the interrogation of victims and witnesses, the development of massive police data-collection systems, and the advantage of two-officer patrol cars versus one-officer vehicles.[45] In each case, the evidence suggests little or no value gained from the more expensive operational option.

Reluctance to Abandon

Once initiated, public sector programs cling to life tenaciously. It is a rare administrator who recognizes and acknowledges that his or her department or agency has outlived its usefulness and leads the movement to have it abolished. More commonly, public administrators commit what Drucker calls the most damning of the administrator's deadly sins, the inability to abandon.

> The only rational assumption is that every public service program will sooner or later—and usually sooner—outlive its usefulness, at least insofar as its present form, its present objectives, and its present policies are concerned. A public service program that does not conduct itself in contemplation of its own mortality will very soon become incapable of performance. In its original guise it cannot produce results any longer; the objectives have either ceased to matter, have proven unobtainable, or have been attained. Indeed, the more successful a public service agency is, the sooner will it work itself out of the job; then it can only become an impediment to performance, if not an embarrassment. [46]

Once the value of an agency or program's output has declined substantially or has been reduced to zero, input must be reduced accordingly if productivity is not to be seriously undermined.

Short Time Horizon

The short time horizon of politicians hoping for reelection and of the typical top administrative official in local government places a premium on projects with a rapid payoff and therefore serves as an impediment to the undertaking of productivity projects having a long lead time prior to realization of major results. Worse still, their short time horizon may induce top management officials to opt for short-term gains at substantial long-term cost. [47] Apparent short-term accomplishments in program expansion, pay increases, or strike avoidance may be secured at long-term cost in the sacrifice of the city's underlying financial strength, its financial reserve, or needed capital investments of a long-term nature. "Faced with the decision to make a capital investment projected to reap benefits in four years or, with the same available resources, to put policemen on the street to fight a rising crime rate today, an elected official who must fight for reelection in two years, not surprisingly, chooses the latter." [48]

Inadequate Performance Evaluation

The absence of adequate performance and program evaluation stems from several other barriers to change, including a lack of ana-

lytic talent, the difficulties of public sector performance measurement, and the lack of accountability by managers for the productivity
of work performed under their supervision. Extensive performance
evaluation systems as well as rigorous program evaluations are expensive and subject affected employees to the risk of possible exposure
of unsatisfactory performance. Consequently, evaluation beyond a
superficial level is often avoided. By such avoidance, organizations
deprive themselves of information that could be of immense value in
targeting and designing productivity-improvement efforts.

The fantasy and reality of program evaluation are poignantly
described by Gerald Barkdoll in the following:

> The fantasy of program evaluation involves three imaginary
> characters: (1) a top executive who supports and uses the re-
> sults of evaluations to make important decisions, (2) a program
> manager who encourages and supports the evaluation of his/her
> program, and (3) a program analyst whose insightful recommen-
> dations produce "slam bang" changes in the efficiency and ef-
> fectiveness of the program.
>
> The reality of program evaluation frequently contrasts mark-
> edly with the fantasy. It includes: (1) a top executive who dis-
> trusts or ignores any evaluation done by anyone else, (2) a pro-
> gram manager who uses guerrilla or subversive tactics to thwart,
> mislead, and discredit evaluations and evaluators, and (3) pro-
> gram analysts whose efforts are equally divided between sur-
> vival and the advocacy of personal agendas with little time left
> for clinical, unbiased, independent assessment. [49]

Overselling Productivity

Overenthusiastic proponents of productivity-improvement programs may threaten the survival of the efforts they promote. [50] The
initial gains from productivity programs are frequently quite modest
and it is only after extended time and effort that cumulative accomplishments reach impressive stages. Once oversold, the expectations
of elected officials and top management become set at unattainable
levels, and the program becomes an easy mark for discrediting by
detractors.

Dominant Preference for the Status Quo

One explanation for failure of public bureaucracies to be innovative holds that dominant social classes have a preference for the status

quo. [51] If the bureaucracy reflects the will of the dominant social class and that class desires no experimentation in the provision of modified services to other classes or gives such experimentation low priority, it would be reasonable to anticipate resistance to change in such programs. Similarly, if the dominant class is satisfied with the status quo in both services provided to its members and the manner of provision, innovation is likely to be rare.

Perceived Threat to Job Security

Employees often fear productivity-improvement efforts as thinly disguised attempts to reduce employment and, therefore, as threats to job security. Such apprehension understandably reduces employee cooperation, potentially threatening program success. To combat such fears, many employers promise that no layoffs will occur as a result of improvement efforts and that any employment reductions will be handled through attrition or employee reassignment.

Absence of Market Pressures

Unlike the private sector, where failure to innovate and control costs may lead to bankruptcy, the public sector is relatively free of such marketlike pressures. [52] Firms competing in the private sector are subjected to a rewards-punishment system under which efficient, innovative companies providing highly desirable products thrive and capture an increasing share of the market, while their less-efficient, less-innovative counterparts face financial demise. Without a profit motive and with few competitors, public administrators lack the major motivational forces of the private sector. The public sector setting typically provides neither the rewards for innovation nor the punishment for failure to innovate that exists in the private sector.

Inadequate Management Commitment to Productivity

Progress in productivity improvement depends not solely upon analysts' skills in identifying problem areas and likely solutions but also upon management's commitment to follow through on productivity-improvement opportunities. The strong support of the chief executive officer is absolutely essential. Moreover, a commitment throughout the top management corps, or at least a healthy portion of it, to productivity improvement greatly improves the prospects for more than modest success. During the celebrated productivity-improvement efforts of the Lindsay administration in New York City, for example, many of the major accomplishments occurred not in Lindsay's first term but in the second, when administrators with a particularly strong commitment to innovation and improvement were placed in key posts.[53]

Risk Avoidance

With relatively few personal or professional rewards for the risk taker who succeeds and the prospect of substantial public criticism and penalties for those who fail, it is not surprising that relatively few administrators in the public sector are willing to expose themselves to the consequences of experimentation with the untested. The "relatively low risk threshold of most public officials"[54] inhibits the search for solutions to public sector problems and even limits the early implementation of innovations developed elsewhere. "Even though American history is full of cases where the opponents of change have later had to admit that the danger they feared never materialized, inertia and the unwillingness to take risks have prevented a more rapid rate of change."[55] Not only does the nature of the public sector discourage administrative or legislative risk taking, it has been suggested that "innovation is seemingly discouraged by the recruitment into civil service jobs of people with high risk avoidance."[56] If such a contention is correct, the threat to change represented by this barrier may be particularly severe.

Policy Rather than Performance Emphasis

Much of the emphasis at the points of high publicity in local government—the controversial items at city council meetings and other front-page fare—is upon the nature of local policies. In contrast, the measurement and management of day-to-day performance, as long as it remains within the relatively wide margin of acceptability, appears to be rather mundane. Consequently, elected officials, chief appointed officials, and their close subordinates tend to seek and find their personal and professional rewards in the area of policy development. As noted by Nancy Hayward and George Kuper, "The success of public administrators is often dependent on making 'good' policy decisions, and bosses don't pay attention to productivity performance indicators."[57] The high-profile nature of policy matters tends to divert the attention of local officials away from productivity-performance indicators and day-to-day operational improvements.

Bureaucratic Socialization Processes

"The socialization of new recruits by socializing agents with little interest in change" solidifies resistance to innovation in a bureaucracy. [58] Productivity-improvement programs must contend with employee opposition to change not necessarily on the grounds that the objective is undesirable but simply on the grounds that any alteration of the status quo is unsavory.

Managerial Alibis

Although managers face numerous obstacles to productivity improvement, many barriers may be found to be surmountable in a given situation if a serious effort is made to deal with them. Many managers, however, choose not to make the effort and cite political problems, the difficulties inherent in public sector personnel management, or some other reason for failure to address a productivity problem. In fact, more often than not incompetent employees can be removed, restrictive work rules can be changed, and new modes of operation can be adopted if a manager is willing to make a strong commitment to those actions. The task involved is sometimes time consuming and personally difficult. Thorough background work and careful documentation are normally required; the managerial responsibility is sometimes unpleasant, since employees are frequently upset by such actions; and there is no guarantee of success 100 percent of the time. Consequently, many managers simply refrain from the difficult and often unpleasant tasks involved in productivity improvement and find it convenient to blame the system for their "inability" to address organizational deficiencies. Hayward and Kuper report a survey of 100 federal managers conducted for the National Center for Productivity and Quality of Working Life in the mid-1970s that "revealed that the barriers so frequently cited as productivity inhibitors, such as civil service regulations and measurement, are in many cases, excuses. Government managers do not shoulder responsibilities and authority that are allowed by the system; presumably because these are unpleasant to exercise."[59] The same criticism may be leveled against administrators in local government.

Absence of Personal Rewards for Innovation and Productivity

Few material incentives exist for managerial innovation and productivity improvement. For chief executives in the public sector, pay increases are more commonly linked to other types of achievement. Few special programs exist to supplement standard civil service step increases for top management positions beneath the chief administrator in recognition of productivity-improvement accomplishments. The unfortunate norm throughout many local government organizations is pay based upon time in service in a given position rather than pay for performance.

Barriers to Monetary Incentive Plans

In addition to civil service and other legal barriers to change that frequently restrict monetary incentive plans, other factors such as employee opposition, political opposition, and funding restrictions may also reduce the likelihood of establishing such plans.[60] Employee opposition frequently focuses upon feared inequities in the administration of monetary incentive plans, particularly when such plans are based upon individual productivity. Group incentives generally have been found to be less objectionable; however, some managers and high-performing employees dislike the possibility of rewarding poor employees for the accomplishments of their fellow workers. Some objections to incentive plans are based upon fundamental beliefs regarding public service and anticipated conflict between those beliefs and an incentive program.

> Some government personnel (especially supervisors and managers) have resisted monetary incentives on the grounds that they are incompatible with the goals of public service. They feel that it is inappropriate to treat public employees like factory workers or salespersons, and they resist the idea of linking service to the public with cash awards to employees. Employees involved in providing social services and other direct help to the public seem especially concerned over the possibility that monetary incentives will lead to clients being viewed primarily in terms of how much they can contribute to an employee's earnings rather than in terms of addressing the client's own specific needs.[61]

Political reluctance to embark upon incentive programs frequently is based upon a desire by legislators to avoid relinquishing control over wage increases, to avoid major cost increases, and to avoid the possibility of adverse citizen reaction. As noted by Greiner and associates, lack of available funds and a desire to return all productivity savings to the legislature for reappropriation constitute further restrictions on the establishment of monetary incentive plans.[62]

Bureaucratic Rigidities and Fragmented Authority

Local government bureaucracies have been created less with innovation in mind than with a desire to ensure good government in the sense of equitable treatment of citizens; adherence to specified steps in the handling of requests, applications, and provision of services; and avoidance of abuse or corruption. The structural design necessary to achieve consistent compliance with these objectives tends to rely heavily upon written procedures and to place major restrictions on flexibility.

> The structure of state and local governments is a reflection of the ideas of the last wave of reformers. Rigid civil-service systems, detailed central approval requirements for almost any deviation from past program patterns, line-by-line budget controls, centralized purchasing, and competitive bidding requirements are all part of the typical structure. It is designed to maintain effective central control, to prevent unauthorized deviations in program, to preclude political decisions in employment and contracting, and to erect safeguards against fraud and embezzlement.
>
> An underlying premise or assumption in all of the above was the belief that in most state and municipal operations, we knew the right way to do things, and that, to some significant degree, we were doing things the right way. All in all, our state and local governments are superbly equipped to do tomorrow what they did yesterday. But these governments are not designed to be highly efficient, responsive, flexible, or innovative. [63]

Not only are local bureaucracies normally quite rigid, but their decision-making authority is typically fragmented, thereby further restricting the likelihood of change. As noted by Hayes,

> The multiple clearances and approvals required and the known or suspected opposition to the changes all give advance notice that the proposed change will demand considerable effort and that it may not survive the process. Within state and local bureaucracies, the most striking characteristic, in this respect, is not resistance to change but the low credibility in the possibility of change. [64]

Effectiveness, Not Efficiency

The tendency of public sector practitioners to overemphasize effectiveness to the point of virtually ignoring efficiency is a further hindrance to well-balanced productivity improvement efforts. Public sector practitioners from judges to building inspectors emphasize, or at least vocalize, quality over quantity, contending that how much they do is less important by far than how well they do it. [65] Sentiment of this sort, often supported by occupational associations, is frequently expressed in resistance to performance measurement or to efforts by outsiders to prescribe acceptable levels of service. Organizationwide fiscal problems are frequently of less concern to such employee groups than is adherence to professionally established service standards.

Supervisory Resistance

Although the successful implementation of productivity-improvement measures may be restricted by the opposition of first-line employees, either individually or as organized units, an even more serious obstacle is supervisory resistance to change. According to Hayes,

> The attitudes of department heads and civil service employees in managerial and supervisory positions probably pose a more widespread problem for productivity improvement than do employee unions. . . . Clearly, many factors are involved including resentment of external interference, reluctance to take risks, low credibility in the possibility of constructive change, the desire to protect subordinates, and more generally, the absence of any tradition of innovative management. [66]

Department heads and other supervisors thrust unwillingly into productivity-improvement programs may feel that their specialty is being intruded upon by nonspecialists; they may feel insecure in their own ability to supervise under a more rigorous work-management mode being proposed by outside analysts; and they may fear that the talk of productivity and effectiveness improvement is a guise and that the real intent is departmental staff reduction, plain and simple. The first staff or budget cut following initiation of a productivity-improvement effort may abruptly sour relations between the department affected and productivity analysts. [67]

Innovations originated outside the department may also threaten supervisors' sense of self-worth as innovators in their own right and be seen as a potential challenge to the work rules and environment that they have established over time. "In many cases, the management of an organization will be more resistant to change than the employees, particularly if the supervisors perceive that the change being made is one which they should have thought of themselves or which is contrary to previous directives for which they are exclusively responsible."[68]

Supervisors may also resist innovations suggested by their subordinates. Clair Vough suggests that the chances for organizational innovation may bear a strong negative relationship to the number of supervisory approvals necessary for implementation.

> The most effective way to kill an innovation—worse still to kill the spirit of innovation—is to require a round of approvals from above. Why? Because an innovation, while an opportunity for the innovator to make points and prove himself, almost always is seen as a threat by a higher manager who has to approve it—whether he's conscious of it or not. The higher manager has a built-in fear of and resistance to experimentation at lower levels. If the experiment works, the innovator will get the credit. If it fails, the person who approved it gets the blame.[69]

The status quo tends to be a comfortable state enjoyed by supervisors as well as by first-line employees. Changes in the status quo may be viewed as personal threats by some supervisors whose narrow view of their function does not include an efficiency-improvement component. Among their many anxieties in the face of impending change are the following:

> Line officers fear staff innovations for a number of reasons. In view of their longer experience, presumably intimate knowledge of the work, and their greater remuneration, they fear being "shown-up" before their line superiors for not having thought of the processual refinements themselves. They fear that changes in methods may bring personnel changes which will threaten the break-up of cliques and existing informal arrangements and quite possibly reduce their area of authority. Finally, changes in techniques may expose forbidden practices and departmental inefficiency. In some cases these fears have stimulated line officers to compromise staff men to the point where the latter will agree to postpone the initiation of new practices for specific periods.[70]

BARRIERS IN PERSPECTIVE

The relative importance of the various productivity barriers that have been described is a topic of debate among practitioners, analysts, and commentators. Many persist in a belief that one of the most serious threats to productivity improvement—perhaps the most serious—is employee opposition to change, and particularly union opposition. Others, including Stanley and Hayes, disagree and cite rather convincing evidence of the overstatement of union power in this regard.

Although many obstacles of a technical variety have been identified, a study by the General Accounting Office reports that the primary barriers to productivity improvement

> are political, not technical, in nature and relate to the lack of strong incentives necessary for State and local managers to overcome the significant internal barriers to change. Technical problems, such as inadquate measurement, systems and lack of trained expertise, constitute important barriers, but are secondary to basic political problems. [71]

Each of the factors noted in this chapter represents a potential barrier to municipal productivity-improvement efforts. Individually, any one factor can be a substantial obstacle to change, but their degree of potency may differ from community to community and from instance to instance. Several in effective combination can stymie movement.

The presence or absence of some of these potential barriers—for example, the extent of federal funding with its peculiar antiefficiency properties, unionization, fragmentation, and the administrative rewards system for innovation and productivity—in the 14 high-quality, full-service cities under examination is explored in Chapter 7. A detailed examination of the presence or absence of all of the factors is beyond the scope of this endeavor.

SUMMARY

In this chapter, 34 common barriers to productivity improvement in local government have been identified and described. Although many are related to technical inadequacies in municipal organizations, there is reason to believe that barriers of a political or psychological nature, especially those that influence initiative and innovation, are more serious. The degree to which selected barriers exist in the 14 study cities and their relevance to productivity will be examined in Chapter 7.

NOTES

1. Clarence E. Ridley and Herbert A. Simon, Measuring Municipal Activities: A Survey of Suggested Criteria for Appraising Admin-

istration (Chicago: International City Managers' Association, 1943), p. x.

2. See, for example, Harry P. Hatry and Donald M. Fisk, Improving Productivity and Productivity Measurement in Local Governments (Washington, D.C.: Urban Institute, 1971), pp. 8-9; Marc Holzer, ed., Productivity in Public Organizations (Port Washington, N.Y.: Kennikat Press, 1976), p. 20; and Multi-Agency Study Team, "Report to the National Productivity Council, November 1979," reprinted in Public Productivity Review 4 (June 1980): 176-77.

3. Charles H. Levine, "More on Cutback Management: Hard Questions for Hard Times," Public Administration Review 39 (March-April 1979): 180. Reprinted with permission from Public Administration Review, copyright 1979 by The American Society for Public Administration, 1225 Connecticut Avenue, N.W., Washington, D.C. All rights reserved.

4. Peter L. Szanton, "The New York City-Rand Institute," in Centers for Innovation in the Cities and States, ed. Frederick O'R. Hayes and John Rasmussen (San Francisco: San Francisco Press, 1972), pp. 189-90.

5. David T. Stanley, Managing Local Government under Union Pressure: Studies of Unionism in Government (Washington, D.C.: Brookings Institution, 1972), p. 73.

6. Walter L. Balk, "Toward a Government Productivity Ethic," Public Administration Review 38 (January-February 1978): 49.

7. See, for example, Multi-Agency Study Team, "Report to the National Productivity Council," p. 170; and General Accounting Office (GAO), State and Local Government Productivity Improvement: What Is the Federal Role? (Washington, D.C.: U.S. Government Printing Office, 1978), p. vi.

8. Peter F. Drucker, "The Deadly Sins in Public Administration," Public Administration Review 40 (March-April 1980): 103-6.

9. Roger Lubin, "Technology and Capital Investment," in Productivity Improvement Handbook for State and Local Government, ed. George J. Washnis (New York: John Wiley & Sons, 1980), p. 329. See also GAO, State and Local Government Productivity Improvement, p. iii.

10. Multi-Agency Study Team, "Report to the National Productivity Council," p. 170; and GAO, State and Local Government Productivity Improvement, p. vi.

11. Reprinted by permission of the publisher, from Productivity in Local Government by Frederick O'R. Hayes (Lexington, Mass.: Lexington Books, D. C. Heath and Company, copyright 1977, D. C. Heath and Company), pp. 287-88.

12. Ibid., p. 287. Reprinted with permission.

13. David N. Ammons and Joseph C. King, "Productivity Improvement in Local Government: Its Place among Competing Priorities," Public Administration Review 43 (March–April 1983): 113–20.

14. See, for example, GAO, State and Local Government Productivity Improvement, pp. 43–44, 49; Nancy Hayward and George Kuper, "The National Economy and Productivity in Government," Public Administration Review 38 (January–February 1978): 4; and Multi-Agency Study Team, "Report to National Productivity Council," p. 170.

15. See, for example, GAO, State and Local Government Productivity Improvement, pp. 22–23.

16. David Rogers, Can Business Management Save the Cities? The Case of New York (New York: Free Press, 1978), p. 4.

17. Price Waterhouse, Productivity Improvement Manual for Local Government Officials (New York: Price Waterhouse, 1977), p. 27.

18. Frederick C. Mosher, Democracy and the Public Service (New York: Oxford University Press, 1968), pp. 197–98.

19. See, for example, Selma J. Mushkin and Frank H. Sandifer, Personnel Management and Productivity in City Government (Lexington, Mass.: Lexington Books, 1979), pp. 92–93; Ira C. Standill, "Gas Utilities," in Productivity Improvement Handbook, ed. Washnis, p. 920; and John M. Greiner et al. , Productivity and Motivation: A Review of State and Local Government Initiatives (Washington, D.C.: Urban Institute, 1981), pp. 361, 379.

20. Walter L. Balk, "Organizational and Human Behavior," in Productivity Improvement Handbook, ed. Washnis, pp. 497–98.

21. Hayes, Productivity in Local Government, pp. 216–17.

22. See, for example, the comments of Jerry Wurf of the American Federation of State, County and Municipal Employees, as reported by Chester A. Newland, "Labor Relations," in Productivity Improvement Handbook, ed. Washnis, p. 506.

23. See, for example, Charles H. Goldstein, "Proposition 13 and Local Government Labor Relations," Western City, July 1979, reprinted in Managing with Less: A Book of Readings, ed. Elizabeth K. Kellar (Washington, D.C.: International City Management Association, 1979), p. 49; and Stanley, Managing Local Government under Union Pressure, pp. 121–22.

24. See, for example, Victor Gotbaum and Edward Handman, "A Conversation with Victor Gotbaum," Public Administration Review 38 (January–February 1978): 19–21.

25. David T. Stanley, Managing Local Government under Union Pressure: Studies of Unionism in Government (Washington, D.C.: Brookings Institution, 1972), p. 20. Reprinted with permission. For similar comments, see James W. Kuhn, "The Riddle of Inflation: A New Answer," Public Interest 27 (Spring 1972): 76.

26. See, for example, Hayes, Productivity in Local Government, p. 86; and Richard D. Bingham, The Adoption of Innovation by Local Government (Lexington, Mass.: D. C. Heath, Lexington Books, 1976), p. 153.

27. Stanley, Managing Local Government under Union Pressure, pp. 91, 97, 106.

28. Hayes, Productivity in Local Government, p. 107.

29. Greiner et al., Productivity and Motivation, pp. 307, 354.

30. Russell L. Smith and William Lyons, "The Impact of Fire Fighter Unionization on Wages and Working Hours in American Cities," Public Administration Review 40 (November-December 1980): 571.

31. Irwin Feller, Donald C. Menzel, and Alfred Engel, Diffusion of Technology in State Mission-Oriented Agencies (State College, Pa.: Pennsylvania State University, Center for the Study of Science Policy, 1974), p. 199.

32. David T. Methé and James L. Perry, "The Impacts of Collective Bargaining on Local Government Services: A Review of Research," Public Administration Review 40 (July-August 1980): 367-68.

33. Stanley, Managing Local Government under Union Pressure, pp. 110-11. Reprinted with permission (see note 25 above).

34. Hayes, Productivity in Local Government, pp. 215, 251-52. Reprinted with permission (see note 11 above).

35. Ibid., pp. 236-37.

36. Stanley, Managing Local Government under Union Pressure, pp. 138-40.

37. David R. Morgan, Managing Urban America: The Politics and Administration of America's Cities (North Scituate, Mass.: Duxbury Press, 1979), p. 253.

38. Ibid., p. 260.

39. Mushkin and Sandifer, Personnel Management and Productivity, p. 96.

40. Balk, "Toward a Government Productivity Ethic," p. 48. Reprinted with permission from Public Administration Review, copyright 1978 by The American Society for Public Administration, 1225 Connecticut Avenue, N.W., Washington, D.C. All rights reserved.

41. Greiner et al., Productivity and Motivation, p. 385.

42. Drucker, "The Deadly Sins in Public Administration," p. 103. Reprinted with permission from Public Administration Review, copyright 1980 by The American Society for Public Administration, 1225 Connecticut Avenue, N.W., Washington, D.C. All rights reserved.

43. Edward K. Hamilton, "Productivity: The New York City Approach," Public Administration Review 32 (November-December 1972): 785. Reprinted with permission from Public Administration

Review, copyright 1972 by The American Society for Public Administration, 1225 Connecticut Avenue, N. W., Washington, D. C. All rights reserved.

44. Saul W. Gellerman, "In Praise of Those Who Leave," Conference Board Record 11 (March 1974): 36.

45. Robert W. Poole, Jr., Cutting Back City Hall (New York: Universe Books, 1980), pp. 37-38, 45-46.

46. Drucker, "The Deadly Sins in Public Administration," p. 105. Reprinted with permission (see note 42 above).

47. Hayes, Productivity in Local Government, p. 219.

48. Hayward and Kuper, "The National Economy and Productivity in Government," p. 3. Reprinted with permission from Public Administration Review, copyright 1978 by The American Society for Public Administration, 1225 Connecticut Avenue, N. W., Washington, D. C. All rights reserved.

49. Gerald Barkdoll, "Type III Evaluations: Consultation and Consensus," Public Administration Review 40 (March-April 1980): 174. Reprinted with permission from Public Administration Review, copyright 1980 by The American Society for Public Administration, 1225 Connecticut Avenue, N. W., Washington, D. C. All rights reserved. See also Carl Swidorski, "Sample Surveys: Help for the 'Out-of-House' Evaluator," Public Administration Review 40 (January-February 1980): 68.

50. George P. Barbour, Jr., "Law Enforcement," in Productivity Improvement Handbook, ed. Washnis, p. 962.

51. Peter Marris and Martin Rein, Dilemmas of Social Reform (Chicago: Aldine, 1973), p. 45.

52. See, for example, Norman I. Fainstein and Susan S. Fainstein, "Innovation in Urban Bureaucracies," American Behavioral Scientist 15 (March-April 1972): 511-31; GAO, State and Local Government Productivity Improvement, p. iii; and Patrick J. Lucey, "Wisconsin's Productivity Policy," Public Administration Review 32 (November-December 1972): 796.

53. Hayes, Productivity in Local Government, pp. 105-6.

54. Alan Walter Steiss and Gregory A. Daneke, Performance Administration: Improved Responsiveness and Effectiveness in Public Services (Lexington, Mass.: D. C. Heath, Lexington Books, 1980), p. 170.

55. Jack L. Walker, "The Diffusion of Innovations among the American States," American Political Science Review 63 (September 1969): 890.

56. Fainstein and Fainstein, "Innovation in Urban Bureaucracies," p. 517.

57. Hayward and Kuper, "The National Economy and Productivity in Government," pp. 3-4. Reprinted with permission (see note 48 above).

58. Fainstein and Fainstein, "Innovation in Urban Bureaucracies," p. 517.

59. Hayward and Kuper, "The National Economy and Productivity in Government," p. 4. Reprinted with permission (see note 48 above).

60. Greiner et al., Productivity and Motivation, pp. 95-104.

61. Ibid., p. 101.

62. Ibid., pp. 95-104.

63. Frederick O'R. Hayes, "Innovation in State and Local Government," in Centers for Innovation in the Cities and States, ed. Frederick O'R. Hayes and John E. Rasmussen (San Francisco: San Francisco Press, Inc., 1972), pp. 7-8. Reprinted with permission.

64. Ibid., p. 8. Reprinted with permission.

65. See, for example, Thomas A. Mills, "Courts," in Productivity Improvement Handbook, ed. Washnis, p. 973; and Richard L. Sanderson, "Housing-Code Enforcement," in Productivity Improvement Handbook, ed. Washnis, p. 1399.

66. Hayes, Productivity in Local Government, p. 252. Reprinted with permission (see note 11 above).

67. See, for example, John R. Hall, Jr., Factors Related to Local Government Use of Performance Measurement (Washington, D.C.: Urban Institute, 1978), pp. 15-16; and Hayes, Productivity in Local Government, pp. 139-40.

68. Price Waterhouse, Productivity Improvement Manual, p. 11.

69. Clair F. Vough, Productivity: A Practical Program for Improving Efficiency (New York: Amacom, 1979), p. 191.

70. Melville Dalton, "Conflicts between Staff and Line Managerial Officers," American Sociological Review 15 (June 1950): 349. Reprinted with permission.

71. GAO, State and Local Government Productivity Improvement, p. 23.

7

COMMUNITY AND ORGANIZATIONAL CHARACTERISTICS AND MUNICIPAL PRODUCTIVITY

Government is not immune to pressure for increased productivity. Citizen resistance to increased taxation is widespread, and moreover, the legal limitations on the local power to tax often create needs for expenditure reductions. But neither the demand nor the need for productivity improvement is likely to be comparable to that in private industry.

The absence of direct competition is one factor. Another is the lack of performance standards and of data on the performance of other governments. Citizen expectations of local government are typically low, and citizens rarely have the information to either identify possible productivity-increasing changes or to demonstrate their feasibility.

Frederick O'R. Hayes*

The absence of adequate performance standards and performance data is a serious impediment to the identification of appropriate productivity-improvement steps for local governments. Furthermore, the absence of uniform performance data for multiple cities makes intergovernmental performance comparison rare. Without such information, citizens and public officials are unlikely to be able to identify on more than a subjective basis the relative strengths and weaknesses of local government performance or to prescribe changes for productivity improvement with any empirically based confidence of success.

---

*Reprinted by permission of the publisher, from Productivity in Local Government (Lexington, Mass.: Lexington Books, D. C. Heath and Company, copyright 1977 D. C. Heath and Company), pp. 12-13.

In this study, the difficulties in intercity performance comparison have been addressed through the development of quality-of-service measures for seven municipal functions and the identification of a group of full-service municipalities with consistently high marks on those measures. Only 14 cities nationwide were found to be comparable in their wide range of excellent municipally provided services in the selected functions. Upon close examination, it is apparent that the cities have many similarities in addition to their high-quality municipal services. More important for this study, they have many notable distinctions from one another. The focus of inquiry in this chapter is upon those distinctions that may be expected to have some bearing on a municipality's Relative Productivity Index score.

OVERVIEW OF THE 14 CITIES

The 14 cities tend to be attractive, desirable places, aesthetically and in terms of their economic health. For the most part, they have managed to avoid the severity of transportation, unemployment, pollution, and crime problems that have befallen so many of their counterparts. They have not, however, been problem free.

The 14 cities tend to have residents who are fairly affluent, to offer those residents abundant amenities given their size, and to be relatively devoid of the variety of industry that might be characterized as dirty. Some are bedroom communities; others tend to house government offices, other public institutions or facilities, or high-technology industries. They also tend to be the home of, or be located close to, major universities.

General Characteristics of the Communities

Sunnyvale, California, is located near the southern tip of San Francisco Bay, 40 miles south of San Francisco and 10 miles northwest of San Jose. Once an agriculturally oriented community, Sunnyvale has evolved dramatically with the development of the Santa Clara Valley electronics and aerospace industries into a high-technology city. Indicative of the nature of the community and the affluence of its residents is the fact that in 1981 the Sunnyvale Chamber of Commerce reported the price range of existing homes as $115,000 to $285,000, noting further that most new construction was of the condominium/townhouse style. The University of California at Berkeley, Stanford University, Santa Clara University, and San Jose State University are all within an hour's drive of Sunnyvale.

Fort Walton Beach, Florida, is located on the coast of the Gulf of Mexico near Pensacola in the northwestern panhandle of the state.

Although Fort Walton Beach began principally as a summer resort area and remains a major tourist spot, its development can be attributed to the establishment of the 800-square-mile Eglin Air Force Base reservation, among the largest of such military reservations in the world.

Gainesville, Florida, located on Florida's north central plain, is 50 miles from the Gulf of Mexico, 60 miles from the Atlantic Ocean, and 70 miles from the Florida-Georgia border. It is the home of the University of Florida, with a 2,000-acre main campus near the city's downtown area. Approximately one-half of the civilian labor force in Gainesville is employed in federal or state government, including the University of Florida.

Saint Petersburg, Florida, is a large, attractive city located on Tampa Bay on Florida's western coast. It is a popular vacation spot as well as the home of many industries. The Pinellas County Industry Council listed the Avionics Division of Honeywell, Inc., as Saint Petersburg's major employer in 1981.

Lake Forest, Illinois, is an affluent suburb of Chicago. Pride in quality development and attention to aesthetics dates to the early attempts of Lake Forest founders to secure the New York firm that had designed Central Park to design Lake Forest. Turned down by their first choice, they secured a St. Louis engineer and landscape architect to design the town in park fashion. Subsequent development has followed a series of planning efforts. Several Lake Forest buildings have been awarded honors for architectural excellence.

Owensboro, Kentucky, located on the Ohio River in the western Kentucky coalfields, is a regional transportation center for the agricultural, coal, and aluminum industries. The area's traditional economic base of tobacco, tobacco processing, distilleries, and agricultural production are being supplemented by developments in the aluminum industry, natural gas transmission, electronic equipment manufacturing, and synthetic fuel production.

Chapel Hill, North Carolina, is located near the center of that state. The home of the University of North Carolina, Chapel Hill is predominantly a university-oriented community. The proximity of other research institutions led to the creation of a 4,600-acre Research Triangle Park nearby, which gives the area a strong research-and-development base.

Greensboro, North Carolina, is located in the rolling piedmont section of North Carolina, 50 miles west of Chapel Hill. Its diversified economic base includes the textile, apparel, electrical and nonelectrical machinery, metals, and tobacco industries. Greensboro is the home of three private colleges, a state technical institute, and two state universities, including the University of North Carolina at Greensboro.

Upper Arlington, Ohio, is a planned residential suburb of Columbus, the state capital. Known initially as the country club district, Upper Arlington has been the place of residence of four Ohio governors. Most of its residents are employed in Columbus in governmental, managerial, technical, or educational capacities. Upper Arlington has no manufacturing industries or industrial zoning, but it does have commercial and office sectors. The campus of Ohio State University in Columbus is located nearby.

Oak Ridge, Tennessee, was developed as a secret community as part of the Manhattan Project in World War II. The local economy continues to revolve around the activities of three major federal facilities involved in various aspects of production and research, primarily in the field of nuclear energy. Located between the Cumberland and Great Smoky mountains, Oak Ridge is near Knoxville and the University of Tennessee. It is the home of the Oak Ridge National Laboratory.

Austin, Texas, located in the state's central hill country, is the state capital and home of the main campus of the University of Texas. Government employment, principally at the state level, is a major part of the community's economic base. Reportedly, seven of every ten working adults in Austin in 1981 were employed in white-collar jobs. [1]

Richardson, Texas, is a relatively affluent, predominantly residential suburb of Dallas. Located contiguous to Dallas, it is 14 miles north of that city's downtown. Many of the area's cultural and educational facilities, including nearby Southern Methodist University, are convenient to Richardson residents.

Newport News, Virginia, is located on the Virginia Peninsula near historic Yorktown and Hampton. Newport News is the home of one of the world's major shipyards, a principal factor in the local economy.

Roanoke, Virginia, is located west of the Blue Ridge Mountains and serves as a regional transportation center. Its major employer is the Norfolk and Western Railway. The Roanoke Valley is considered to be Virginia's western center for industry, trade, and medical facilities.

Form of Government

All 14 of the study cities operate under the council-manager form of government. This form differs from the strong mayor and commission forms of local government in that executive power is vested in a city manager rather than in a popularly elected mayor or in a commission with dual executive-legislative responsibilities. The council-manager form of government is generally considered less politically charged than the other forms, though the city manager serves at the pleasure of the city council and, for a variety of reasons, long tenure in office is relatively rare.

The origin of the council-manager form of government is normally associated with the appointment of Charles E. Ashburner as the first city manager of Staunton, Virginia, in 1908, and the advocacy of Richard S. Childs, which led to the adoption of the manager plan by the National Municipal League in 1915 as part of its model city charter. [2] Enthusiasm for scientific management in the 1920s, the growing reform movement and its emphasis on the need for greater efficiency in government and the elimination of corruption, and the support of prominent scholars of the period led to rapid adoption of the council-manager plan. By the 1950s the zeal for efficiency and reform had waned, but America's move to suburbia rejuvenated enthusiasm for the council-manager plan as new communities looked to the technical skills of city managers to solve the problems of rapid development. [3]

The council-manager plan was promoted as an effective means of separating legislative and administrative functions, with the city council having responsibility for the former and the city manager handling the latter. In practice, however, each party inevitably takes frequent excursions into the prescribed domain of the other, with the city manager's trips into the policy-making arena normally gaining greater attention and more-publicized expressions of resentment by elected legislators. A study by Ronald Loveridge reveals a fundamental disagreement over the manager's appropriate role in policy innovation. [4] Managers tend to perceive their roles as including policy innovation and advocacy, while council members tend to prefer a city-manager role more limited to the execution of council policy. Despite the apparent preference of most council members, the nature of the city manager's executive and advisory roles frequently thrusts the manager into the forefront of policy recommendation and development, as well as execution. Undoubtedly, some managers enjoy that aspect of their responsibilities more than do others. In a survey of city managers in cities of more than 100,000 population, however, Deil Wright found that managers tended to spend more time on, and to perceive a greater contribution through, the performance of managerial duties, rather than policy-related or community-leadership functions. [5]

Several studies have been conducted contrasting the different forms of local government. Some have examined the tendency for particular types of communities to opt for one form over others; others have attempted to identify differences in program and policy emphases associated with the various forms; and still others have explored differences in taxation and expenditure-level tendencies. For example, Robert Alford and Harry Scoble found positive associations between the council-manager form of government and growing, mobile cities with white, Anglo-Saxon, protestant populations; between the mayor-council form and industrial cities with ethnically and religiously diverse populations; and between the commission form of government and nonmobile cities with little ethnic and religious diversity, low education level, low white-collar composition, and a declining population. [6] Oliver Williams and Charles Adrian associate council-manager government with the goals of economic growth and/or amenities rather than with maintenance of traditional services or conflict arbitration. [7] Robert Lineberry and Edmund Fowler examined 200 cities of 50,000 population or greater and found tax and expenditure effort to be lower among reformed cities (those with the council-manager form and nonpartisan, at-large elections) even when taking socioeconomic characteristics into account. Socioeconomic cleavages within communities were found to be reflected in the policy preferences of unreformed cities more than in reformed cities. [8] Bernard Booms found that expenditures in Ohio and Michigan cities with populations between 25,000 and 100,000 tended to be lower in council-manager cities, leading him to suggest the possibility of greater efficiency with that form of government. [9]

The impact of the council-manager form of government vis-à-vis other forms is difficult to assess in any absolute sense. Richard Stillman notes that "despite all the heated political debate over the advantages and disadvantages of the plan itself, no empirical evidence so far indicates that council-manager government is any better or worse than other forms of municipal government at coping with the ills that beset our urban centers."[10] Harold Stone, Don Price, and Kathryn Stone examined city-manager government and concluded that absolute judgment on impact was impossible, suggesting that in some instances the use of the manager plan may have reduced unit costs while increasing the quantity and quality of services and perhaps raising the total cost to the taxpayer. [11]

Regardless of the debate among academicians over the impact of council-manager government, the council-manager form has flourished. In 1982 approximately 48 percent of all U.S. communities with populations of 10,000 or greater operated under the council-manager plan. [12] Although about half of the U.S. cities in the population range from which the 14 high-quality, full-service cities in this study were drawn are council-manager cities, all 14 of the study cities operate under that plan. Such clustering may be less the result of management prowess that elevated the quality of services overall in those 14 cities than the product of upper-middle-class community values that favor high-quality services in the functions selected and recognize the council-manager form of government as a system through which such values, for one reason or another, are likely to be protected. As noted by Emmette Redford,

> Decisions on administrative organization reflect the expectation that certain kinds of interest will be promoted by the kind of organization chosen. . . . There is no such thing as a neutral decision on these matters—even the decision to have a presumably neutral agency is a decision that certain interests shall prevail. [13]

It would be an overstatement to contend, based upon the screening process employed in this study to identify high-quality, full-service cities, that the highest quality of service is delivered only in communities with council-manager government. Cities operating under other forms of government came close to making the final list—some were eliminated not for failure to comply with the quality standards but for failure to meet the full-service-municipality criterion. Excellent services were provided for local residents in such instances, but not by a single, municipal entity. Still, the domination of the list by cities with the council-manager form of government is noteworthy.

Differences from the National Average

Descriptive statistics for the high-quality, full-service municipalities differ in important ways from national averages (Table 7.1). Based upon 1970 and 1975 census information, a reasonably consistent pattern emerges in which the high-quality, full-service cities reflect higher income, less unemployment, and more adequate housing of greater value than the national average. [14] In addition, the study cities tend to have lower percentages of elderly persons and persons of foreign stock, a lower percentage of owner-occupied housing, and a slightly greater percentage of blacks than the national average.

Comparison of per capita income in the high-quality, full-service cities with nearby major cities and with state averages further confirms the relative affluence of residents in most of the study cities (Table 7.2). With few exceptions, the 1974 per capita income in the study cities was higher than that of the closest major city and the state average. In the case of Upper Arlington the difference was enormous, with per capita income in that city almost twice the level of per capita income in Columbus and the state as a whole. The weighted average per capita income for the 12 high-quality, full-service cities for which data were available was 10 percent greater than the national average per capita income.

TABLE 7.1

Comparison of Community Characteristics in the High–Quality–
Service Cities with the United States in General

	High–Quality–Service Cities, Unweighted Average (N = 12)[a]	U. S. Summary
Percentage of population 65 years of age or older	8.8[b]	10.5[c]
Percent black population, 1970	11.7	11.1
Percent of population of foreign stock, 1970	9.3	16.5
Percentage of civilian labor force unemployed, 1970	3.4	4.4
Per capita income, 1974 (in dollars)	5,369	4,572
Median family income, 1969 (in dollars)	10,756	9,586
Percentage of families with money income in 1969 below the poverty level	8.4	10.7
Percentage of families with money income in 1969 below 125 percent of the poverty level	12.0	15.0
Percentage of families with money income in 1969 of $15,000 or more	27.5	20.6
Percentage of owner-occupied housing, 1970	60.9	62.9
Percentage of housing lacking some or all plumbing facilities, 1970	1.8	5.5
Percentage of housing with a ratio of more than one person per room, 1970	5.2	8.0
Median value of owner-occupied single family housing, 1970 (in dollars)	20,206	17,130
Median gross rent, renter-occupied housing, 1970 (in dollars)	122	110

[a]Information unavailable for two cities.
[b]1970 data.
[c]1975 data.

Source: U.S., Department of Commerce, Bureau of the Census, County and City Data Book, 1977 (Washington, D.C.: U.S. Government Printing Office, 1978).

TABLE 7.2

Comparison of 1974 per Capita Income in 14 High-Quality, Full-Service Cities, Nearby Major Cities, State Averages, and the National Average

	Per Capita Income, 1974 (dollars)	Percentage Difference from Comparison City	Percentage Difference from State Average	Percentage Difference from National Average
Sunnyvale, Calif. [a]	6,081	+1.5	+18.9	+33.0
San Francisco, Calif.	5,990			
California	5,114			
Fort Walton Beach, Fla. [a]	n.a.	n.a.	n.a.	n.a.
Mobile, Ala.	4,195			
Florida	4,815			
Gainesville, Fla. [a]	4,274	-7.4	-11.2	-6.5
Jacksonville, Fla.	4,615			
Florida	4,815			
Saint Petersburg, Fla. [a]	4,940	+13.3	+2.6	+8.0
Tampa, Fla.	4,362			
Florida	4,815			
Lake Forest, Ill. [a]	n.a.	n.a.	n.a.	n.a.
Chicago, Ill.	4,689			
Illinois	5,107			
Owensboro, Ky. [a]	4,123	-2.9	+11.1	-9.8
Evansville, Ind.	4,244			
Kentucky	3,712			
Chapel Hill, N.C. [a]	5,012	+13.4	+29.3	+9.6
Durham, N.C.	4,421			
North Carolina	3,875			

Greensboro, N.C. [a]	5,016	+3.5	+29.4	+9.7
Winston-Salem, N.C.	4,847			
North Carolina	3,875			
Upper Arlington, Ohio [a]	8,471	+95.5	+85.7	+85.3
Columbus, Ohio	4,333			
Ohio	4,561			
Oak Ridge, Tenn. [a]	5,605	+38.6	+46.7	+22.6
Knoxville, Tenn.	4,044			
Tennessee	3,821			
Austin, Tex. [a]	4,379	+21.6	+4.6	-4.2
San Antonio, Tex.	3,601			
Texas	4,188			
Richardson, Tex. [a]	6,423	+21.5	+53.4	+40.5
Dallas, Tex.	5,285			
Texas	4,188			
Newport News, Va. [a]	4,657	+10.0	-0.9	+1.9
Norfolk, Va.	4,233			
Virginia	4,701			
Roanoke, Va. [a]	5,448	+10.0	+15.9	+19.2
Richmond, Va.	4,952			
Virginia	4,701			
High-quality, full-service cities, unweighted average [b]	5,369	—	—	+17.4
High-quality, full-service cities, weighted average [c]	5,030	—	—	+10.0
United States, average	4,572	—	—	—

[a] High-quality, full-service city.

[b] Includes only the 12 high-quality, full-service cities for which data are available.

[c] Weighted using 1975 population figures; includes only the 12 high-quality, full-service cities for which data are available.

— = not applicable; n.a. = information not available

Source: U.S., Department of Commerce, Bureau of the Census, County and City Data Book, 1977 (Washington, D.C.: U.S. Government Printing Office, 1978).

CHARACTERISTICS EXAMINED

Considerable research has been directed toward variations in state and local government expenditure levels; however, unless scope and quality of services are taken into consideration, expenditure levels may reveal relatively little about productivity.[15] Perhaps of greater relevance to productivity analysis is the growing literature on innovation and its determinants.

Innovation, defined in different research projects in a variety of ways but often simply referring to a process or product that is new to the organization or jurisdiction under study, would seem to have much in common with productivity improvement.[16] Although an innovation could be a process or product that provides no productivity gains (as when an automated process is adopted that offers no apparent quality-of-service advantage and simply shifts an equivalent input requirement from labor to equipment), innovation, like productivity improvement, requires willingness and ability to alter the status quo. The applicability of innovation research to productivity-improvement research, however, is dependent in part upon the choice of innovations being examined. For example, it may be easy to conceive of a city that is innovative in the use of library security systems as also being concerned with the efficient use of resources throughout the organization. The linkage between the construction of public housing, examined as an innovation in some research, and productivity improvement seems less direct. Care must be exercised, therefore, in translating innovation determinants to productivity research. Nevertheless, the lessons of innovation research are instructive.

Based upon previous research, George W. Downs, Jr., has identified numerous organizational attributes associated with innovativeness as well as attributes of innovations themselves that are thought to influence adoptability.[17] Among the many organizational attributes identified are such characteristics as functional specialization, the existence of conflict-reducing mechanisms, participative decision making, resource availability (or slack), contact with information sources, and the presence of a crisis. Among the attributes of the innovations themselves that are thought to determine adoptability are perceived efficiency, returns to investment, clarity of results, perceived relative advantages, and the degree of commitment held for the particular innovation. Other factors found to be positively related to the adoption of innovations in other studies include city size and the degree of importance placed on the innovation by the chief administrator.[18] Richard Bingham notes that innovation research frequently emphasizes the importance of intergovernmental relations, professionalism, private sector influence, and/or slack resource availability.[19]

Frederick Hayes contends that productivity improvement in municipal government requires innovation in organizations that normally exhibit little receptivity to new ideas.[20] Under these conditions, he states, innovation (and therefore productivity improvement) requires leadership willing to take risks; managerial vision as well as analytic and evaluative capabilities; staff and employee cooperation; accommodation with the city council, unions, community groups, and other external participants; and managerial capacity for implementation.

In this chapter many organizational and community characteristics, including several identified in innovation research, are explored in an effort to identify their relationship with municipal productivity. The characteristics examined may be divided into the following categories: characteristics of the chief executives, characteristics of the organizations, managerial approaches, organizational emphases, municipal finances, city council characteristics, citizen participation, and general community characteristics.

PROFILE OF THE CHIEF EXECUTIVES

The importance of administrators, particularly the chief administrator, is often stressed in innovation research. Hayes notes that the principal factor that explains why innovations occur in some governments and not in others "is likely to be the varied incidence of entrepreneurial and innovating characteristics among mayors and city managers."[21] Everett Rogers and Floyd Shoemaker contend that innovators tend to be more educated, more cosmopolitan, more professionally oriented, and more likely to be opinion leaders than noninnovators.[22] In a review of 203 studies relating education to innovation, they report that approximately 74 percent of the studies conclude that early adopters of innovations tend to have more education than do late adopters.

Although an apparently strong relationship exists between individual characteristics and innovation, there is reason to believe that situational factors and organizational characteristics are also of considerable importance.[23] Which of the two factors, the individual or the environment, is of greater importance remains unclear. Bingham contends that other basic factors can be overridden by strong administrative attitudes toward an innovation,[24] while Downs observes that high agency autonomy, an environmental factor, positively impacts the degree to which executive ideology is a strong predictor of innovation.[25]

In this analysis, numerous city-manager characteristics in the 14 high-quality, full-service municipalities were explored. Age, education, salary, tenure, and recognition for innovation were all examined, as well as each city's record of turnover among managers and its practice of promoting managers from within the organization versus hiring from the outside. Data sources were various publications of the International City Management Association (ICMA), including The Municipal Year Book, various membership directories, and Urban Data Service reports on salaries.

The city managers in the 14 study cities tended to be somewhat older and to have achieved a higher level of formal education than their counterparts in other cities (Table 7.3). A survey conducted by the ICMA in June 1980 indicated that the average age for city managers was 42 years and that 47 percent of city managers held graduate degrees.[26] A review of the city managers serving the 14 study cities at that time reveals an average age of 44 and graduate degrees held by eight managers, or 57 percent.

In order to get a more complete image of the typical city manager in each of the 14 cities under study, 20 years of history (from 1963 through 1982) were examined.[27] For each city the characteristics of the city manager in each year were recorded as if each year's service were provided by a separate city manager. In all, 280 years of experience (20 years times 14 cities) were examined. City managers with a graduate degree served 48 percent of those years. The average age was 46 years. These 20-year characteristics, compared with the 1980 "snapshot" reported in Table 7.2, suggest little change among the study cities regarding managers' average age (a 20-year average age of 46 compared with a 1980 average of 44) but a rather substantial shift toward managers with greater formal education (a 20-year average of 48 percent had graduate degrees compared with a 1980 average of 57 percent).

TABLE 7.3

Comparison of Age and Education of City Managers in the 14 High-Quality, Full-Service Cities with Age and Education of City Managers in General

	High-Quality, Full-Service Cities, 1980	ICMA Survey, 1980
Average age (years)	44	42
Graduate degree (percent)	57	47

Sources: International City Management Association, Directory of Members, 1981-1982 (Washington, D.C.: ICMA, 1981); and idem, "Our Profession: Today's Profile," ICMA Newsletter (supp. 2), November 2, 1981. Adapted by permission.

The hiring practices of city councils were found to differ sharply in regard to their tendencies, on the one hand, to recruit city managers from outside the organization or, on the other, to either promote from within or hire city managers who had served their city previously in some other capacity and left to join another organization for some period of time. Two cities, Lake Forest and Greensboro, were served during the 20 years reviewed only by city managers with previous experience in those cities. Three cities, the three Florida cities, were served only by city managers who had acquired all of their previous municipal experience elsewhere. Hiring practices in the remainder of the cities fell between the two extremes, with 47 percent of the 280 years examined being served by city managers with previous experience in a different position within the same city government. Approximately a third of the cities exhibited a balanced practice of hiring from both outside and within the organization. Those five cities were served during 6 to 14 of the 20 years examined (30 percent to 70 percent of the period) by a city manager with previous service in a lesser position in the same city government.

From 1963 through 1982 the 14 cities had an average of 3.43 different city managers apiece. The most by any city was five; the fewest, two. A slightly different period of time was examined for each of the cities in an effort to review tenure patterns. Incumbent city managers in 1982 were eliminated from consideration, since their tenure was incomplete. At the other end of the time span, prior service in the same post was included in the computation for city managers serving in 1963 (for example, a city manager serving a particular community from 1960 through 1965 would be given credit for six years rather than simply the three-year period from 1963 through 1965). The tenure patterns so computed reflect relatively lengthy service for city managers. The mean tenure was 11.4 years. The average was influenced by extremely long periods of service by some managers, in some cases by incumbents in 1963. For three cities the mean tenures were 24, 23, and 19 years. The briefest mean tenure for any of the study cities was 5.3 years.

The city managers in the 14 cities tended to be relatively well compensated, with an average salary in 1981 of $48,252 for the 12 city managers for whom salary information was readily available.[28] Their salaries were approximately 7 percent more than those of their average counterparts within the same city size and region. Their salaries were an average of 362 percent greater than the 1979–80 salary index for entry-level police officer, fire fighter, and clerk-typist positions in the same cities.

The city managers serving the 14 cities tended to be regarded highly by their peers. One measure of such regard is receipt of an ICMA Management Innovation Award for special achievement in the

TABLE 7.4

Pearson Product-Moment Correlation between Characteristics of the
City Manager and the Relative Productivity Index

Characteristic	N	r
Balanced practice of promoting city managers from within and hiring from outside the organization, 1963-82[a]	14	.605**
Employment of an ICMA Management Innovation Award recipient	14	-.435*
Deviation of city-manager salary from average salary index for selected employee classifications in same city	12[b]	-.421*
Number of different managers, 1963-82	14	.358
Number of city managers 1963-82 who served in city being examined at least seven years	14	.327
Number of city managers 1963-82 who served in city being examined at least six years	14	.265
Previous service by city manager in another position in the same city	14	.246
Deviation of city-manager salary from median city-manager salary for city size and region	12[b]	.224
Deviation of city-manager salary from mean city-manager salary for city size and region	12[b]	.217
Average age of city manager, 1963-82	14	-.206
Number of city managers 1963-82 who served in city being examined at least eight years	14	.180
Median tenure, 1963-82 (excluding incumbent)	14	-.084
Salary, 1981	12[b]	.073

Characteristic	N	r
Number of city managers 1963–82 who served in city being examined at least five years	14	.063
Number of city managers 1963–82 who served in city being examined at least ten years	14	.062
Number of city managers 1963–82 who served in city being examined at least 15 years	14	-.061
Number of city managers 1963–82 who served in city being examined at least 20 years	14	.057
Mean tenure, 1963–82 (excluding incumbent)	14	.026
Average education, 1963–82[c]	14	-.010
Number of city managers 1963–82 who served in city being examined at least nine years	14	-.006

r = Pearson product-moment correlation

*p < .10 (one-tailed test)
**p < .025 (one-tailed test)

[a]If during 30 percent to 70 percent of the years from 1963 through 1982 the city had a city manager who held a previous position in that organization, the city was coded 1; otherwise, it was coded 0 for purposes of computing the correlation with the Relative Productivity Index.

[b]N = 12 owing to nonreporting by two cities.

[c]Each year in which a city had a city manager with a graduate degree was scored 1. Other years were scored 0. The average education level of the city managers from 1963 to 1982 for a given city is the mean of those scores.

Sources: International City Management Association, The Municipal Year Book, vols. 30–49 (Washington, D.C.: ICMA, 1963–82); idem, Directory of Members (Washington, D.C.: ICMA, various editions); idem, "Salaries of Municipal Officials for 1981," Urban Data Service Report 13, no. 3; and idem, Salaries $25,000 and Over for City Managers/Chief Administrative Officers as of 1 January 1981 (Washington, D.C.: ICMA, 1981).

implementation of programs demonstrating innovation in effective problem solving. Of the 94 Management Innovation Awards granted by the ICMA from 1968, the year of the award's inception, through 1981, a total of eight, or 8.5 percent, were awarded to six city managers with service in six, or approximately 43 percent, of the high-quality, full-service cities.

In what fashion and to what degree are these city-manager characteristics related to municipal productivity? Pearson product-moment correlations were computed to determine the relationship between selected characteristics and the Relative Productivity Index scores for the 14 cities. Three characteristics were found to be significantly related to the index at $p < .10$ (Table 7.4). Although statistical significance for purposes of inference seems less essential in this study than in some others (since the 14 cities constitute the universe of high-quality, full-service cities rather than a sample), it is possible that some inferences regarding statistically significant findings may be made to cities with similar high-quality services but a narrower range of functions or to cities that narrowly missed the high-quality-service standards. Furthermore, the common statistical significance thresholds provide a degree of confidence that the observations and relationships are unlikely to be chance occurrences that would not have existed had the observations been made at a different point in time. For this inquiry, the conventional significance threshold of .05 is relaxed somewhat to .10 in recognition of the relatively small number of study cities (N = 14) and the statistical ramifications of dealing with a small number of observations.

A negative relationship was found between the percentage deviation of the city manager's salary from the salary index for police officer, fire fighter, and clerk-typist entry-level salaries in the same organization and that organization's Relative Productivity Index score. Cities with large deviations tended to rank lower on the Relative Productivity Index. With a correlation of -.421, the relationship is significant at the .10 level.

Those cities that have employed a recipient of an ICMA Management Innovation Award also tend to rank lower on the Relative Productivity Index (r = -.435; significant at $p < .10$). Innovation is considered necessary for effective productivity improvement, so this result is somewhat surprising. It is useful, however, to consider the nature of the ICMA awards. Although some Management Innovation Awards are granted for productivity improvement, many are awarded for new programs and program enhancements. While it is true that the managers so recognized are considered to be progressive in their field, the orientation that typically leads to Management Innovation Awards may differ in most instances from the quiet pursuit of efficiency in everyday departmental activities.

The strongest correlation between any of the city-manager characteristics and the Relative Productivity Index ($r = .605$; significant at $p < .025$) was for the tendency to have a balanced practice in the hiring of city managers from within and outside the organization. Those cities that from 1963 through 1982 were served between 30 percent and 70 percent of the time by city managers who had previously held a lesser position within the same organization tended to have a higher score on the Relative Productivity Index than did cities with an imbalance, relatively speaking, of service either by city managers promoted from within or returning to the organization or by city managers hired from outside the organization.

Although lacking statistical significance at the .10 level, correlations for city-manager age and tenure are also worthy of mention. A negative correlation was found for age, indicating that the more productive cities among the 14 tended to be served by younger city managers. In combination, the correlations pertaining to tenure suggest a modest, positive association between relative productivity and a moderate rate of turnover among city managers. The strongest correlations between tenure and relative productivity were found for the number of different managers serving a given city and the number of city managers with at least seven years of service, both of which were positively related to the Relative Productivity Index. The first suggests the desirability of occasional turnover and the influx of new ideas; the second reveals the importance of stability in organizational leadership and council-manager relations. Relative productivity correlations tend to move toward zero for cities with numerous managers with shorter tenure periods (for example, five years) and for cities with several managers with longer tenure (for example, ten years) or one or more with extremely long tenure (for example, 20 years).

PROFILE OF THE ORGANIZATIONS

Various management writers have characterized organizations according to the nature of interaction within and between various levels of the organization as evidenced in communication patterns, confidence in subordinates, participatory or nonparticipatory decision making, teamwork, and degree of centralization or decentralization. Douglas McGregor characterized two distinct management perspectives, which influence interaction patterns, as theory X and theory Y.[29] Managers operating under theory X perceive employees to be lacking in creativity, opposed to change, indifferent to the organization's goals, and motivated by threat of punishment. Managers subscribing to theory Y, on the other hand, tend to believe that work can be made enjoyable, that employees desire responsibility, that individual and organizational goals can be made to coincide, that employees are intelligent and can be flexible and creative, and that they can be motivated by nonmonetary as well as monetary factors.

Robert Blake and Jane Mouton contribute the idea that managers and their organizations may be characterized according to a two-dimensional "managerial grid" designating management's concern for production and its concern for people. [30] The best management, according to Blake and Mouton, is team management, in which high concern for production coexists with high concern for people.

Another useful distinction among organizations is offered by the work of Rensis Likert. Identifying four organizational types, Likert defined a series of continua on which an organization's operating characteristics may be identified as exploitive-authoritative (system 1), benevolent-authoritative (system 2), consultative (system 3), or participative group (system 4). [31] For example, if an organization's information flow is always downward, it is considered to be system 1. If information flow is just mostly downward, it is a system 2 organization; if down and up, system 3; and if down, up, and with peers, system 4.

In this analysis, 11 of Likert's continua were used in a questionnaire mailed to the assistant city manager or assistant to the city manager in the 14 high-quality, full-service municipalities (see sample questionnaires, Appendix B). Respondents were asked to rank their organization along each continuum. None of the continua were labeled by system numbers or descriptive titles (such as exploitive-authoritative) and the direction of some of the continua were reversed in the questionnaire to avoid a patterned response. Each respondent was assured of the confidentiality of individual responses.

In addition to survey responses on the Likert continua, information was secured from personnel directors regarding department-head education and degree of municipal unionization (see sample questionnaires, Appendix B). Responses were secured from all 14 cities for both questionnaires.*

Responses by assistant city managers to the questions regarding the profile of their organizations indicate that the 14 municipalities tend to operate in the system 3 and system 4 range, or what Likert terms consultative or participative group fashion (Figure 7.1). The mean score for most operating characteristics lies at the approximate

---

*A survey of four city officials—city manager, assistant city manager or assistant to the city manager, personnel director, and city clerk—from each of the 14 high-quality, full-service cities provided much of the basic data for this study. The survey was conducted from November 1981 to March 1982. Follow-up letters and telephone calls produced a response rate of 100 percent.

juncture between system 3 and system 4. Exceptions are the slightly lower mean ratings for the extent to which personnel at all levels feel responsibility for organizational goals (continuum 2b) and the extent to which decision making is dispersed rather than concentrated at the top of the organization (continuum 5a), and the somewhat higher mean rating for the amount of cooperative teamwork present within the organizations (continuum 4).

In most of the organizations, supervisors were perceived to have substantial confidence in subordinates, rewards were reportedly mixed with occasional punishment, and a fairly substantial proportion of personnel were perceived to feel responsibility for organization goals. In terms of the communication processes in the 14 cities, information was typically reported to flow downward and upward; downward communication was normally accepted but, if not, was sometimes openly questioned; and the information was perceived to be generally accurate but sometimes influenced by what top management wanted to hear. Teamwork was reported to be fairly substantial; however, broad policy decisions were generally thought to be made at the top of the organization with more specific decisions being made at lower levels. The decision-making process was perceived to provide some motivation for implementation of decisions and goal setting was reported to normally occur following some discussion with subordinates. Finally, control data pertaining to accounting, productivity, costs, and so forth, tended to be used for self-guidance, coordinated problem solving, and some policing, but with emphasis normally on rewards rather than on punishment.

In addition to responses to the Likert organization profile questions, information was also obtained regarding the extent of unionization within the municipal organizations and the formal education level of department heads. Unionization of fire department employees was more extensive than for other employee groups among the 14 cities, with formal employee unions for fire department personnel reported in seven cities, informal employee associations in four cities, and no permanently organized effort for fire department employees reported in three cities. Formal employee unions were reported for police department employees in four cities, for public works employees in four cities, for office workers in two cities, and for other employees in three cities. The least organized workers, either formally or informally, were office workers, with ten cities reporting no permanently organized effort by this category of employees. Two cities indicated formal unions in all five categories (fire, police, office workers, public works, and other), while three indicated no permanently organized effort in any of the five categories.

Department heads in the 14 cities were reportedly well educated (Table 7.5). On average, approximately 73 percent had a college degree, with many also having a graduate degree.

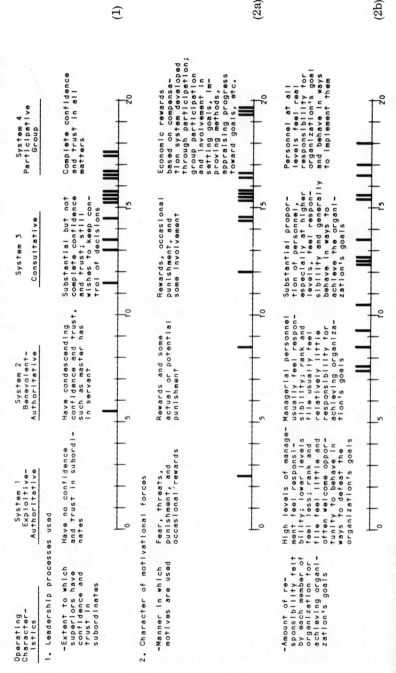

FIGURE 7.1

Distribution of Answers for High-Quality, Full-Service Cities on Likert Organization Profile Questions

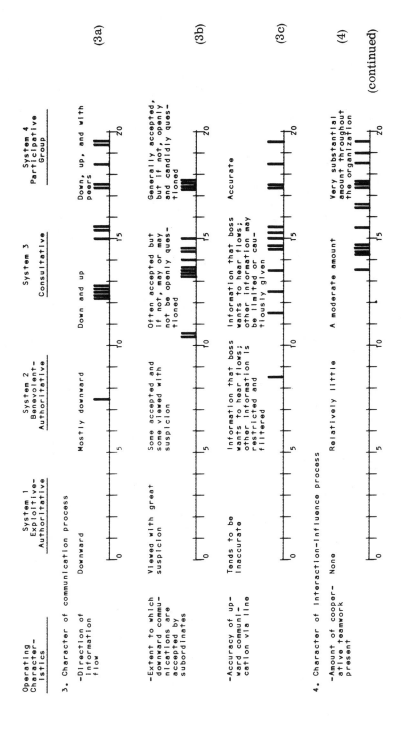

Operating Characteristics	System 1 Exploitive-Authoritative	System 2 Benevolent-Authoritative	System 3 Consultative	System 4 Participative Group	
3. Character of communication process					
—Direction of Information flow	Downward	Mostly downward	Down and up	Down, up, and with peers	(3a)
—Extent to which downward communications are accepted by subordinates	Viewed with great suspicion	Some accepted and some viewed with suspicion	Often accepted but if not, may or may not be openly questioned	Generally accepted, but if not, openly and candidly questioned	(3b)
—Accuracy of upward communication via line	Tends to be inaccurate	Information that boss wants to hear flows; other information is restricted and filtered	Information that boss wants to hear flows; other information may be limited or cautiously given	Accurate	(3c)
4. Character of interaction-influence process					
—Amount of cooperative teamwork present	None	Relatively little	A moderate amount	Very substantial amount throughout the organization	(4)

(continued)

FIGURE 7.1 (continued)

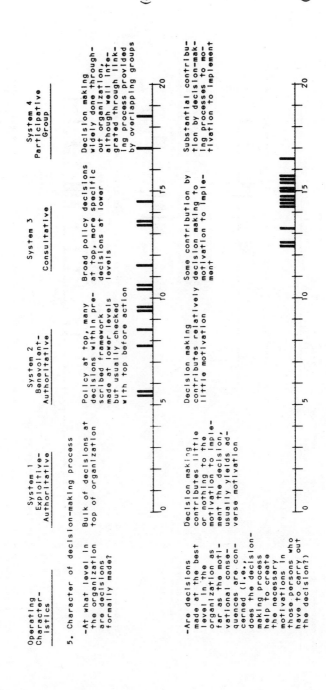

Operating Character- istics	System 1 Exploitive- Authoritative	System 2 Benevolent- Authoritative	System 3 Consultative	System 4 Participative Group
5. Character of decision-making process				
-At what level in the organization are decisions formally made?	Bulk of decisions at top of organization	Policy at top, many decisions within prescribed framework made at lower levels but usually checked with top before action	Broad policy decisions at top, more specific decisions at lower levels	Decision making widely done throughout organization, although well integrated through linking process provided by overlapping groups

(5a)

-Are decisions made at the best level in the organization as far as the motivational consequences are concerned (i.e., does the decision-making process help to create the necessary motivations in those persons who have to carry out the decision?)	Decision making contributes little or nothing to the motivation to implement the decision, usually yields adverse motivation	Decision making contributes relatively little motivation	Some contribution by decision making to motivation to implement	Substantial contribution by decision-making processes to motivation to implement

(5b)

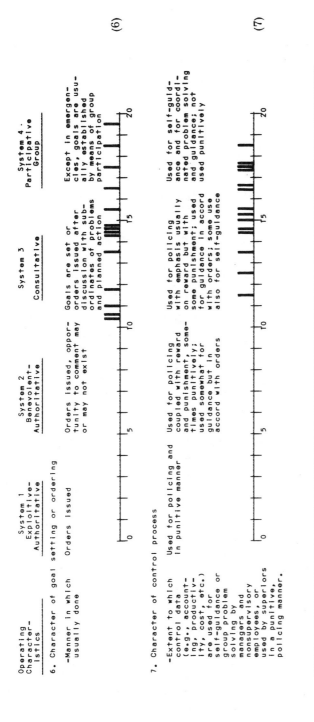

Note: The continua on which the study cities were rated were developed by Rensis Likert. See Rensis Likert, The Human Organization: Its Management and Value (New York: McGraw-Hill, 1967). Used with permission.

175

TABLE 7.5

Formal Education Level of Department Heads in the 14 High–Quality,
Full–Service Cities

Education Level	Unweighted Mean
Percentage with graduate degree	30. 6
Percentage with college degree but no graduate degree	42. 4
Percentage with some college but no degree	11. 2
Percentage with high school diploma but no college	15. 6
Percentage with less than high school education	0. 2
Total	100. 0

Note: As estimated by personnel directors in the 14 cities.

Source: Compiled by the author.

Only three of the characteristics revealed by the raw Likert question scores, unionization information, or information on the formal education level of department heads were found to be significantly correlated with the Relative Productivity Index at the . 10 level (Table 7. 6). The percentage of department heads with a high school diploma but no college was found to be correlated negatively with the Relative Productivity Index (r = -. 383; significant at p < . 10). Surprisingly, the extent to which information within an organization was perceived by respondents to flow upward and with peers, as well as downward, was negatively correlated with the index (r = -. 426; significant at p < . 10) and the extent to which cooperative teamwork was perceived to be present was also negatively correlated with the Relative Productivity Index (r = -. 581; significant at p < . 025).

A possible explanation for the negative correlation between multidirectional communication flow and the Relative Productivity Index pertains to the importance of clarity of information for organizational efficiency and effectiveness.[32] It is possible that an emphasis on downward communication could enhance information clarity. The implications of this finding, however, should not be overstated. None of the 14 organizations reported exclusively downward information flow and only one reported flow to be mostly downward. The results suggest only that some productivity advantages may exist with moderation in the extent of multidirectional communication flow.

TABLE 7.6

Pearson Product–Moment Correlation between Organizational
Characteristics and the Relative Productivity Index

Characteristic	N	r
Amount of cooperative teamwork present	14	-.581**
Extent to which information flows upward and with peers as well as downward	14	-.426*
Percentage of department heads with high school diploma but no college[a]	14	-.383*
Extent to which goal setting is participatory	14	-.329
Extent of unionization, office workers	14	-.301
Formal education level of department heads, aggregate index[b]	14	.281
Accuracy of upward communication via line	13	-.256
Extent to which decision making is dispersed rather than concentrated at the top	14	-.233
Extent to which control data (for example, accounting, productivity, and so forth) are used for self-guidance or group problem solving rather than for punishment	14	.213
Percentage of department heads with some college but no degree[a]	14	.175
Extent to which downward communications are accepted by subordinates	14	-.168
Percentage of department heads with college degree but no graduate degree[a]	14	.154
Extent of unionization, public works employees	14	-.132
Extent of unionization, aggregate	14	-.116
Extent of unionization, other employees	14	-.116

(continued)

TABLE 7.6 (continued)

Characteristic	N	r
Extent to which personnel at all levels feel responsibility for organizational goals	14	-.114
Extent of unionization, fire department employees	14	.107
Extent of confidence in subordinates	14	.103
Extent to which decision-making process contributes to motivation to implement	13	-.090
Percentage of department heads with graduate degree[a]	14	.066
Extent of unionization, police department employees	14	-.051
Overall profile of organizational characteristics[c]	12	-.050
Extent of motivation through rewards rather than punishment	14	-.031
Percentage of department heads with less than high school education[a]	14	.014

r = Pearson product-moment correlation

$p < .10$ (one-tailed test)

$p < .025$ (one-tailed test)

[a]The figure indicated is the correlation between the percentage and the Relative Productivity Index, not the percentage itself.

[b]The aggregate index of department-head education level for each city was determined by multiplying the percentage of department heads at a given education level, as estimated by the personnel director, times a score for that level and adding all the products together. The scoring of education levels was as follows: less than high school diploma = 0; high school diploma = 1; some college = 2; college degree = 3; graduate degree = 4.

[c]The overall profile of organization characteristics is the average score of responses to Likert questions in the following seven categories: leadership processes, character of motivational forces, character of communication process, character of interaction-influence process, character of decision-making process, character of goal setting, and character of control process. Where more than one question was asked in a given category, the mean response was used in the computation of the profile.

Source: Compiled by the author

Caution should also be exercised in interpreting the finding regarding teamwork and productivity, since all of the organizations reported either a moderate or a substantial amount of teamwork. None of the respondents reported relatively little or no teamwork, so there is no basis upon which to conclude that teamwork has no place in a productive organization—only that moderation may be conducive to productivity. Moderation may be especially important at the initial stages of developing ideas for productivity improvement. Group review can be deadly for raw ideas. Furthermore, Hayes reports that group decision processes frequently extend the time prior to implementation.[33] Properly focused, however, group involvement can refine concepts, improve plans, and enhance the likelihood of success. Carefully directed teamwork, with involvement at the proper stages of development, differs substantially from aimless committee work and incessant rap sessions. The distinction is an important one.

Although failing to achieve statistical significance at the .10 level, a consistent pattern of negative correlations with relative productivity is evident for a particular group of characteristics. Negative correlations for participative goal setting, the extent to which decision making is dispersed rather than concentrated at the top, and the extent to which personnel at all levels feel responsible for organizational goals, coupled with the statistically significant negative correlation for multidirectional communication flow, suggest some support for the findings of Robert Yin, Karen Heald, and Mary Vogel that successful innovations tend to occur more frequently in centralized organizations[34]—support, that is, to the extent that innovation and productivity are related.

In addition to examining the raw scores from the Likert questions another approach was taken using standardized Z scores of the organization profile responses. Assuming that each organization among the 14 examined has relative strengths and weaknesses as well as some aspects of organizational relationships that are emphasized and some that receive little emphasis, it is useful to examine how the 11 operating characteristics were rated in relationship to each other within each municipality. A mean of all the operating-characteristic ratings was calculated for each city. Z scores were then computed for the 11 ratings in each city. Each Z score reflects an operating-characteristic rating in terms of its distance in standard deviations from the mean score for all operating characteristics in a particular city. The more positive the Z score, the more system 4-like the operating characteristic was perceived to be relative to other characteristics; the more negative the Z score, the less system 4-like. On average, the amount of cooperative teamwork present had the greatest Z score, at .772. The lowest average Z score was −1.243, for the extent to which decision making was perceived to be dispersed rather than concentrated at the top of the organization.

TABLE 7.7

Pearson Product-Moment Correlation between Elements of
Standardized Organizational Profile (Z Scores of Organizational
Characteristics) and the Relative Productivity Index

Element	N	r
Extent to which the use of control data (for example, accounting, productivity, and so forth) for self-guidance or group problem solving rather than for punishment is emphasized or perceived as a relative strength	14	.596***
Extent to which confidence in subordinates is perceived as a relative strength	14	.493**
Extent to which information flowing upward and with peers as well as downward is emphasized or perceived as a relative strength	14	-.409*
Extent to which cooperative teamwork is emphasized or perceived as a relative strength	14	-.309
Extent to which decision-making dispersal, rather than concentration at the top, is emphasized or perceived as a relative strength	14	-.278
Extent to which the contribution of the decision-making process to motivation to implement is emphasized or perceived as a relative strength	13	.224
Extent to which the accuracy of upward communication via the line is perceived as a relative strength	13	-.150
Extent to which the acceptance of downward communications is perceived as a relative strength	14	.121
Extent to which a feeling of responsibility for organizational goals by personnel at all levels is perceived as a relative strength	14	-.042
Extent to which motivation through rewards rather than punishment is emphasized or perceived as a relative strength	14	.025
Extent to which participatory goal setting is emphasized or perceived as a relative strength	14	-.004

r = Pearson product-moment correlation

*p < .10 (one-tailed test)
**p < .05 (one-tailed test)
***p < .025 (one-tailed test)

Source: Compiled by the author.

Examining the relative strengths, weaknesses, and organizational emphases through the use of Z scores reveals three factors that are significantly related to the Relative Productivity Index at the .10 level (Table 7.7). The extent to which an organization's multidirectional information flow was perceived as a relative strength was negatively correlated with the Relative Productivity Index ($r = -.409$; significant at $p < .10$). On the other hand, the degree to which an organization's confidence in subordinates was perceived as a relative strength was found to be positively related to the index ($r = .493$; significant at $p < .05$). Furthermore, the extent to which emphasis was placed upon the use of control data for self-guidance or group problem solving, rather than for punishment, was strongly correlated in a positive fashion with the Relative Productivity Index ($r = .596$; significant at $p < .025$).

MANAGEMENT APPROACHES

Management approaches refer to some of the particular techniques used by organizations in pursuing their objectives. Such techniques include contracting for services,[35] volunteerism, pay flexibility, and other employee incentives;[36] and the establishment of a special unit within the organization with special responsibility for productivity improvement.[37] The techniques employed may have a distinctly behavioral flavor (for example, organizational development, job enrichment, employee motivation, and so forth), an industrial engineering emphasis (for example, work measurement, job simplification, procedures improvement, and so forth), or some blend of the two.

Information on employee incentives in the 14 study cities, their use of volunteerism, the existence of special productivity-improvement efforts, and the tendency of those cities attempting productivity improvement to emphasize either behavioral or industrial engineering techniques was obtained by surveying personnel directors. Information regarding contracting for services, pay flexibility for administrators, and the organizational structure of productivity-improvement efforts was secured by means of a questionnaire mailed to the city managers (see sample questionnaires, Appendix B). As with other city officials, questionnaire responses were received from all 14 city managers.

Survey responses revealed a wide variety of management approaches in the 14 cities. Various types of incentives were found to be used in certain cities and in certain functional areas more extensively than in others. For example, six cities reported the use of suggestion awards, while the other eight indicated that a suggestion-award program was not in use at the time of the survey. Five cities reported the use of safety incentives, while nine cities indicated that no such program existed in their organization. Attendance incentives (such as annual bonuses for unused sick leave, conversion of unused sick leave to additional terminal leave, and so forth) were reportedly available for fire department employees in six cities, for police department employees in five cities, for public works employees in five cities, and for other employees in four cities. Four cities reported the use of attendance incentives in all four employee categories, while seven cities reported the availability of no attendance incentives for any employee group.

Education incentives were reported for all four employee categories included on the questionnaire (fire, police, public works, and other) in 11 cities. One city reported the availability of education incentives for three of the employee groups and two cities reported availability for two of the groups. Two cities reported work-hour variation (for example, flextime, four-day workweek, and so forth) for at least some of the employees in all four of the employee groups, while 5 of the 14 cities reported no work-hour variation other than typical shift arrangements in public safety functions within their organizations. The standard workweek in 13 of the cities was reported to be 40 hours. In one city the standard was 37.5 hours per week.

Relatively modest use of task systems and job enrichment techniques was found among the 14 cities. Not surprisingly, no task-system usage was reported for any of the fire or police departments. Seven cities reported the use of task systems for some public works department employees; two reported task systems for some "other" employees; and five cities reported no use of task systems. The reported use of job enrichment techniques was especially low. One city reported job enrichment techniques for all four employee groups; one reported job enrichment for one of its employee groups; and twelve cities reported no use of job enrichment techniques whatsoever.

Another type of incentive, directed specifically toward managerial employees, involves managerial rewards. Eleven city managers indicated some flexibility available to them in granting managerial awards, while three indicated no such flexibility. Specific types of reward flexibility included total flexibility to establish pay levels within specified pay ranges, reported by seven city managers; the ability to advance deserving administrators extra steps within their specified pay range, reported by five city managers; nonmonetary recognition, reported by five city managers; and the ability to grant one-time bonuses, in two cities, Lake Forest and Newport News. Several cities offered more than one type of managerial incentive.

Volunteerism has been suggested as a potential means of meeting citizen demands for services while minimizing resource requirements. The reported use of volunteers differs among the 14 cities. Personnel directors in two cities, for example, perceived greater-than-average use of volunteers in their communities' municipal libraries. Only average use of library volunteers was reported in 6 cities, less-than-average in 1 city, and no library volunteerism in 5 of the 14 cities. Average use of volunteers was reported in the fire departments of 4 cities, less than average in 2 cities, and no fire department volunteerism in 8 of the 14 cities. Greater-than-average use of volunteers in a police department setting was reported for Austin and Greensboro, while at the other extreme, no police department volunteerism was reported for 7 of the 14 cities. In the parks activity, greater-than-average volunteerism was reported for Greensboro, while 10 cities reported no use of volunteers in their parks programs. The remaining cities had intermediate levels of parks volunteerism reported.

Contracting with private companies or other governmental entities for the provision of municipal services is a technique frequently identified as a potential means of reducing costs. Once again, considerable variation among the cities was reported in the use of this management approach for the delivery of services. For example, Sunnyvale, Gainesville, and Oak Ridge reported that primary refuse-collection services were provided through a contractor, Austin reported supplemental services through a contractor, and the other ten cities reported no contracting for refuse collection. Lake Forest and Richardson reported that primary legal services to the city were provided by contract, six cities reported supplemental services by contract, and six cities reported no contracting for legal services. Five cities reported primary custodial services provided through contract, three reported supplemental services, and six reported no custodial service contracting.

The manner in which internally operated functions were staffed was explored through an examination of employment levels in police and fire departments as well as through a review of the use of civilians in those operations. On average, the 14 cities employed approximately 37 police and fire personnel per 10,000 population in 1980 (unweighted average). Again on average, approximately 87 percent of all police and fire employees were uniformed personnel.

Finally, the existence of a special productivity-improvement effort in the cities was explored. City managers were asked how the productivity-improvement effort in their organization was structured. Three indicated that their city's effort was unstructured and that improvements occurred as opportunities arose. Three others reported that productivity-improvement efforts were decentralized, with department heads being held accountable for improvements on a regular basis. The other eight city managers reported that primary productivity efforts were centralized through a special office or unit with responsibility for serving as a catalyst for organizationwide productivity improvement. Of those eight, four reported the productivity-improvement unit's existence in the budget office, two in a department of management services, and two in the city manager's office. [38]

Personnel directors were also asked about the existence of a perceptible productivity-improvement effort in their municipality. Eleven responded that such an effort existed, while three perceived nothing special to be occurring in that regard. Of the eleven reporting special efforts, seven characterized those efforts as mostly of a behavioral nature, two reported a primarily industrial engineering approach, and two reported approximately equal amounts of each.

Relatively few of the management approaches examined were found to be significantly correlated with the Relative Productivity Index (Table 7.8). Of the various incentives, only three were found to be significant at the .10 level. Mixed results were found in the use of task systems, with a positive correlation for public works task systems ($r = .386$; significant at $p < .10$) and a negative correlation for the "other employees" category ($r = -.382$; significant at the $p < .10$ level). Among the managerial rewards, the one-time bonus was found to be highly correlated in a positive fashion with the index ($r = .637$; significant at the .025 level). Although lacking statistical significance at the .10 level, small negative correlations with the Relative Productivity Index were found for job enrichment techniques and suggestion awards and small positive correlations for work-hours variation, education incentives, and safety incentives. Mixed results were found for attendance incentives. An aggregate score on the extent of usage of employee incentives in general was found to be virtually unrelated to the Relative Productivity Index ($r = .09$).

Volunteerism was found to have a significant correlation with the index only for the use of volunteers in the police department, and that correlation was negative ($r = -.437$; significant at the .10 level). The use of library volunteers had a fairly strong positive relationship to the index ($r = .359$) but fell just short of significance at the .10 level.

The direction of correlation between the use and extent of contracting and the Relative Productivity Index fluctuated from service area to service area. The only statistically significant relationship at the .10 level was found in contracting for legal services. Cities that contracted for legal services tended to be among the more productive of the cities ($r = .373$; significant at the .10 level). Extent of contracting for legal services was even more strongly correlated to the Relative Productivity Index ($r = .597$; significant at the .025 level). Although lacking statistical significance at the .10 level, positive correlations with the Relative Productivity Index were found

TABLE 7.8

Pearson Product-Moment Correlation between Selected Management
Approaches and the Relative Productivity Index

Management Approach	N	r
Use of attendance incentives		
Fire department employees	14	-.073
Police department employees	14	.077
Public works department employees	14	.072
Other employees	14	.137
Aggregate	14	.056
Use of education incentives		
Fire department employees	14	.000
Police department employees	14	.000
Public works department employees	14	.102
Other employees	14	.349
Aggregate	14	.249
Use of job enrichment techniques		
Fire department employees	14	-.106
Police department employees	14	-.067
Public works department employees	14	-.106
Other employees	14	-.106
Aggregate	14	-.101
Use of suggestion awards	14	-.289
Use of safety incentives	14	.288
Use of task system		
Fire department employees	14	.000
Police department employees	14	.000
Public works department employees	14	.386*
Other employees	14	-.382*
Aggregate	14	.123
Use of work hours variation (flextime, four-day workweek, and so forth)		
Fire department employees	14	.327
Police department employees	14	.032
Public works department employees	14	.039
Other employees	14	.210
Aggregate	14	.174
Use of attendance incentives, education incentives, job enrichment, suggestion awards, safety incentives, task system, work-hours variation	14	.090
Managerial reward flexibility	14	-.058

(continued)

TABLE 7.8 (continued)

Management Approach	N	r
Managerial rewards		
Extra steps in pay range	14	-.051
Total flexibility within pay range	14	.017
One-time bonus	14	.637**
Nonmonetary recognition	14	.307
Other rewards	14	.095
Aggregate	14	.333
Standard workweek (number of hours)	14	-.242
Use of volunteers[a]		
Library	14	.359
Fire department	14	-.025
Police department	14	-.437*
Recreation	14	-.055
Parks	14	.027
Other	14	.041
Aggregate	14	-.028
Use of contracting[b]		
Street construction	14	.236
Street maintenance	14	-.291
Park maintenance	14	-.041
Recreation services	14	-.219
Police	14	-.267
Fire	14	.000
Library	14	-.267
Refuse collection	14	-.232
Legal services	14	.373*
Planning services	14	-.108
Custodial services	14	.061
Other	14	.219
Aggregate	14	-.071
Extent of contracting[c]		
Street construction	14	.358
Street maintenance	14	-.328
Park maintenance	14	-.041
Recreation services	14	-.219
Police	14	-.267
Fire	14	.000
Library	14	-.267
Refuse collection	14	-.259
Legal services	14	.597**
Planning services	14	-.129

Management Approach	N	r
Extent of contracting (continued)		
Custodial services	14	.124
Other	14	.175
Aggregate	14	.056
Labor intensity[d]	14	-.057
Ratio of uniformed to total police and fire personnel	14	-.098
Existence of centralized structure for productivity improvements	14	.066
Existence of a perceptible special productivity-improvement effort	14	.136
Extent to which behavioral approaches to productivity improvement are emphasized over industrial-engineering approaches	11	.454*

r = Pearson product-moment correlation

*p < .10 (one-tailed test)
**p < .025 (one-tailed test)

[a]Personnel directors were asked to indicate the extent to which volunteers were being used in various departments in their cities. Their perceptions, which were then correlated with the Relative Productivity Index, were coded as follows: no use of volunteers = 0; less-than-average use = 1; average use = 2; greater-than-average use = 3.

[b]City managers were asked to indicate whether or not their cities were contracting for services from a private company or another governmental entity in specified functions. Their responses, which were then correlated with the Relative Productivity Index, were coded as follows: yes = 1; no = 0.

[c]City managers were asked to indicate the extent of contracting for specified functions in their cities. Their responses, which were then correlated with the Relative Productivity Index, were coded as follows: no contracting = 0; supplemental contracting = 1; primary service provision through contracting = 2.

[d]The labor intensity measure used is public safety personnel per 10,000 population in 1980. Staffing levels for police and fire personnel are readily available in International City Management Association (ICMA), The Municipal Year Book 1981, vol. 48 (Washington, D.C.: ICMA, 1981), pp. 94-146. Reliable comparison information in other services is less available.

Source: Compiled by the author.

for cities contracting for street construction, custodial services, and undefined "other" services. Negative correlations, also lacking statistical significance and in some instances quite weak, were found for cities contracting for street maintenance, park maintenance, recreation services, police, library, refuse collection, and planning services.

Extremely weak negative correlations with the Relative Productivity Index, lacking statistical significance at the .10 level, were found for labor intensity in the public safety functions and for the ratio of uniformed to total police and fire personnel. The weakness of the correlations implies virtually independent relationships.

Only one of the factors related to special productivity-improvement efforts was found to be significantly correlated with the Relative Productivity Index. Cities that were perceived to emphasize a behavioral approach to productivity improvement tended to have higher index scores than those emphasizing an industrial engineering approach ($r = .454$; significant at $p < .10$). The relationships between the Relative Productivity Index and the existence of perceptible, special productivity-improvement efforts and a centralized productivity-improvement structure were positive but quite weak.

ORGANIZATIONAL EMPHASES

Productivity-improvement efforts flourish only when given emphasis by top management.[39] Some studies have, in fact, concluded that productivity improvement is most likely to occur when a sense of urgency, or even a crisis, has elevated its priority.[40] Productivity improvement must compete with other local issues or problems for the time and attention of city officials, and its preeminence is not a certainty. In a recent survey of local government administrators, it was ranked fourth as a pressing concern among ten major issues.[41]

In this analysis, the city managers of the 14 high-quality, full-service municipalities ranked the same ten issues included in the previously mentioned national survey. In this way not only could the relative priority of productivity improvement among the study cities be established, but the findings could also be compared with the priorities of local government administrators nationally. Each city manager was asked to rank the ten problems or issues in the list provided, with the most pressing issue being rated 1 and the least pressing issue rated 10. As a group, the 14 city managers ranked productivity improvement the number one priority, narrowly ahead of the fiscal crisis. Public safety was ranked third, followed by capital improvements, economic development, quality of life, community relations, intergovernmental relations, staff development, and labor relations, in that order.

TABLE 7.9

Comparison of Priority of Local Government Problems or Issues, as Perceived by City Managers of the 14 High-Quality, Full-Service Cities versus a National Sample of Local Government Administrators

Local Government Problem or Issue	High-Quality Full-Service Cities			National Sample of Local Government Administrators		
	Priority	Average Score	N	Priority	Average Score	N
Productivity improvement	1	3.64	14	4	4.45	273
The fiscal crisis	2	3.71	14	1	3.20	279
Public safety	3	4.29	14	5	5.78	266
Capital improvements	4	4.71	14	2	3.58	279
Economic development	5	5.29	14	3	4.22	276
Quality of life	6	5.71	14	8	6.67	263
Community relations	7	6.29	14	6	6.02	266
Intergovernmental relations	8	6.79	14	10	7.03	266
Staff development	9	7.07	14	7	6.34	265
Labor relations	10	7.50	14	9	6.72	267

Source: Compiled by the author. Comparison figures for National Sample from David N. Ammons and Joseph C. King, "Productivity Improvement in Local Government: Its Place among Competing Priorities," Public Administration Review 43 (March–April 1983): 113–20. Reprinted with permission from Public Administration Review, copyright 1983 by The American Society for Public Administration, 1225 Connecticut Avenue, N.W., Washington, D.C. All rights reserved.

The aggregate ranking of priorities by managers in the study cities differs in several respects from that of the national survey of local government administrators (Table 7. 9). The two rankings, however, possess certain underlying similarities. The same five issues that constitute the top half of the national priority ranking also comprise the top half of the priority list of the 14 city managers. Accordingly, the bottom halves are also comprised of the same set of issues. The order of the issues, however, differs between the two lists. Nationally, the fiscal crisis, capital improvements, economic development, productivity improvement, and public safety, in that order, were found to be the most pressing among the ten issues. The top four issues were all directly related to finances.

Public safety ranked ahead of two of the financial issues in the priorities for the study cities. Perhaps the general affluence of the 14 communities influences a relative emphasis upon service delivery and amenities (for example, public safety and quality of life, which also received a higher ranking than in the national sample) and less emphasis on strictly financial matters compared with the national sample. The fact that productivity improvement may be perceived to have more of a service-improvement component than other financial issues (the fiscal crisis, capital improvements, and economic development) may explain its movement to the head of the aggregate list for the 14 city managers.

Although productivity improvement earned the number one aggregate ranking and received fairly consistent high marks as a pressing issue, it was ranked number one by only one of the fourteen city managers Thirteen managers assigned higher priority to another issue. Six city managers ranked productivity improvement as the number two issue, and none of the managers ranked it lower than number seven.

In contrast to the consistently high rating for productivity improvement, none of the managers ranked labor relations higher than number three among the issues, and six ranked it either ninth or tenth. The perceived priority of the quality-of-life issue, on the other hand, was widely split, with three city managers ranking the issue number one and two city managers ranking it number ten.

Positive correlations between issue rankings and the Relative Productivity Index were found for productivity improvement ($r = .285$), capital improvements, staff development, and intergovernmental relations, though none of the correlations was significant at the .10 level (Table 7. 10). All other correlations were negative, though many approached zero, with only the priority given to labor relations having a significant correlation ($r = -.392$; significant at $p < .10$). As the perception of labor relations as a pressing issue increased, a city's score on the Relative Productivity Index tended to decline.

TABLE 7.10

Pearson Product-Moment Correlation between Organizational
Emphases and the Relative Productivity Index

Organizational Emphasis	N	r
Relative significance of the following issues as perceived by the city manager		
Labor relations	14	-.392*
Productivity improvement	14	.285
Capital improvements	14	.260
Staff development	14	.204
The fiscal crisis	14	-.149
Intergovernmental relations	14	.105
Public safety	14	-.093
Community relations	14	-.071
Quality of life	14	-.064
Economic development	14	-.004

r = Pearson product-moment correlation

*$p < .10$ (one-tailed test).

Source: Compiled by the author.

FINANCIAL REVIEW

In many respects the condition and nature of municipal financial
resources—the variety of revenue sources, the mix or balance of
revenues, and the degree of reliance on certain sources—may constitute important elements in the environment in which the local legislative body and city management function. Each of these factors and its
relevance to relative productivity is examined in this analysis. Specific attention is directed toward each city's total general revenues
(consisting of general fund revenues and federal revenue-sharing receipts), intergovernmental revenues, property tax revenues, sales
tax revenues, and income tax revenues. In addition, each city's general obligation debt service and municipal appropriation to local
schools are examined. Data were obtained from financial statements
and budget documents of the 14 cities.

The average annual per capita general revenue for the 14 municipalities in fiscal years 1979 and 1980, including general fund revenues
and federal revenue sharing, was $275. On average, per capita prop-

erty tax revenues, sales tax revenues, and intergovernmental revenues were approximately $101, $28, and $57, respectively. The
average general obligation debt service per capita was approximately
$24.

On average, the ratio of property and sales tax revenues to total
general revenues for the 1979 and 1980 fiscal years was approximately
45 percent. The average ratio of property tax revenues alone to total
general revenues was about 36 percent, while the ratio of sales tax
revenues to total general revenues was approximately 10 percent. The
average ratio of intergovernmental revenues to total general revenues
was approximately 20 percent. On the expenditure side, the average
ratio of general obligation debt service to total general revenues for
the 14 cities was approximately 8 percent.

Eight of the financial characteristics of a per capita or ratio
nature were found to be significantly correlated with the Relative Productivity Index at the .10 level (Table 7.11). The ratio of sales tax
revenues to total general revenues, property and sales tax revenues
per capita, and sales tax revenues per capita were all found to be
positively correlated to the index ($r = .426, .415,$ and $.372$, respectively; significant at $p < .10$). The ratio of adjusted general obligation debt service (removing general obligation debt service on behalf
of the local schools) to total general revenues was found to be positively correlated with relative productivity ($r = .484$; significant at
the .05 level), while the ratio of intergovernmental revenues to property
tax revenues was negatively correlated with the index ($r = -.501$; significant at $p < .05$). The strongest correlations with the Relative Productivity Index were for the ratio of property and sales tax revenues
to total general revenues ($r = .655$; significant at $p < .025$), the ratio
of property tax revenues to total general revenues ($r = .557$; significant at $p < .025$), and the ratio of general obligation debt service to
total general revenues ($r = .552$; significant at $p < .025$).

The mix of revenue sources and the degree of reliance upon
particular sources appear to have an impact on municipal productivity.
Three relationships seem to exist.

The greater a community's reliance on what are typically the
most highly visible forms of own-source revenues (those that tend to
impact most directly and to the greatest degree the greatest number
of local citizens), the more efficient it tends to be in its operations;
The greater a community's debt service relative to revenues,
the more efficient it tends to be in its operations; and
The greater a community's reliance on intergovernmental revenues, the less efficient it tends to be in its operations.

The first point implies the existence of special pressures or incentives for frugality when there is a clear perception that expendi-

TABLE 7.11

Pearson Product-Moment Correlation between Municipal
Finances and the Relative Productivity Index

Financial Characteristic	N	r
Ratio of property and sales tax revenues to total general revenues	14	.655***
Ratio of property tax revenues to total general revenues	14	.557***
Ratio of general obligation debt service to total general revenues	14	.552***
Ratio of intergovernmental revenues to property tax revenues	14	-.501**
Ratio of adjusted general obligation debt service to total general revenues[a]	14	.484**
Ratio of sales tax revenues to total general revenues	14	.426*
Property and sales tax revenues per capita	14	.415*
Sales tax revenues per capita	14	.372*
Property tax revenues per capita	14	.364
Ratio of intergovernmental revenues to total general revenues	14	-.335
Adjusted general obligation debt service per capita[a]	14	.322
General obligation debt service per capita	14	.298
Intergovernmental revenues per capita	14	-.219
Ratio of sales tax revenues to property tax revenues	14	.216
Sales and income tax revenues per capita	14	.207
Ratio of sales and income tax revenues to total general revenues	14	.170
Ratio of city appropriations to schools to total general revenues	14	.160
Ratio of sales and income tax revenues to property tax revenues	14	-.114
General revenues per capita	14	.100

r = Pearson product-moment correlation
*p < .10 (one-tailed test)
**p < .05 (one-tailed test)
***p < .025 (one-tailed test)
[a]Excluding any debt service on behalf of city schools.

Note: Except where otherwise specified, financial information
used in the computations is the mean of revenues, expenditures,
debt service, and so forth for the 1979 and 1980 fiscal years for each
city. General revenues refers to general fund revenues and federal
revenue-sharing receipts.

Source: Compiled by the author.

tures for municipal services, while providing one type of benefit, also deprive the citizenry of the use of those resources for private purposes. The second point is subject to at least two interpretations. A heavy debt service requirement may place a strain on resources and encourage frugality. Conceivably, heavy debt service could also reflect the acquisition or construction of more efficient equipment or facilities designed to hold down expenditures.

The third point has many possible explanations. First, the use of state and federal funds normally imposes extensive reporting and procedural requirements, often including requirements regarding wage rates, hiring practices, and the use of minority or other special categories of contractors. Such requirements can drive total costs up substantially. Second, the lure of state or federal funds can induce a local government to acquire equipment and facilities with ongoing operating expenses that otherwise might not have been incurred. Third, intergovernmental funding may increase expenditures even in nonaided functions by making it easy for local governments to reallocate their resources to those other functions.[42] Finally, a different sense of frugality may apply when a project's funding source can be clearly identified as intergovernmental rather than local. Rigorous cost-benefit analysis may seem less essential when the money comes from Washington or the state capital.

CITY COUNCIL CHARACTERISTICS

The leadership of the local governing body as well as top management is important in establishing the environment in which a municipal organization functions. City council attitudes, owing perhaps in part to individual backgrounds and the nature of local politics, may influence the establishment of a climate for, against, or indifferent toward innovation and productivity improvement. City councils with time horizons that extend only until the next election, with more interest in how grants are distributed among neighborhoods than how efficiently they are spent,[43] or with little appreciation of the value of effective management techniques can undermine municipal productivity.[44]

In this inquiry, the degree of each city's reformism (in other words, the extent to which it conforms to the reformists' ideal of council-manager government, nonpartisan election, and election at large rather than by ward or district) is examined, as well as characteristics such as occupation, education, and tenure of council members; the size of the city council; and pay for serving as a council member. Information on reformism, council size, and council pay was obtained from The Municipal Year Book 1979. The data source

TABLE 7.12

Governmental Structure of the High-Quality, Full-Service Cities

City	Form of Government	Election	
		Partisan or Nonpartisan	At Large or District
Sunnyvale, Calif.	Council-manager	Nonpartisan	All nominated and elected at large
Fort Walton Beach, Fla.	Council-manager	Nonpartisan	Some nominated by district, some at large; all elected at large
Gainesville, Fla.	Council-manager	Nonpartisan	All nominated and elected at large
Saint Petersburg, Fla.	Council-manager	Nonpartisan	Some nominated by district, some at large; all elected at large
Lake Forest, Ill.	Council-manager	Nonpartisan	Some but not all nominated and elected by ward or district
Owensboro, Ky.	Council-manager	Nonpartisan	All nominated and elected at large
Chapel Hill, N.C.	Council-manager	Nonpartisan	All nominated and elected at large
Greensboro, N.C.	Council-manager	Nonpartisan	All nominated and elected at large
Upper Arlington, Ohio	Council-manager	Nonpartisan	All nominated and elected at large
Oak Ridge, Tenn.	Council-manager	Nonpartisan	All nominated by district and elected at large
Austin, Tex.	Council-manager	Nonpartisan	All nominated and elected at large
Richardson, Tex.	Council-manager	Nonpartisan	Some nominated by district, some at large; all elected at large
Newport News, Va.	Council-manager	Partisan	All nominated and elected at large
Roanoke, Va.	Council-manager	Nonpartisan	All nominated and elected at large

Source: International City Management Association (ICMA), The Municipal Year Book 1979, vol. 46 (Washington, D.C.: ICMA, 1979), pp. 111-43. Adapted by permission.

for individual characteristics of council members was a questionnaire sent to city clerks/secretaries (see sample questionnaires, Appendix B). Responses were received from all 14 cities.

All 14 of the high-quality, full-service cities operate under the council-manager form of government. Most but not all have city councils elected at large on a nonpartisan basis (Table 7.12). Nine of the fourteen cities have city councils nominated and elected entirely at large. Three have city councils to which some members have been nominated by district and some at large, with all elected at large. One city has a system by which council members are nominated by district and elected at large. Only one city, Lake Forest, has any of its council members nominated and elected by ward or district—and only part of the Lake Forest city council is elected in that manner. Only 1 of the 14 cities, Newport News, has party affiliations listed on its ballot for city council.

Using a reformism index in which each of the reform ideals of council-manager government, a totally at-large system of nomination and election, and nonpartisan elections is awarded one point, 8 of the 14 cities have a perfect reform score of three.* Scoring partisan elections as 0 and applying gradients between 0 and 1 on the at-large criterion results in an average reformism index score for the 14 cities of 2.79—a score that indicates high but not perfect conformance to the reformists' ideal.†

Most of the council members in the 14 cities were reportedly in the occupational category of executive-proprietor-manager-professional-administrator, though there is also substantial representation from the small-businessman-clerk-salesman-teacher-technician category. Very few city council members came from the skilled-semiskilled-unskilled employee category.

More than three-fourths of the council members in the 14 cities (79.6 percent) were reported to have a college degree. Moreover, almost half (44.7 percent) were reported to have graduate degrees.

The average city council size was between seven and eight members. The average tenure of council members serving at the time of

---

*Those eight cities are Sunnyvale, California; Gainesville, Florida; Owensboro, Kentucky; Chapel Hill, North Carolina; Greensboro, North Carolina; Upper Arlington, Ohio; Austin, Texas; and Roanoke, Virginia.

†Scoring for the at-large criterion was as follows: all nominated and elected at large = 1; some nominated by district, some nominated at large, but all elected at large = 0.75; nominated by district and elected at large = 0.50; some but not all nominated and elected by ward or district = 0.25; all nominated and elected by ward or district = 0.

TABLE 7.13

Pearson Product-Moment Correlation between City Council
Characteristics and the Relative Productivity Index

Characteristic	N	r
Reformism index[a]	14	-.650**
Reformism, nonpartisan elections	14	-.435*
Reformism, at-large elections	14	-.401*
Occupation level of council members (mean)[b]	14	.367*
Formal education level of council members (median)[c]	14	.347
Formal education level of council members (mean)[c]	14	.325
Occupation level of council members (median)[b]	14	.317
Average tenure of current council members (median)	14	-.302
Number of council members	14	.258
Level of pay received by council members	14	-.207
Average tenure of current council members (mean)	14	-.153
Reformism, council-manager form	14	.000

r = Pearson product-moment correlation

*p < .10 (one-tailed test)
**p < .025 (one-tailed test)

[a]The reformism index is the sum of three scores assigned to
each city based upon its conformance to the reformists' ideal type:
council-manager form of government, at-large elections, and nonpartisan elections. Scoring was as follows: council-manager form
of government (yes = 1; no = 0); at large or ward elections (all nominated and elected at large = 1; some nominated by district, some
nominated at large, but all elected at large = 0.75; nominated by district and elected at large = 0.50; some but not all nominated and
elected by ward or district = 0.25; all nominated and elected by ward
or district = 0); nonpartisan election (yes = 1; no = 0).

[b]Skilled, semiskilled, unskilled employee = 1; small businessman, clerk, salesman, teacher, technician, and similar occupations
= 2; executive, proprietor, manager, professional, administrator =
3. Homemaker coded by spouse's occupation. Retirees coded by
former occupation.

[c]Less than high school diploma = 1; high school diploma = 2;
some college = 3; college degree = 4; graduate degree, medical degree, law degree = 5.

Source: Compiled by the author.

the survey was between five and six years. Most council members
received modest levels of compensation, with some receiving no pay
at all and, at the other extreme, two of the cities compensating their
council members in the $10,000-to-$12,000-per-year range. [45]

Four of the city council characteristics were found to be significantly correlated with the Relative Productivity Index at the .10
level (Table 7.13). The occupation level of council members was
positively correlated with the index (r = .367; significant at p < .10).
Nonpartisan and at-large elections were negatively correlated with
the Relative Productivity Index (r = -.435 and -.401, respectively;
significant at p < .10). The strongest correlation was the negative
relationship between relative productivity and the reformism index
(r = -.650; significant at the .025 level). Although the negative correlation is surprising given the fact that greater efficiency in government was part of the reformers' aim, it should be noted that all of
the 14 cities tend to conform in most respects to the reformists'
ideal, and this finding indicates only that those cities that conform
somewhat less than others, though remaining more reformed than unreformed, tend to possess higher scores on the Relative Productivity
Index.

Although lacking statistical significance at the .10 level, the
formal education level of city council members and the number of
members on the council were found to be positively correlated with
the Relative Productivity Index (r = .347 and .258, respectively).
The average tenure of city council members and the level of pay provided for city council service were negatively correlated with the index
(r = -.302 and -.207, respectively).

CITIZEN PARTICIPATION

Citizen participation is a valued principle in local government.
Citizen participation and citizen approval of government actions are
important elements in at least the first three of the four local government goals of responsiveness, equity, effectiveness, and efficiency. [46]
The impact of citizen involvement on the fourth objective, efficiency,
is a question deserving further examination.

Local governments' tendencies to solicit and receive structured
citizen involvement, especially of an advisory nature, and the impact
of such involvement on municipal productivity is explored to a modest
degree in this inquiry. [47] Information regarding the number of city-
council-appointed citizen boards and commissions, total membership
on those boards, and the number of ad hoc citizen advisory groups
appointed by the city council in a typical year were obtained from city
clerks. In addition, the records of the National Municipal League's

All-America City award, recognizing community achievements through citizen involvement, were examined to ascertain which of the 14 cities had been accorded that honor. These measures of citizen participation were then compared with the Relative Productivity Index to determine any apparent associations.

The number of permanent citizen boards and commissions varies widely among the 14 cities, ranging from a low of only 4 permanent boards in one city to a high of 52 boards in another. Total membership on such boards and commissions similarly spans a wide range from an estimated low of 28 persons in one city to a high of 410 persons in another. One city reports the appointment of no ad hoc citizen advisory groups in a typical year; eight report the appointment of one to three such groups, as a rule; four report the appointment of four to six ad hoc groups; and one reports the appointment of seven or more ad hoc citizen advisory groups in a typical year.

A separate measure of citizen participation is provided by examination of the list of recipients of the All-America City award. That award is granted annually to cities that have had noteworthy community achievements through citizen participation. Through 1981, 6 of the 14 cities had received All-America City recognition.*

Three citizen-participation factors were found to have statistically significant correlations with the Relative Productivity Index at the .10 level (Table 7.14). The number of permanent citizen boards and commissions per 10,000 population was positively correlated with the index ($r = .409$; significant at $p < .10$). On the other hand, the number of ad hoc advisory groups appointed per year and All-America City recognition were negatively correlated with relative productivity ($r = -.481$ and $-.470$, respectively; significant at $p < .05$).

The absence of a consistently positive correlation between citizen participation and municipal productivity should not be particularly surprising. As noted by Robert Crain and Donald Rosenthal, high levels of citizen participation, especially common in high-status communities, tend to escalate controversy, promote decentralized decision making, and often result in governmental immobility.[48] Productivity-improvement efforts often produce a substantial measure of controversy on their own, with little need of further assistance from interest groups. An environment that tends to amplify controversy can stymie changes from the status quo. Furthermore, even the type

---

*The cities included in this study that, as of 1981, had received All-America City recognition are Sunnyvale (1980), Gainesville (1970), St. Petersburg (1972), Owensboro (1952), Greensboro (1966), and Roanoke (1952, 1978, and 1981). Honorable mention had also been granted to Sunnyvale (1958) and St. Petersburg (1978).

TABLE 7.14

Pearson Product-Moment Correlation between Measures of Citizen
Participation and the Relative Productivity Index

Measure of Citizen Participation	N	r
Number of ad hoc citizen advisory groups appointed by the city council in a typical year[a]	14	-.481**
All-America City recognition	14	-.470**
Number of permanent citizen boards and commissions per 10,000 population	14	.409*
Total membership on boards and commissions per 10,000 population	14	.228
Number of permanent citizen boards and commissions appointed by the city council	14	.189
Total membership on boards and commissions	14	-.010

r = Pearson product-moment correlation
*p < .10 (one-tailed test)
**p < .05 (one-tailed test)
[a]None = 0; 1 to 3 = 1; 4 to 6 = 2; 7 or more = 3 for computational
purposes.

Source: Compiled by the author.

of citizen participation represented by the appointment of citizen
boards and commissions may reflect the degree to which the community possesses an activist citizenry and also the degree to which
public opinion is perceived to be of value. Special interests are
likely to be pursued vigorously in communities where such activism
and perceptions thrive. But special interests rarely, if ever, coal-
esce behind a drive for productivity improvement. More often special interest groups and individuals pursue program expansion, facility improvement, and other outlays rather than greater efficiency.
    As observed by Charles Wise, two types of accountability,
each desirable in its own right, tend to be pursued simultaneously
in local government: process accountability and outcome accountability. Process accountability stresses the importance of codes of
ethics, sunshine laws, and citizen participation. Outcome accountability emphasizes the importance of measuring agency output and impacts. Wise notes that "steps taken to make a decision process more
participative and thus more accountable may well result in less efficient provision of services."[49]

COMMUNITY CHARACTERISTICS

Several general community characteristics in addition to those identified in Table 7. 1 were examined in an effort to detect any significant relationship with the Relative Productivity Index. Characteristics examined in addition to those previously identified include the 1980 presidential vote in the county in which each city is located, governmental fragmentation, population change, education level, racial and age composition, population per square mile, government employment, federal presence, retail sector impact, manufacturing sector impact, a city's tendency to be a regional service center, city age, black student population, and rate of housing construction.

In 1980 the highest percentage of votes for the Democratic presidential candidate, Jimmy Carter, among the study cities was reported at 53 percent, for the counties in which Gainesville and Chapel Hill are located. The lowest percentage, 27 percent, was reported for the county in which Fort Walton Beach is located. The highest percentage vote for the Republican candidate, Ronald Reagan, was 70 percent of the total vote in the county in which Fort Walton Beach is located, and the lowest percentage was 38 percent in the counties in which Chapel Hill is located.

Local government fragmentation, reflected by the number of local governments in the Standard Metropolitan Statistical Area (SMSA) per 10,000 population, ranged from a low of 0. 26 local governmental entities per 10,000 population in the Newport News-Hampton SMSA to a high of 1. 83 in the Columbus SMSA, in which Upper Arlington is located. The average was 0. 96 local governmental entities per 10,000 population. [50]

Community growth among the 14 cities was reflected in the percentage of 1970 housing that had been constructed since 1960 and the percentage of population change from 1970 to 1980. The percentage of housing in 1970 that had been constructed during the previous ten years ranged from a low of 13. 8 percent in Roanoke to a high of 69 percent in Richardson. Population change from 1970 to 1980 ranged from an 8 percent decline in Upper Arlington to a 50 percent increase in Richardson.

The 14 cities were found to have generally well-educated populations. On average, approximately 66 percent of the persons 25 years of age and older had a formal education consisting at least of four years of high school.* Only 4 percent of the persons in that age category had less than five years of schooling. The study cities had an

---

*The averages reported for these and other characteristics are unweighted means for the 14 study cities.

average black student enrollment figure of approximately 19 percent
in elementary and high schools in 1970.

On average, approximately 87 percent of the population in the
14 cities was white in 1970 and approximately 32 percent was less than
18 years of age. The average population per square mile in 1975 for
the cities was 3,180 persons. An average of 23 percent of the civilian
labor force in the cities was employed in government at various levels
in 1970. The federal presence, represented by the ratio of local federal government employees in 1975 to the 1980 population, was an
average of 1.3 percent.

On average, the retail sector impact, represented by total retail sales in 1972 divided by the 1970 population, was approximately
$2,700. The manufacturing sector impact, represented by the value
added by manufacturing in 1972 divided by the 1970 population, was
an average of approximately $2,200. The tendency for the cities to
serve as regional service centers was explored by examining the ratio
of total sales from eating and drinking places in 1972 to the 1970 population; the average was approximately $202 per resident. The aver-
age 1980 population for the 14 cities was 102,150. The average city
age, in years since incorporation, was 91 as of 1980.

Of the many community characteristics examined, only four
were found to have statistically significant correlations with the Relative Productivity Index at the .10 level (Table 7.15). Federal presence
and population per square mile had negative correlations with the index
($r = -.469$ and $-.417$, respectively; significant at $p < .10$). Community
growth, on the other hand, was found to have a positive relationship
with relative productivity. Percentage of population change from 1970
to 1980 had a correlation of .393 with the Relative Productivity Index
(significant at $p < .10$). Percentage of 1970 housing constructed during the preceding ten years had a correlation of .538 with the index
(significant at $p < .05$).

Although lacking statistical significance at the .10 level, several
other relationships warrant mention. Moderate correlations were
found between a community's population age profile and the Relative
Productivity Index. Cities with greater percentages of their population less than 18 years old tended to do better on the index; those
with greater percentages of senior citizens tended to rank lower.

The pattern of correlations between personal income and the
Relative Productivity Index suggests greater productivity for communities with a large middle class. Negative correlations with the index
were found for the highest-income category (percentage of families
with money income in 1969 of $25,000 or more), the two lowest-income
categories (percentage below the poverty level and percentage below
125 percent of the poverty level), and per capita income. A positive
correlation ($r = .184$), on the other hand, was found for the middle-

TABLE 7.15

Pearson Product–Moment Correlation between Selected Community Characteristics and the Relative Productivity Index

Characteristic	N	r
Percentage of 1970 housing constructed since 1960	12	.538**
Federal presence[a]	11	-.469*
Population per square mile, 1975[b]	12	-.417*
Percentage population change from 1970 to 1980	14	.393*
Percentage of population 65 years of age or older, 1970	12	-.299
Retail-sector impact[c]	12	-.265
Percentage of families with money income in 1969 of $25,000 or more	12	-.256
Percentage of population less than 18 years of age, 1970	12	.235
Per capita income, 1974	12	-.221
Percent black students in elementary and high schools, 1970	10	.208
Percentage of families with money income in 1969 of $15,000–$24,999	12	.184
Percentage of persons 25 years of age and older with less than five years of school, 1970	12	-.178
Percentage of owner-occupied housing, 1970	12	-.139
Ratio of county's Democratic votes to total county votes in 1980 presidential election	14	-.132
Percentage of housing lacking some or all plumbing facilities, 1970	12	-.130
Median value of owner-occupied, single-family housing, 1970	12	.117
Percentage of families with money income in 1969 below the poverty level	12	-.112
Percentage of population of foreign stock, 1970	12	-.110
Median gross rent, renter-occupied housing, 1970	12	.104
Ratio of county's Independent Party votes to total county votes in 1980 presidential election	14	.097
Percent black population, 1970	12	.095
Percentage of families with money income in 1969 below 125 percent of poverty level	12	-.093
Ratio of county's Republican votes to Democratic votes in 1980 presidential election	14	.090
Ratio of county's Republican votes to total county votes in 1980 presidential election	14	.088

Percentage of persons 25 years of age and older with four years of high school or more, 1970	12	.085
Percent white population, 1970	12	-.072
Manufacturing-sector impact[d]	9	-.068
Percentage of housing with a ratio of more than one person per room, 1970	12	.062
Median family income, 1969	12	-.061
Percentage of civilian labor force employed in government, 1970	12	.043
Percentage of civilian labor force unemployed, 1970	12	-.036
Population, 1980[e]	14	.010
Fragmentation: local governments in SMSA per 10,000 population, 1977	13	-.050
City age (years since incorporation)	14	-.005
Tendency to be regional service center[f]	11	-.003

r = Pearson product-moment correlation

*p < .10 (one-tailed test)
**p < .05 (one-tailed test)

[a] Ratio of local federal government employees (December 1975) to the 1980 population.

[b] The County and City Data Book, 1977 lists the 1975 population per square mile as 326 for Oak Ridge, Tennessee. Much of Oak Ridge is uninhabited federal reservation property. The inhabited portion, including federal laboratory and industrial facilities, is estimated by city officials at 27.9 square miles. An adjusted figure of 966 persons per square mile, based upon this estimate for the sake of comparability, was used in the computation of the Pearson product-moment correlation.

[c] Ratio of total retail sales (1972) to the 1970 population.

[d] Ratio of value added by manufacturing (1972) to the 1970 population.

[e] Since population was one of the independent variables in the regression equation that generated the Relative Productivity Index, a correlation of approximately 0.0 should not be surprising.

[f] Ratio of sales at eating and drinking places (1972) to the 1970 population.

Sources: Richard P. Nathan and Mary M. Nathan, America's Governments (New York: John Wiley & Sons, 1979), pp. 21-105 (governmental fragmentation); survey of city clerks (city age); U.S., Department of Commerce, Bureau of the Census, County and City Data Book, 1977 (Washington, D.C.: U.S. Government Printing Office, 1978) (census information); and The World Almanac and Book of Facts, 1982 (New York: Newspaper Enterprise Association, 1981), pp. 254-84 (1980 voting information).

income category (percentage of families with money income in 1969 of $15,000 to $24,999).

A strong retail sector was found to be negatively related to the Relative Productivity Index, though not at the $p < .10$ level of significance. Extremely weak associations with the index were found for race and ethnicity, education level of the general population, housing factors, presidential voting patterns, manufacturing sector impact, and employment factors. The Relative Productivity Index scores were found to be virtually independent of a city's tendency to serve as a regional service center, measured by the volume of its restaurant business per resident.

CLOSER EXAMINATION OF STRONGEST
CORRELATIONS BETWEEN ORGANIZATIONAL
AND COMMUNITY CHARACTERISTICS AND
RELATIVE PRODUCTIVITY

Computation of the Pearson product-moment correlations between the many variables examined in this study and the Relative Productivity Index provides a means of determining which of the variables appear to have the strongest simple (zero-order) relationship with relative productivity. Thirty-six variables, some of which are close variations of one another, were found to have statistically significant correlations at the .10 level. Most, but not all, of those variables maintain that level of statistical significance when Kendall or Spearman's correlation coefficients are used (Table 7.16).

The Pearson, Kendall, and Spearman correlation coefficients for each variable differ somewhat from one another in magnitude and significance, but the most dramatic difference occurs in the coefficients for the correlation between the Relative Productivity Index and the number of permanent citizen boards and commissions per 10,000 population. The Pearson correlation coefficient is .409, while the Kendall and Spearman coefficients indicate virtually no relationship at all ($r = -.044$ and $r = -.002$, respectively). The degree to which this discrepancy draws into the question the positive correlation indicated by the Pearson coefficient strengthens the argument that citizen participation is unlikely to lead to greater efficiency.

Although numerous variables with apparently strong correlations with relative productivity have been identified, the lengthiness of the list tends to exaggerate the substantive significance of this finding. Upon closer examination it becomes apparent that many of the variables are related to one another and possess only modest correlation with the Relative Productivity Index once other variables are controlled. A stepwise regression process allows an examination of the

TABLE 7.16

Coefficients of Correlation between Relative Productivity Index and Principal Explanatory Variables

Variable	N	Pearson Correlation Coefficient	Kendall Correlation Coefficient	Spearman Correlation Coefficient
Ratio of property and sales tax revenues to total general revenues (PSTT)	14	.655***	.522***	.702***
Reformism index (RFM)[a]	14	-.650***	-.476***	-.588***
Availability of one-time bonuses for managerial performance (B)	14	.637***	.430**	.507**
Balanced practice of promoting city managers from within and hiring from outside the organization, 1963–82 (BAL)[b]	14	.605***	.597***	.703***
Extent of contracting for legal services (LLSC)	14	.597****	.544***	.613***
Extent to which the use of control data (accounting, productivity, and so forth) for self-guidance or group problem solving rather than for punishment is emphasized or perceived as a relative strength (AQ11)	14	.596***	.442***	.638***
Amount of perceived cooperative teamwork present (Q7)	14	-.581***	-.380**	-.433*
Ratio of property tax revenues to total general revenues (PTT)	14	.557***	.425***	.638***
Ratio of general obligation debt service to total general revenues (DSTT)	14	.552***	.456***	.593***
Percentage of 1970 housing constructed since 1960 (RCH)	12	.538**	.260	.368
Ratio of intergovernmental revenues to property tax revenues (ITP)	14	-.501**	-.411***	-.485**

Extent to which confidence in subordinates is emphasized or per-ceived as a relative strength (AQI)	14	.493**	.376**	.563***
Ratio of adjusted general obligation debt service to total general revenues (ADSTT)	14	.484**	.339**	.507**
Number of ad hoc advisory groups appointed by city council in a typical year (AHAG)	14	-.481**	-.433**	-.514**
All-America City recognition (AAC)	14	-.470**	-.411**	-.484**
Federal presence (FP)[d]	11	-.469*	-.359*	-.474*
Extent to which behavioral approaches to productivity improve-ment are emphasized over industrial-engineering approaches (BIE)	11	.454*	.334*	.397
Use of volunteers in the police department (PDV)	14	-.437*	-.275	-.414*
Reformism, nonpartisan elections (NPE)	14	-.435*	-.322*	-.379*
Employment of an ICMA Management Innovation Award recipient (MIA)	14	-.435*	-.304*	-.359
Ratio of sales tax revenues to total general revenues (STT)	14	.426*	.436***	.587***
Extent to which information perceived to flow up and with peers, as well as downward (Q4)	14	-.426*	-.361**	-.425*
Deviation of city-manager salary from average salary index for selected employee classifications in same city (CMSALDV3)	12	-.421*	-.199	-.336
Population per square mile, 1975 (PPSM)[e]	12	-.417*	-.260	-.340
Property and sales tax revenues per capita (PASTPC)	14	.415*	.420***	.504**
Number of permanent citizen boards and commissions per 10,000 population (CBCPTT)	14	.409*	-.044	-.002
Extent to which information flow upward and with peers, as well as downward, is emphasized or perceived as a relative strength (AQ4)	14	-.409*	-.177	-.211

(continued)

TABLE 7.16 (continued)

Variable	N	Pearson Correlation Coefficient	Kendall Correlation Coefficient	Spearman Correlation Coefficient
Reformism, at-large elections (ALE)	14	-.401*	-.307*	-.374*
Percentage population change from 1970 to 1980 (POPCH70)	14	.393*	.322*	.399*
Emphasis upon labor relations as a high-priority issue (LR)	14	-.392*	-.223	-.259
Use of task system for public works department employees (TSPW)	14	.386*	.361*	.426*
Percentage of department heads with high school diploma but no college (HSD)	14	-.383*	-.252	-.392*
Use of task system for "other" employees (TSO)	14	-.382*	-.387*	-.456*
Contracting for legal services (LSC)	14	.373*	.426**	.502**
Sales tax revenues per capita (AVGSTPC)	14	.372*	.351**	.439*
Occupation level of council members (ACO)^f	14	.367*	.203	.290

*p < .10 (one—tailed test)
**p < .05 (one—tailed test)
***p < .025 (one—tailed test)

^{a}The reformism index is the sum of three scores assigned to each city based upon its conformance to the reformists' ideal type: council—manager form of government, at—large elections, and nonpartisan elections. Scoring was as follows: council—manager form of government (yes = 1; no = 0); at—large or ward elections (all nominated and elected at large = 1; some nominated by district, some nominated at large, but all elected at

208

large = 0.75; nominated by district and elected at large = 0.50; some but not all nominated and elected by ward or district = 0.25; all nominated and elected by ward or district = 0); nonpartisan election (yes = 1; no = 0).

[b]If during 30 percent to 70 percent of the years from 1963 through 1982 the city had a city manager who held a previous position in that organization, the city was coded 1; otherwise, it was coded 0 for purposes of computing the correlation with the Relative Productivity Index.

[c]Excluding any debt service on behalf of city schools.

[d]Ratio of local federal government employees (December 1975) to the 1980 population.

[e]The County and City Data Book, 1977 lists the 1975 population per square mile as 326 for Oak Ridge, Tennessee. Much of Oak Ridge is uninhabited federal reservation property. The inhabited portion, including federal laboratory and industrial facilities, is estimated by city officials at 27.9 square miles. An adjusted figure of 966 persons per square mile, based upon this estimate for the sake of comparability, was used in the computation of the correlations.

[f]Skilled, semiskilled, unskilled employee = 1; small businessman, clerk, salesman, teacher, technician, and similar occupations = 2; executive, proprietor, manager, professional, administrator = 3. Homemaker coded by spouse's occupation. Retirees coded by former occupation.

Note: Parentheses in variable list contain the variable labels.

Sources: Financial reports and budgets from the cities; "ICMA 1981 Annual Award Winners," Public Management 63 (August 1981): 2–12 (and previous awards issues; "International City Management Association (ICMA), Directory of Members (various editions); ICMA, "Salaries of Municipal Officials for 1981," Urban Data Service Report 13, no. 3 (March 1981); ICMA, Salaries $25,000 and Over for City Managers/Chief Administrative Officers as of 1 January 1981 (Washington, D.C.: ICMA, 1981); ICMA, The Municipal Year Book, vols. 30–49 (Washington, D.C.: ICMA, 1963–82; National Municipal League, Citizens Forum on Self-Government, All-America Cities Award Competition (New York: National Municipal League, 1981); survey of city managers, city clerks, personnel directors, and assistant city managers; and U.S., Department of Commerce, Bureau of the Census, 1980 Census of Population and Housing: Advance Reports (Washington, D.C.: Government Printing Office, 1981).

relative significance of the relationships between the potential explanatory variables and the Relative Productivity Index by entering the variables that explain the greatest amount of variance in the dependent variable into the regression equation one at a time. In this manner variables that have little direct relationship with relative productivity, but instead derive their apparent association through a correlation with other variables, may be exposed.

A stepwise regression procedure was employed using the Relative Productivity Index as the dependent variable and the ratio of property and sales tax revenues to total general revenues (PSTT), the variable with the greatest Pearson correlation coefficient with relative productivity ($r = .655$), as the first independent variable. In order to reduce the problem of multicollinearity, several variables based in large measure on the same data as the primary independent variable (PSTT) were excluded from the stepwise regression (AVGPTPC, AVGSTPC, PASTPC, PTT, and STT). As indicated in Table 7.17, the second most important variable for explaining variation in the Relative Productivity Index is the extent to which the use of control data (accounting, productivity, and so forth) for self-guidance or group problem solving, rather than for punishment, is emphasized or perceived as a relative strength within an organization (AQ11). (These two variables, PSTT and AQ11, are virtually unrelated to each other among the study cities, with a Pearson correlation coefficient of only 0.0004. The relationship between the Relative Productivity Index and AQ11 therefore remains strong even when controlling for PSTT.) The R^2 for the regression equation, indicating the amount of variance explained, increased from .432 using PSTT as the only independent variable to .784 using both PSTT and AQ11.

Controlling for the property and sales tax variable (PSTT) and the use of control data variable (AQ11), none of the other variables was found to be significant at the .10 level. Therefore, using $p = .10$ as the cutoff, the following equation appears to best explain variation in the Relative Productivity Index:

$$RPI = -0.31318 + 0.553(PSTT) + 0.12609(AQ11)$$

where RPI is the Relative Productivity Index, PSTT is the ratio of property and sales tax revenues to total general revenues, and AQ11 is the extent to which control data for self-guidance or group problem solving, rather than for punishment, are emphasized or perceived as a relative strength within a given organization. The R^2 value of .784 for this equation indicates that approximately 78 percent of the variation in the Relative Productivity Index is explained by the two variables selected.

TABLE 7.17

Variables Identified through Stepwise Regression as Having Strongest Independent Association with the Relative
Productivity Index
(N = 14)

Variable	r	b	beta	Cumulative R^2
Ratio of property and sales tax revenues to total general revenues (PSTT)	.655*	.553*	.655	.432
Extent to which the use of control data (accounting, productivity, and so forth) for self-guidance or group problem solving, rather than for punishment, is emphasized or perceived as a relative strength (AQ11)	.596*	.126*	.596	.784
(Constant)		-.313		

r = Pearson product-moment correlation; b = regression coefficient; beta = standardized b; and R^2 = proportion of variation explained.

*Significant at p < .025.

Note: Included in the stepwise process were most of the variables having a zero-order correlation with the Relative Productivity Index significant at the p < .10 level (see Table 7.16). Excluded were five variables (AVGPTPC, AVGSTPC, PASTPC, PTT, and STT) that are derivations of the primary independent variable, PSTT. Criterion for entry: p < .10.

Source: Compiled by the author.

SUMMARY OF FINDINGS

The 14 cities identified for the wide scope and consistently high quality of their municipal services are similar to one another in many respects. Their relative affluence and tendencies to conform to the reformists' ideal of council-manager form of government and non-partisan, at-large election of council members are especially apparent. But there are also substantial differences among the cities. Multiple characteristics on which the cities differ were explored, with statistically significant correlations with the Relative Productivity Index at the $p < .10$ level discovered in many instances. Closer examination controlling for correlations with other independent variables revealed that only two of the potential explanatory variables had independent correlations with the Relative Productivity Index significant at the .10 level. Those two variables—the ratio of property and sales tax revenues to total general revenues and the extent to which the use of control data for self-guidance or group problem solving, rather than for punishment, is emphasized or perceived as a relative strength —were found to account for approximately 78 percent of the variation in the Relative Productivity Index.

These findings suggest the relative insignificance, at least on a general basis independent of other factors, of the impact of a wide variety of organizational and community characteristics on municipal productivity. More important, they reveal the primacy of financial condition, represented by the resource mix and presumably the pressure that reliance on the property tax and sales tax places on local government to be productive, and of progressive management control for productivity in local government.

NOTES

1. Scarboro Research Corporation, 1981 Austin Market Survey, as cited in Austin Fast Facts (Austin, Tex.: Research Department, Austin American-Statesman, 1981), p. 2.
2. Ukiah, California, could legitimately lay claim to being the first council-manager city, since the post of chief executive officer, selected by the city council, was established in that city in 1904. See Richard J. Stillman, II, The Rise of the City Manager: A Public Professional in Local Government (Albuquerque, N. Mex.: University of New Mexico Press, 1974), pp. 14-15.
3. Ibid., pp. 20-23.
4. Ronald O. Loveridge, "The City Manager in Legislative Politics: A Collision of Role Conceptions," Polity 1 (Winter 1968): 213-36.

5. Deil Wright, "The City Manager as a Development Administrator," in Comparative Urban Research, ed. Robert Daland (Beverly Hills, Calif.: Sage, 1969), pp. 203-48.

6. Robert R. Alford and Harry M. Scoble, "Political and Socioeconomic Characteristics of American Cities," in International City Managers' Association (ICMA), The Municipal Year Book 1965, vol. 32 (Chicago: ICMA, 1965), pp. 82-97.

7. Oliver P. Williams and Charles R. Adrian, "Community Types and Policy Differences," in City Politics and Public Policy, ed. James Q. Wilson (New York: John Wiley & Sons, 1968), pp. 17-36.

8. Robert L. Lineberry and Edmund P. Fowler, "Reformism and Public Policies in American Cities," American Political Science Review 61 (September 1967): 701-17.

9. Bernard H. Booms, "City Governmental Form and Public Expenditure Levels," National Tax Journal 19 (June 1966): 187-99.

10. Stillman, The Rise of the City Manager, p. 102.

11. Harold A. Stone, Don K. Price, and Kathryn H. Stone, City Manager Government in the United States (Chicago: Public Administration Service, 1940), p. 260.

12. ICMA, Directory of Recognized Local Governments 1982 (Washington, D.C.: ICMA, 1982), p. 11.

13. Emmette S. Redford, Democracy in the Administrative State (New York: Oxford University Press, 1969), pp. 29-30.

14. U.S., Department of Commerce, Bureau of the Census, County and City Data Book, 1977 (Washington, D.C.: U.S. Government Printing Office, 1978). Owing to delays in the release of 1980 census information, the majority of the census data used in this study is 1970 and 1975 information, as reported in the above.

15. In a study of 243 central cities, Dye and Garcia found the functional scope of city government to be the most important single determinant of the level of municipal taxation and expenditures. Thomas R. Dye and John A. Garcia, "Structure, Function, and Policy in American Cities," Urban Affairs Quarterly 14 (September 1978): 103-22.

16. See, for example, Richard D. Bingham, The Adoption of Innovation by Local Government (Lexington, Mass.: D. C. Heath, Lexington Books, 1976), p. 3; Jack L. Walker, "The Diffusion of Innovations among the American States," American Political Science Review 63 (September 1969): 881; and Robert K. Yin, Karen A. Heald, and Mary E. Vogel, Tinkering with the System: Technological Innovations in State and Local Services (Lexington, Mass.: D. C. Heath, Lexington Books, 1977), pp. 43-44.

17. George W. Downs, Jr., Bureaucracy, Innovation, and Public Policy (Lexington, Mass.: D. C. Heath, Lexington Books, 1976), pp. 16, 19.

18. John P. Frendreis, "Innovation Characteristics as Correlates of Innovation Adoption in American Cities," Midwest Review of Public Administration 12 (June 1978): 67-86.

19. Bingham, The Adoption of Innovation by Local Government, p. 9.

20. Frederick O'R. Hayes, Productivity in Local Government (Lexington, Mass.: D. C. Heath, Lexington Books, 1977), p. 14.

21. Reprinted by permission of the publisher, from Productivity in Local Government by Frederick O' R. Hayes (Lexington, Mass.: Lexington Books, D. C. Heath and Company, copyright 1977, D. C. Heath and Company), p. 15.

22. Everett M. Rogers and F. Floyd Shoemaker, Communication of Innovations: A Cross-Cultural Approach (New York: Free Press, 1971), pp. 347-85.

23. Some researchers contend that leadership characteristics that work well in one situation may be less suitable in another; hence, individual characteristics might be perceived to be less important than the environment or situation in determining the success of the leader and his or her ability to influence events, including the adoption of innovations. For a review of some of the premises of the arguments supporting the situational character of leadership, see Larry B. Hill and F. Ted Hebert, Essentials of Public Administration (North Scituate, Mass.: Duxbury Press, 1979), pp. 287-89.

24. Bingham, The Adoption of Innovation by Local Government, p. 104. Furthermore, George Barbour cites an example of the impact of leadership on a particular innovative program in one of the fourteen study cities. Total Performance Management (TPM) was implemented in Sunnyvale, California, under the direction of the city manager. When he moved to Long Beach, he established TPM in that city. Following his departure from Sunnyvale, the program at that location declined. George P. Barbour, Jr., "Key Factors Influencing Productivity of State and Local Government Activities," Public Productivity Review 4 (September 1980): 276.

25. Downs, Bureaucracy, Innovation, and Public Policy, pp. 109-10.

26. ICMA, "Our Profession: Today's Profile," ICMA Newsletter (supp. 2), November 2, 1982.

27. As noted by A. W. Steiss and Gregory Daneke, current conditions may be the result of decisions made several years earlier. Alan Walter Steiss and Gregory A. Daneke, Performance Administration: Improved Responsiveness and Effectiveness in Public Service (Lexington, Mass.: D. C. Heath, Lexington Books, 1980), p. 61. Therefore, a profile of the city manager in each city based upon 20 years of history is desirable.

28. ICMA, Salaries $25,000 and Over for City Managers/Chief Administrative Officers as of 1 January 1981 (Washington, D. C.: ICMA, 1981).

29. Douglas McGregor, The Human Side of Enterprise (New York: McGraw-Hill, 1960).

30. Robert R. Blake and Jane Srygley Mouton, The New Managerial Grid (Houston: Gulf, 1978).

31. Rensis Likert, The Human Organization: Its Management and Value (New York: McGraw-Hill, 1967).

32. See, for example, Donald S. Van Meter and Carl E. Van Horn, "The Policy Implementation Process: A Conceptual Framework," Administration and Society 6 (February 1975): 465-66.

33. Hayes, Productivity in Local Government, p. 200.

34. Yin, Heald, and Vogel, Tinkering with the System, pp. 74-75. For a review of the debate over whether centralization is positively or negatively related to innovation, see Downs, Bureaucracy, Innovation, and Public Policy, pp. 89-91. Wilson and Zaltman, Duncan, and Holbek have hypothesized that centralization and the initiation of innovation are negatively related but that centralization is positively related to implementation. See James Q. Wilson, "Innovation in Organization: Notes toward a Theory," in Approaches to Organizational Design, ed. James Thompson (Pittsburgh, Pa.: University of Pittsburgh Press, 1966), pp. 193-218; and Gerald Zaltman, Robert Duncan, and Jonny Holbek, Innovations and Organizations (New York: John Wiley & Sons, 1973), p. 146.

35. Contracting for municipal services is an option receiving increasing attention from practitioners and scholars. See, for example, Donald Fisk, Herbert Kiesling, and Thomas Muller, Private Provision of Public Services: An Overview (Washington, D. C.: Urban Institute, 1978); and R. Scott Fosler, "State and Local Government Productivity and the Private Sector," Public Administration Review 38 (January-February 1978): 22-27.

36. For a review of motivation theories and practical incentives, especially as they apply to productivity improvement in local government, see John M. Greiner et al., Productivity and Motivation: A Review of State and Local Government Initiatives (Washington, D. C.: Urban Institute, 1981); National Commission on Productivity and Work Quality, Employee Incentives to Improve State and Local Government Productivity (Washington, D. C.: U. S. Government Printing Office, 1975); and National Center for Productivity and Quality of Working Life, Employee Attitudes and Productivity Differences between the Public and Private Sector (Washington, D. C.: U. S. Government Printing Office, 1978), p. 6.

37. For discussions regarding the usefulness of a separate productivity-improvement unit, the advantages of a centralized versus

decentralized approach, desirable size and background of a productivity staff, and the advantages and disadvantages of placement within the municipal budget agency, see John R. Hall, Jr., Factors Related to Local Government Use of Performance Measurement (Washington, D.C.: Urban Institute, 1978), p. 24; Hayes, Productivity in Local Government; idem, "Implementation Strategies to Improve Productivity," in Productivity Improvement Handbook for State and Local Government, ed. George J. Washnis (New York: John Wiley & Sons, 1980), pp. 25–38; and John S. Thomas, So, Mr. Mayor, You Want to Improve Productivity (Washington, D.C.: National Commission on Productivity and Work Quality, 1974), p. 13.

38. These findings are generally consistent with a survey of 404 cities in which 46 percent reported the existence of a special staff unit organized to analyze municipal operations. The most common titles for such units incorporated the words budget and research or management and budget. See Rackham S. Fukuhara, "Productivity Improvement in Cities," in ICMA, The Municipal Year Book 1977, vol. 44 (Washington, D.C.: ICMA, 1977), p. 195.

39. See, for example, Hayes, Productivity in Local Government, pp. 110–11; and National Center for Productivity and Quality of Working Life, Improving Governmental Productivity: Selected Case Studies (Washington, D.C.: U.S. Government Printing Office, 1977), p. 12.

40. David Rogers, Can Business Management Save the Cities? The Case of New York (New York: Free Press, 1978), pp. 249–52; and Peter L. Szanton, "The New York City-Rand Institute," in Centers for Innovation in the Cities and States, ed. Frederick O'R. Hayes and John E. Rasmussen (San Francisco: San Francisco Press, 1972), pp. 186–88.

41. David N. Ammons and Joseph C. King, "Productivity Improvement in Local Government: Its Place among Competing Priorities," Public Administration Review 43 (March–April 1983): 113–20.

42. Roy Bahl, Metropolitan City Expenditures (Lexington, Ky.: University of Kentucky Press, 1969), pp. 87–88; Richard D. Gustely, Municipal Public Employment and Public Expenditure (Lexington, Mass.: D. C. Heath, Lexington Books, 1974), p. 75; and Seymour Sacks and Robert Harris, "The Determinants of State and Local Government Expenditures and Intergovernmental Flows of Funds," National Tax Journal 17 (March 1964): 75–85.

43. Nicholas P. Retsinas, Mary K. Menno, and William Witte, "Community Development," in Productivity Improvement Handbook, ed. Washnis, p. 1321.

44. Hayes, Productivity in Local Government, pp. 161–62.

45. Gainesville city council members reportedly received $10,282 per year and Austin city council members received $12,006

per year in 1977-78. See ICMA, The Municipal Year Book 1979, vol. 46 (Washington, D.C.: ICMA, 1979), pp. 111-43.

46. The four urban service goals of responsiveness, equity, effectiveness, and efficiency were identified by David R. Morgan in Managing Urban America: The Politics and Administration of America's Cities (North Scituate, Mass.: Duxbury Press, 1979), p. 150.

47. Uninvited involvement, prompted in many cases by a citizen's objection to a government action, is not examined in this study, but could be a useful area of inquiry. Coleman suggests that such objections are important stimuli to citizen participation. See James S. Coleman, Community Conflict (New York: Free Press, 1957).

48. Robert L. Crain and Donald B. Rosenthal, "Community Status as a Dimension of Local Decision Making," American Sociological Review 32 (December 1967): 970-85.

49. Charles R. Wise, "Productivity in Public Administration and Public Policy," Policy Studies Journal 5 (Autumn 1976): 100-1.

50. The number of local governments per 10,000 population within SMSAs is based upon information from the 1977 Census of Governments reported in Richard P. Nathan and Mary M. Nathan, America's Governments (New York: John Wiley & Sons, 1979), pp. 21-105. Fort Walton Beach was excluded from the examination of governmental fragmentation owing to the absence of relevant data.

8

CONCLUSION

In the preceding chapters, the topic of municipal productivity has been taken from its broadest definitional aspects to the identification of specific factors statistically associated with relative productivity in a narrow stratum of U.S. cities. Numerous productivity definitions were found to exist, with an absence of unanimity among scholars and practitioners over a single definition best suited for the public sector. A general appreciation of the importance of efficiency and effectiveness, however, was found to be a recurring element in many definitions. The Hayward definition of governmental productivity as the "efficiency with which resources are consumed in the effective delivery of public services,"[1] with emphasis on quality as well as quantity of services and relating the value of all resources consumed to outputs or results, was adopted for purposes of this study.

Attention has been devoted to the considerable difficulty in measuring municipal performance—and especially municipal productivity. Numerous productivity-improvement efforts in local governments have been undertaken and many have reportedly achieved excellent results. The absence of adequate means for making valid interorganizational comparisons, however, has restricted the ability of researchers to verify most such results and to assess the significance of various factors potentially relevant to the successful institutionalization of productivity-enhancing practices.

A major problem for previous municipal productivity research has been the service-quality variable. The question of quality is especially troublesome in intercity comparisons, where one city's apparent relative efficiency may, in fact, be attributable entirely to its provision of lower-quality, cheaper municipal services. Similarly, a narrow scope of services may lead to a false impression of efficiency. In this study, both factors have been addressed by the identification of 14 cities well matched in terms of the scope and quality of their municipal services.

Many barriers to productivity improvement are common to local government. Some cities are plagued by productivity barriers to a much lesser degree than many of their counterparts, but no local government can escape them altogether. To enhance productivity, the impact of the obstacles must be minimized.

In order to assess relative productivity among the high-quality, full-service cities identified in this study, a Relative Productivity Index was developed by means of statistical regression, using municipal expenditures for selected functions as the dependent variable and a salary index and variations of city population as the independent variables. The Relative Productivity Index provides a measure of each city's actual expenditure deviation from its regression-based projected expenditure. High relative productivity is attributed to those cities spending less than the projected amount, and low relative productivity is attributed to those spending more than the projection.

Organizational and community characteristics of the 14 study cities were examined and correlated with the Relative Productivity Index. Several factors were found to have simple (zero-order) Pearson product-moment correlations with the index, but upon closer examination only two characteristics were found to be strongly correlated with relative productivity when other factors were controlled. Those characteristics—one financial and one managerial—were the ratio of property and sales tax revenues to total general revenues and the extent to which the use of control data (accounting reports, productivity records, and so forth) for self-guidance and group problem solving rather than for punishment was emphasized or perceived as a relative strength of the organization.

COMMENTS ON THE FINDINGS

The results of this inquiry suggest the primacy of two factors as important determinants of relative municipal productivity. As important as such a finding may be for practical application as well as for further research, the lack of statistical significance between relative productivity and various managerial techniques and characteristics formally or informally hypothesized to be relevant by many scholars and practitioners may be just as important.

Ratio of Property and Sales Tax
Revenues to Total General Revenues

The factor found to have the greatest degree of association with the Relative Productivity Index was the ratio of property and sales tax revenues to total general revenues in the various study cities. Property and sales taxes represent the principal forms of own-source revenue for most local governments. Their relationship to relative productivity suggests a psychology among local government actors —city council members, administrators, actively involved citizens, and perhaps the general citizenry as well—that differentiates among sources of revenues, placing higher value on revenues raised locally (especially those with a high profile and widespread impact) and demanding greater efficiency in their expenditure. Conceivably such differentiation could influence the acceptability of administrative practices, service delivery techniques, and expenditure levels, depending upon funding source, and even permit acquiescence to wastefulness in projects funded primarily through intergovernmental revenues. Such a frame of mind could reduce the inclination to say no to citizen requests for special projects or facilities, even when the need is extremely modest at best, if intergovernmental revenue is the major funding source.

Some writers have suggested that the pain of forced budget cuts is the primary motivator of productivity improvement.[2] Others have countered that slack conditions enhance the likelihood of innovation;[3] that organizational wealth or slack might at least be a better predictor of how early innovations are adopted, if not how extensively;[4] and that a sound financial base is crucial to state and local government productivity improvement.[5] Empirical evidence does little to sort out the apparent contradictions over the impact of scarcity and slack on innovation and productivity. While management strategies emphasizing productivity improvement have been reported to be more likely found among cities without financial problems than among those with financial problems,[6] a General Accounting Office survey indicates that resource scarcity is used by some cities as the justification for establishing a productivity-improvement program and by others as the reason for failure to establish such a program.[7] Perhaps the relevant factor is not the presence or absence of resources but the sense of possession that comes through heavy reliance on high-profile, own-source revenues with widespread impact on the local citizenry.

Lyle Fitch notes that "fiscal stress in the modern American community is often more psychological than economic."[8] Fiscal stress in fact may be more related to one's perception of whether one's own resources are being tapped too extensively than to objective measures of financial capacity. The 14 study cities tend to be relatively affluent. An assumption, however, that an affluent community is less concerned with frugality in local government spending may be in error. There is really no reason to expect a wealthy individual to be any more frivolous than a poor one in the sense that less value is expected on the dollar. The important factor appears to be the perception of whose dollar is being spent.

Based upon this examination of 14 high-quality, full-service cities, there is reason to believe that municipal productivity would be advanced by greater reliance by local governments on own-source revenues. Such a prescription should not be misconstrued as simply a call for reduced federal and state aid to local governments. Intergovernmental revenues serve important purposes in the mitigation of adverse local impacts of federal projects and in the reallocation of maldistributed resources between suburb and central city, which should not be abandoned casually for the sake of marginal productivity gains. To the extent possible, however, intergovernmental revenues should be altered from their prevailing form in which they tend to be perceived, at best, as less manageable than locally raised resources in the sense that they are governed by excessive regulations and are undependable from year to year and, at worst, as supplemental gifts, which unless claimed, will only be spent somewhere else.

Perhaps the purest sense in which intergovernmental revenues may be modified to be perceived in a manner similar to own-source revenues is through revision of the methods for compensating local governments for the impact of federal facilities. The placement of federal facilities is normally sought for the jobs and wages they offer to the local economy. Such placement, however, is often a mixed blessing, since federal property is not subject to local property taxes. In some cases federal payments are made in lieu of local taxes, but normally such payments are much less than what would have been received from a similar but privately owned property.

To remedy inequities in the municipal support provided by public and private institutions, serious consideration should be given to the waiver of federal-property-tax immunity or to payments in lieu of taxes based on full tax equivalency of federally owned real properties, as recommended by the Advisory Commission on Intergovernmental Relations (ACIR).[9] Under such an approach, the careful placement of federal programs and facilities in locations most in need of aid would not only provide the desired service to that place but would also expand employment opportunities and the local tax base. The federal government would not be an outside benefactor but would instead become part of the community, providing support indistinguishable from own-source revenues. The ACIR found "no inherent constitutional barriers to either the direct imposition of nondiscriminatory state/local taxes on federal real property or an equivalent payment in lieu of taxes on real property owned by the U.S. government. In both cases, only statutory consent of Congress is required."[10]

Another avenue for introducing intergovernmental revenues into the local resource mix in a manner that would minimize the differentiation from own-source revenues is the replacement of many of the current criteria for award of funds with criteria for program results and managerial efficiency. This would not necessarily mean that citizens in a given locale would be denied services because of inefficient local government management; however, they might receive the services from a private provider rather than from the local government for that reason. The federal government pursues many federal objectives through the funding of local delivery of specified services. To the extent possible, competitiveness should be nurtured among alternate service providers, including private entities, other local governments, the state government, and the federal government as a direct service provider itself. If a municipal government cannot compete successfully under such conditions, its scope should be narrowed. If a municipal government can compete successfully, it will have earned the federal dollars it receives and, ideally, should be awarded the resources under a contract with the flexibility to apply any excess revenues, or "profit," to other local programs, as long as the contracted results are achieved. Under such circumstances there would be little basis for treating intergovernmental revenues differently than own-source revenues.

Remaining federal grants should be restructured to substitute result requirements for procedural requirements to the extent possible and to incorporate positive productivity incentives.[11] One possible approach might involve the awarding of demonstration grants in stages, with fewer and fewer grant recipients at the second and subsequent stages of the program based upon demonstrated productivity at the preceding stage.

A gradual reduction in the degree of local government dependence on intergovernmental revenues could be practicable if local taxation authority were expanded. The major sources of locally raised revenues, the property tax and the sales tax, are inequitable and inadequate. Not only do they tend to be regressive forms of taxation, placing disproportionate burdens on the smaller resources of the poor than upon the more substantial resources of the wealthy, but they are also often limited to prescribed ceilings by local charter or state law. Greater reliance on own-source revenues for municipal services should be accompanied by a relaxation of tax limits and the lifting of restrictions against the use of more progressive means of generating needed revenues, including income taxation by local government.

Further research on a scale broader than 14 cities should be undertaken to confirm the existence of a special psychology in local government—a psychology that places a premium on high-impact, locally raised revenues and thereby promotes greater productivity among cities relying most heavily upon such revenues—before major changes in intergovernmental relations are pursued. The results of this analysis, however, are clear enough to call strongly for such expanded research.

Progressive Application of
Management Control

After controlling for the ratio of property and sales tax revenues to total general revenues, the only other variable of the many examined that retained statistical significance at the $p < .10$ level was the extent to which the use of control data, such as accounting, productivity, and cost information, for self-guidance and group problem solving rather than for punishment was emphasized or perceived to be a relative strength of the organization. This factor may be divided into two relevant components.

First, a nonneutral response regarding the use of control data (one that emphasizes use of such information for self-guidance and problem solving, system 4, or at the other extreme, use for policing and punishment, system 1) may imply the existence of a more sophisticated control-data system than would a more neutral response (system 2 or system 3).[12] At the very least it implies the active use of whatever control-data system is available. Nine of the fourteen organizations were placed in the participative group category (system 4) on this item. The other five municipalities were rated in the system 3 category, implying the use of control data in a progressive manner but an unwillingness on the part of the respondent to make a strong claim in this regard.

Second, the importance of using control data in a progressive, reinforcing manner is apparent. Some of the respondents rated their organization more system-4-like than other respondents—perhaps appropriately in every case, perhaps inappropriately in some. The point here, however, is not simply an intercity comparison of raw scores for organizational traits but a comparison of perceptions of organizational characteristics in terms of relative strengths, weaknesses, and emphases (for example, to what extent is a given characteristic perceived as a relative strength in Greensboro vis-à-vis other characteristics in the other 13 cities?). Through the use of standardized Z scores, it is possible to compare the extent to which respondents perceived the use of control data within each organization as more system-4-like than other operating characteristics within the same organization. Those municipalities in which such an approach is emphasized as a relative strength tend to have greater relative productivity.

This finding emphasizes the importance of adequate control-data systems and a progressive rather than repressive approach to accountability. Accurate information by which to judge performance is important. Perhaps even more important is the manner in which such information is used.

Other Factors

When the two principal explanatory variables were controlled, none of the other factors examined was found to be significantly related to the Relative Productivity Index at the .10 level. Community factors such as racial and ethnic composition, found in other research to be important determinants of expenditure patterns and public regardingness,[13] were not found to be good predictors of the efficiency with which municipal funds were spent. Also lacking direct significance to relative productivity were organizational factors such as teamwork, communication processes, decision-making processes, education level of department heads, various city manager characteristics, employee unionization, the use of a wide variety of employee incentives and popular management techniques, volunteerism, contracting for services, various city council characteristics, and degree of reformism. Further research with a larger sample might establish the relevance of some of these factors to municipal productivity; however, their independent importance was not apparent in this analysis.

The absence of a finding of statistical significance between relative productivity and management techniques popularly perceived to improve productivity should not be construed to be a criticism of their effectiveness. This study, limited as it was to a small number of cities, simply failed to verify the productivity advantages of those techniques. It remains possible that a given technique may be quite effective under the conditions of heavy reliance on own-source revenues and progressive application of management control but much less effective absent those conditions. Overall effectiveness ratings would be diluted under such circumstances by those instances of less-than-optimum conditions for success. Even more fundamentally, variation in the effectiveness of a given technique may simply be a factor of managerial skill.

The small number and rather exclusive nature of the cities that have been examined here render the findings tentative and exploratory. Further research to confirm these findings on a larger scale and to examine the many hypotheses suggested is clearly in order.

MUNICIPAL PRODUCTIVITY IMPROVEMENT
IN PERSPECTIVE

The need for improved productivity in local government and the assumed desire of local officials to effect such improvement tend to be taken for granted by proponents of productivity improvement. It is important to recognize, however, that communities and their goals differ. Whether local governments are differentiated in terms of roles[14] or goals,[15] it is apparent that some local governments are likely to emphasize the need for productivity improvement to a greater degree than others.

Assuming a desire for productivity improvement, what advice can be given for the establishment of a system conducive to that end? Many writers on municipal productivity prescribe a major role for the federal government. Although a secondary role far less important than that of local government associations and local governments themselves seems most appropriate, federal involvement is nevertheless needed.

Local governments tend to be disjointed and isolated from one another, especially in their approach to technological research and development. Since the benefits to a single community often fail to justify the substantial costs of developing the prototype for an important productivity-enhancing process or tool, federal funding of research and development would be an important contribution.[16] Federal loans for major productivity-improvement projects, with repayments from savings in operating costs, could also be a major boon.[17] As noted previously, the federal government could also advance the cause of municipal productivity by the substitution of requirements for quantifiable program results in place of detailed procedural requirements in federally funded, locally administered programs, as recommended by the General Accounting Office.[18] Furthermore, the federal government should examine its role in intergovernmental relations and the impact that the current approach to financial assistance has upon municipal productivity in order to restructure the system for maximum productivity in the use of public funds.

State and national associations of local governments and local government occupations could also take steps to enhance the likelihood of productivity improvement in local government. Such associations could be instrumental in recognizing communities and individuals responsible for significant productivity improvement and, by so doing, could help overcome the reluctance of many officials to risk challenging the status quo. Associations could furthermore assume greater responsibility for objective program evaluation, either directly or through grants, and could also support applied productivity research in local governments.

Numerous writers have prescribed specific steps for local governments desiring to improve their productivity. Harry Hatry and Donald Fisk, for example, recommend such measures as the rotation of managers among agencies within a government, increased hiring of managers from outside the organization, provision of adequate responsibility and increased opportunity for early promotion, increased experimentation, expanded technological capabilities, improved planning and evaluation, better information dissemination on programs elsewhere, consideration of measures to achieve improved economies of scale, increased use of the private sector, establishment of adequate incentives and satisfactory working conditions for employees, mechanization of revenue collection, improved capabilities of local legislative bodies, improved labor-management relations, increased training of employees, and improvements in federally imposed procedures.[19] Many writers recommend the establishment of special productivity-improvement units within local governments, with Frederick Hayes suggesting that such units should be able to offset their expenses with an equivalent level of identified savings in the first year and aggregate savings well in excess of expenditures thereafter.[20]

The advice of Hatry, Fisk, Hayes, and many others regarding the importance of establishing suitable analytic capabilities within local governments, preferably in a special unit with responsibility for productivity improvement, appears to be well founded. The results of this study of 14 high-quality, full-service cities indicate that such a productivity-improvement unit would be well advised to adopt an overall strategy emphasizing opportunities for savings in own-source revenues or opportunities for program enhancement in activities supported by such resources. Among the principal tactics for productivity improvement should be the strengthening of management information systems; cooperative goal setting focusing upon tangible, measurable objectives; and increased accountability for program results, with emphasis on special rewards for excellence in performance.

This study has failed to provide significant support for the use of gimmicks or relatively simple special approaches to productivity improvement in local government. The incentive—or perhaps the pressure—of managing one's own resources and the progressive application of management control appear from this analysis to be principal keys to municipal productivity.

USEFULNESS OF THE RELATIVE PRODUCTIVITY
INDEX FOR FURTHER RESEARCH

The Relative Productivity Index offers a potentially useful means of examining relative productivity and community and organizational characteristics associated with it in all municipal service-quality strata—not just the one selected for this study. Further research focusing upon a different service-quality stratum, including perhaps a larger number of municipalities, could test the applicability of this study's findings in other settings and perhaps lead to a greater ability to generalize relevant associations.

The approach taken here to intercity productivity comparisons provides a means of controlling for quality-of-service differences among municipalities. Comparison of cities in any quality stratum is possible and potentially quite useful, both for the sake of providing revealing comparative information for those cities included and also for the possibility of instilling a sense of competitiveness that could have important productivity-improvement ramifications. In actual application, however, the procedure requires considerable effort in data collection, reconciliation of different financial reporting formats and categories, compilation of data, computation of relevant statistics, and analysis of results. Sponsorship of the project by a respected agency or association would perhaps minimize data-collection problems and make it possible to prevail upon the municipalities themselves to conform to a uniform format in reporting financial and performance data. Under such conditions, many of the difficulties could be minimized and important information pertaining to municipal productivity obtained.

NOTES

1. Nancy S. Hayward, "The Productivity Challenge," Public Administration Review 36 (September-October 1976): 544.

2. Robert Quinn, cited in Frederick O'R. Hayes, Productivity in Local Government (Lexington, Mass.: Lexington Books, 1977), p. 280.

3. See, for example, Jack L. Walker, "The Diffusion of Innovations among the American States," American Political Science Review 63 (1969): 883; and Robert K. Yin, Karen A. Heald, and Mary E. Vogel, Tinkering with the System: Technological Innovations in State and Local Services (Lexington, Mass.: Lexington Books, 1977), p. 71.

4. George W. Downs, Jr., Bureaucracy, Innovation, and Public Policy (Lexington, Mass.: Lexington Books, 1976), p. 96.

5. Hayward, "The Productivity Challenge," p. 549.

6. General Accounting Office (GAO), State and Local Government Productivity Improvement: What Is the Federal Role? (Washington, D. C.: U.S. Government Printing Office, 1978), p. 19.

7. Ibid., p. 25.

8. Lyle Fitch, "Metropolitan Financial Problems," Annals of the American Academy of Political and Social Science 314 (November 1957): 73.

9. Advisory Commission on Intergovernmental Relations, Payments in Lieu of Taxes on Federal Real Property (Washington, D. C.: U.S. Government Printing Office, 1981), p. 19.

10. Ibid., p. 8.

11. GAO, State and Local Government Productivity Improvement, pp. 62, 66.

12. Different organizational traits have been characterized by Likert as being in one of four distinguishable systems. See Rensis Likert, The Human Organization: Its Management and Value (New York: McGraw-Hill, 1967), pp. 3-12.

13. See, for example, Michael Aiken and Robert Alford, "Community Structure and Innovation," American Political Science Review 64 (1970): 843-64; Edward Banfield and James Q. Wilson, City Politics (Cambridge, Mass.: Harvard University Press, 1963), pp. 35-44; and Robert L. Lineberry and Edmund P. Fowler, "Reformism and Public Policies in American Cities," American Political Science Review 62 (1967): 701-16.

14. Oliver Williams and Charles Adrian have identified four local government roles as (1) promoting economic growth, (2) providing amenities, (3) maintaining traditional services, and (4) arbitrating conflicting interests. See Oliver P. Williams and Charles R. Adrian, "Community Types and Policy Differences," in City Politics and Public Policy, ed. James Q. Wilson (New York: John Wiley & Sons, 1968), pp. 17-36.

15. David Morgan has identified the four common urban service goals of local government as (1) efficiency, (2) effectiveness, (3) equity, and (4) responsiveness. See David R. Morgan, Managing Urban America: The Politics and Administration of America's Cities (North Scituate, Mass.: Duxbury Press, 1979), p. 150.

16. Hayes, Productivity in Local Government, p. 212.

17. For a description of such an approach on the state level in New Jersey, see Richard F. Keevey, "State Productivity Improvements: Building on Existing Strengths," Public Administration Review 40 (September-October 1980): 451-58.

18. GAO, State and Local Government Productivity Improvement, p. 62.

19. Harry P. Hatry and Donald M. Fisk, Improving Productivity and Productivity Measurement in Local Governments (Washington, D. C.: Urban Institute, 1971), pp. 49-59.

20. Frederick O'R. Hayes, "Resources for Productivity Programs," in Productivity Improvement Handbook for State and Local Government, ed. George J. Washnis (New York: John Wiley & Sons, 1980), pp. 39-47.

APPENDIX A

EXPENDITURE LEVELS
AMONG THE CITIES

Productivity comparisons among cities should be more than a simple contrasting of relative expenditure levels. Unless service quality, service quantity, and principal raw material costs (especially the cost of labor in the delivery of municipal services) are taken into account, total-expenditure comparisons reveal very little about relative proficiency in the efficient and effective provision of public services. Quality of service is an important factor, for a city providing a better service than its counterparts may be expected, ceteris paribus, to incur greater expenses as well. Other factors, such as the number of service recipients and the cost of labor as reflected in local wage rates, also influence total expenditures and should be considered in assessing relative productivity levels.

The 14 cities in this study were matched for their consistently high quality of municipal services in seven functional areas. Population, wages, and expenditure levels in selected functions for the 1979 and 1980 fiscal years were used to establish relative productivity levels in Chapter 5. The tables on the following pages report expenditures in applicable service functions for each of the 14 cities.

A few preliminary comments regarding data compilation are appropriate. The absence of uniformity in the reporting of detailed expenditure information complicates cross-city comparisons of financial data. Descriptive labels for expenditure categories may be identical for two or more cities and yet convey different meanings and cluster different sets of services. Furthermore, unusual developments in a community, such as the construction of major new facilities, can temporarily distort expenditure patterns. For these reasons, several steps were taken to promote uniformity in tabulating the expenditures of the 14 study cities. These steps included the following:

I. Guidelines were established governing the selection of data sources and the inclusion or exclusion of expenditure categories and municipal service functions. The guidelines were as follows:

A. Where available, budget documents indicating actual expenditures in previous years and generally providing a more complete description of services rendered were used to supplement the general expenditure information of annual financial reports. In all cases, however, actual expenditures were tabulated rather than budgeted amounts.

B. Major capital expenditures that appeared to be of a nonroutine nature—especially those included in a special capital-expenditures activity or account—have been omitted from the tabulation. Smaller or more routine capital outlays reported within functional activities have been included as operational expenses.

C. Debt service has been omitted from the tabulation. The magnitude of such expenditures may be more a matter of when a given capital improvement was constructed than the quality of services or manner of municipal operations.

D. Although used as a performance measure in the identification of high-quality-service cities, street maintenance activities have been excluded from expenditure analysis. Intercity differences in reporting practices for direct and overhead expenses in street maintenance make reliable intercity financial comparisons unwieldy. Furthermore, even temporary changes in development activity within a given city can seriously distort this expenditure category.

E. For purposes of this study, general government expenses are considered to be those incurred in the conduct of a set of administrative staff functions common to all city governments. Special care was required in the tabulation of these expenditures, since general government often carries a somewhat different meaning from one city to another. Not only are intercity definitional differences common, many cities are internally inconsistent in the application of the general government label in two major financial documents: their financial statement and their annual budget. For this study, the cities' reported, lump-sum expenditures for general government as defined by the cities themselves were simply accepted only when more detailed financial data were unavailable. In instances where details were available, expenditures for the following functions were included as general government activities: assistant manager or administrator, auditor, budget, city attorney, city clerk, city manager or chief administrator, city treasurer, data processing, elections, employee or labor relations, finance and accounting, governing body, grants administration, personnel, printing, public information, purchasing, tax assessor and collections, and directly related functions. Among the excluded expenditures that conceivably could have been included in a differently defined general government function were those for airport, bad debts, building and grounds maintenance, central warehousing, city engineer, community development, Community Development Block Grant (CDBG) projects, Comprehensive Employment Training Act (CETA) projects or administration, contributions to community agencies, cultural affairs, data processing or accounting services for utility funds or agencies other than those identified as general government, economic development, housing assistance, insurance (other than group life and health insurance for general government employees), motor pool, municipal court, office on aging, office of energy and technology, planning (often a public works function), public service employment, public works and other line activities, real estate management, risk management, transportation, and workers' compensation.

F. Library expenditures include all costs reported for the library function, including auxiliary or special services.

G. Parks and recreation expenditures include only those costs commonly associated with the traditional parks-and-recreation function in most cities. Park maintenance, arts and crafts, athletics programs, swimming pools, tennis courts, senior citizen programs, and the operation of recreation centers are common examples. Excluded from the tabulation are the less common (but by no means unique) expenditures for such functions as convention center operation and promotion, golf courses, museums, and the operation of professional baseball facilities.

H. Public safety expenditures include only those for the police and fire functions. Excluded are civil defense, building code and health inspections, and ambulance services, each of which is listed as a public safety function in at least some cities.

I. Refuse collection and disposal expenditures include all costs reported for commercial and residential services.

J. Where identifiable from available documents, net rather than gross expenditures have been reported for general government activities. The use of net expenditures helps to produce equity between cities in instances in which a given function is performed in one city by line departments and in another city by a general government office with charges levied against line departments benefiting from the service. The use of net expenditures also minimizes the possibility of double-counting expenditures in general government, a collection of activities in which interdepartmental services and charges are especially common (for example, the use of gross expenses of the data processing department plus gross expenses of the accounting department, including charges for data processing services, would double-count data processing). Gross expenditures, where available, are reported for all other services.

K. The total General Fund expenditure is reported simply to provide a sense of perspective regarding the magnitude of total operations. Excluded are General Fund allocations for local school support.

II.   Expenditures were tabulated for the 14 study cities using the above-stated guidelines.

III.   The tabulations for the 14 cities were sent in initial draft form to the respective city managers along with a copy of the guidelines in an effort to correct any misinterpretation of financial data. Each was requested to provide feedback confirming the accuracy of the tabulations or noting any incorrect figures or instances of noncompliance with the specified guidelines. Replies were received from the city manager or a finance or budgetary official in all 14 cities, five specifying corrections to be made and nine confirming the accuracy of the tabulations.

IV.   Corrections, where feedback indicated they were necessary, were made prior to the use of expenditure data in the study.

The resulting expenditure tables are provided on the following pages.

TABLE A.1

Municipal Expenditures by Function in Sunnyvale, California, Fiscal Year 1979
(in dollars)

Selected Functions	Expenditure
General government[a]	1,737,953
Library	1,160,276
Parks and recreation[b]	3,436,399
Public safety	9,116,330
Refuse collection and disposal	2,882,222
General Fund total	20,839,237[c]

Fiscal year = July 1, 1978, to June 30, 1979.

[a]General government expenditures reported are listed by Sunnyvale as planning and management and include city council, city manager, and departments of administration and finance.

[b]Golf course expenditures ($389,795) not reported for the sake of comparability with other cities.

[c]The General Fund total includes more than the selected functions listed here.

Sources: City of Sunnyvale, California, Resource Allocation Plan (1980–81); and idem, Comprehensive Annual Financial Report (1979).

TABLE A.2

Municipal Expenditures by Function in Sunnyvale, California, Fiscal Year 1980
(in dollars)

Selected Functions	Expenditure
General government[a]	1,996,434
Library	1,018,341
Parks and recreation[b]	3,667,208
Public safety	9,830,172
Refuse collection and disposal[c]	3,512,500
General Fund total	22,442,967[d]

Fiscal year = July 1, 1979, to June 30, 1980.

[a]General government expenditures include fiscal planning and control ($167,215); accounting ($234,611); revenue billing and collection ($359,087); purchasing and stores ($169,839); community relations ($100,430); city council ($58,590); boards and commissions ($23,418); municipal elections ($14,878); management ($143,042); policy and systems ($77,648); management services administration ($80,937); legal services ($233,460); official records ($91,834); personnel services ($179,869); and productivity improvement ($61,576).

[b]Golf course expenditures ($477,376) not reported for the sake of comparability with other cities.

[c]Street-sweeping costs ($216,097) not reported for the sake of comparability with other cities.

[d]The General Fund total includes more than the selected functions listed above.

Sources: City of Sunnyvale, California, Comprehensive Annual Financial Report (1980); idem, Resource Allocation Plan (1980–81); and idem, Resource Allocation Plan (1981–82).

TABLE A.3

Municipal Expenditures by Function in Fort Walton Beach, Florida, Fiscal Year 1979
(in dollars)

Selected Functions	Expenditure
General government[a]	730,351
Library	120,627
Parks and recreation[b]	492,991
Public safety[c]	1,462,720
Refuse collection and disposal	556,731
General Fund total	4,748,339[d]

Fiscal year = October 1, 1978, to September 30, 1979.

[a]Includes legislative ($15,000), executive ($141,216), financial and administrative ($290,007), legal counsel ($66,382), and other general government services ($217,746). The sum of $20,980 in special revenue funds was spent for general government services in fiscal year 1979, of which $5,414 was Community Development Block Grant. The remaining $15,566 is not specified as to legislative, executive, or other expenditure categories and therefore is not included for purposes of this study.

[b]Includes parks and recreation department ($451,303) and tennis center ($41,688). Excludes golf course department ($314,792). The sum of $28,057 in special revenue funds was spent for culture/recreation in fiscal year 1979; however, it is not specified as to parks and recreation, library, golf courses, or museum and therefore is not included for purposes of this study.

[c]Includes law enforcement ($853,887); fire control ($605,740); and detention/correction ($3,093). Excludes protective inspections.

[d]The General Fund total includes more than the selected functions listed above.

Source: City of Fort Walton Beach, Florida, Annual Financial Report Fiscal Year Ended September 30, 1979.

TABLE A.4

Municipal Expenditures by Function in Fort Walton Beach, Florida, Fiscal Year 1980
(in dollars)

Selected Functions	Expenditure
General government[a]	766,432
Library	135,779
Parks and recreation[b]	552,679
Public safety[c]	1,633,571
Refuse collection and disposal	642,018
General Fund total	5,397,740[d]

Fiscal year = October 1, 1979, to September 30, 1980.

[a]Includes legislative ($15,200); executive ($140,340); financial and administrative ($307,251); legal counsel ($36,905); and other general government services ($266,736). The sum of $58,598 in special revenue funds was spent for general government services in fiscal year 1980, of which $7,330 was Community Development Block Grant. The remaining $51,268 is not specified as to legislative, executive, or other expenditure categories and therefore is not included for purposes of this study.

[b]Includes parks and recreation department ($511,862) and tennis center ($40,817). Excludes golf course department ($566,450). The sum of $25,221 in special revenue funds was spent for culture/recreation in fiscal year 1980; however, it is not specified as to parks and recreation, library, golf courses, or museum and therefore is not included for purposes of this study.

[c]Includes law enforcement ($1,067,898); fire control ($540,041); and detention/correction ($25,632). Excludes protective inspections.

[d]The General Fund total includes more than the selected functions listed above.

Source: City of Fort Walton Beach, Florida, Annual Financial Report Fiscal Year Ended September 30, 1980.

TABLE A.5

Municipal Expenditures by Function in Gainesville, Florida, Fiscal Year 1979
(in dollars)

Selected Functions	Expenditure
General government[a]	1,329,588
Library[b]	761,236
Parks and recreation[c]	956,020
Public safety[d]	7,906,871
Refuse collection and disposal	1,679,452
General Fund total	18,615,248[e]

Fiscal year = October 1, 1978, to September 30, 1979.

[a]General Fund activities included as general government are city commission; clerk of the commission; city manager; city attorney; finance; purchasing; and personnel, less bad debts and contributions to community agencies ($143,282) and utility operating expenses ($651,154). Special Fund expenditures include Gainesville Comprehensive Survey ($16,000); management by objectives ($59,714); other projects ($44,467); and other ($2,760).

[b]Library expenditures include General Fund ($721,778) and special funds ($39,458).

[c]Parks and recreation expenditures include General Fund ($920,663) and special funds ($35,357).

[d]Public safety expenditures include General Fund ($7,844,147) and special funds ($62,724).

[e]The General Fund total includes more than the selected functions listed above.

Sources: City of Gainesville, Florida, Financial Report: Fiscal Year Ended September 30, 1980, pp. 36–46; and information from the City of Gainesville accounting manager.

TABLE A.6

Municipal Expenditures by Function in Gainesville, Florida, Fiscal Year 1980
(in dollars)

Selected Functions	Expenditure
General government[a]	1,670,188
Library[b]	856,318
Parks and recreation[c]	978,216
Public safety[d]	8,630,281
Refuse collection and disposal	1,921,511
General Fund total	21,397,196[e]

Fiscal year = October 1, 1979, to September 30, 1980.

[a]General Fund activities included as general government are city commission; clerk of the commission; city manager; city attorney; finance; purchasing; personnel; and internal auditor, less bad debts and contributions to community agencies ($590,252) and utility operating expenses ($682,617). Special Fund expenditures include Gainesville Comprehensive Survey ($42,673); other projects ($16,325); and other ($5,311).

[b]Library expenditures include General Fund ($833,262) and special funds ($23,056).

[c]Parks and recreation expenditures include General Fund ($945,424) and special funds ($32,792).

[d]Public safety expenditures include General Fund ($8,506,641) and special funds ($123,640).

[e]The General Fund total includes more than the selected functions listed above.

Sources: City of Gainesville, Florida, Financial Report: Fiscal Year Ended September 30, 1980, pp. 36–46; and information from the City of Gainesville accounting manager.

TABLE A.7

Municipal Expenditures by Function in Saint Petersburg, Florida, Fiscal Year 1979
(in dollars)

Selected Functions	Expenditure
General government[a]	4,232,000
Library[b]	1,129,000
Parks and recreation[c]	4,743,000
Public safety	22,044,000
Refuse collection and disposal[d]	8,394,000
General Fund total	45,073,000[e]

Fiscal year = October 1, 1978, to September 30, 1979.

[a]Includes mayor and city council, city manager, legal, employee relations, labor relations, budget and management, data processing—General Fund operations, grants administration, internal audit, finance, purchasing, and administrative services. Not included are human relations, risk management, data processing—Internal Service Fund, utility accounting, central stores, economic development, and Office on Aging.

[b]Library expenditures include General Fund ($1,103,000) and special funds for Senior Citizen Bookreach ($26,000).

[c]Includes leisure services administration, recreation, parks, and landscape and design. Omitted for the sake of comparability with other cities are administration of a professional baseball facility, the Bayfront Center, a marina, golf courses, a pier complex, and the Edgewater Beach Inn.

[d]Includes expenditures from Sanitation Operating Fund ($8,171,000) and General Fund ($223,000).

[e]The General Fund total includes more than the selected functions listed above.

Source: City of Saint Petersburg, Florida, Approved Operating Budget (1980-81).

TABLE A.8

Municipal Expenditures by Function in Saint Petersburg, Florida, Fiscal Year 1980
(in dollars)

Selected Functions	Expenditure
General government[a]	4,197,000
Library[b]	1,209,000
Parks and recreation[c]	5,281,000
Public safety[d]	23,009,000
Refuse collection and disposal	10,296,000
General Fund total	44,667,000[e]

Fiscal year = October 1, 1979, to September 30, 1980.

[a]Includes mayor/city council, city manager, legal, employee relations, labor relations, budget and management, intergovernmental relations, internal audit, finance—General Fund, purchasing, and administrative services—General Fund. Not included are Internal Service Fund expenditures, risk management, utility accounting, central stores, administrative services—Internal Service Fund, economic development, real estate management, Office on Aging, and Office of Energy and Technology.

[b]Library expenditures include a special grant for Senior Citizen Bookreach ($1,000).

[c]Includes leisure services administration, recreation (excluding pier operation), and parks. Omitted for the sake of comparability with other cities are pier operation, baseball (professional) facilities, the Bayfront Center, marina, golf courses, and the Edgewater Beach Motel.

[d]Public safety expenditures include General Fund ($22,971,000), special grants for crime prevention for the elderly ($22,000), and miscellaneous police grants ($16,000).

[e]The General Fund total includes more than the selected functions listed above.

Sources: City of Saint Petersburg, Florida, 1982 Recommended Program Budget; and idem, Recommended Operating Budget (1981-82).

TABLE A.9

Municipal Expenditures by Function in Lake Forest, Illinois, Fiscal Year 1979
(in dollars)

Selected Functions	Expenditure
General government[a]	561,411
Library[b]	287,534
Parks and recreation[c]	722,216
Public safety[d]	1,816,136
Refuse collection and disposal	356,511
General Fund total	3,935,629[e]

Fiscal year = May 1, 1978, to April 30, 1979.

[a]Included are city council, city manager, fiscal and administrative services (except fire and police commission) and law.

[b]Does not include $114,680 designated for library capital equipment in fiscal year 1979. According to the Lake Forest director of finance, this expenditure was for the final costs incurred in a two-year project to construct an addition to the library building and should be considered a capital improvement rather than operating expenses.

[c]Parks and forestry and recreation are included; golf ($206,818) is excluded for the sake of comparability with other cities.

[d]Police; fire (except civil defense [$7,876] and emergency medical services and training [$75,509]); and police and firemen's pensions.

[e]The General Fund total includes more than the selected functions listed above.

Sources: City of Lake Forest, Illinois, Annual Budget (1981); idem, Annual Report (April 30, 1980), especially p. 77; and information from the Lake Forest director of finance.

TABLE A.10

Municipal Expenditures by Function in Lake Forest, Illinois, Fiscal Year 1980
(in dollars)

Selected Functions	Expenditure
General government[a]	660,255
Library	341,590
Parks and recreation[b]	850,891
Public safety[c]	1,962,467
Refuse collection and disposal	374,086
General Fund total	4,641,153[d]

Fiscal year = May 1, 1979, to April 30, 1980.

[a]Included are city council, city manager, city clerk, finance, computer services, fiscal and administrative services (except fire and police commission), budget and systems, and law.

[b]Parks and forestry and recreation are included; golf ($222,323) is excluded for the sake of comparability with other cities.

[c]Police, fire (except civil defense [$1,060] and ambulance service and training [$71,033]); and police and firemen's pensions.

[d]The General Fund total includes more than the selected functions listed above.

Source: City of Lake Forest, Illinois, Annual Report (April 30, 1980), pp. 15, 50-51, 77.

TABLE A. 11

Municipal Expenditures by Function in Owensboro, Kentucky, Fiscal
Year 1979
(in dollars)

Selected Functions	Expenditure
General government[a]	791,790
Library	365,929
Parks and recreation[b]	1,043,077
Public safety[c]	3,765,883
Refuse collection and disposal[d]	1,560,297
General Fund total	10,032,226[e]

Fiscal year = June 1, 1978, to May 31, 1979.

[a]General Fund activities included as general government are
those listed in the Annual Financial Report as administration—city
commission, finance, personnel, and administrative. Omitted from
the Owensboro general government listing are Comprehensive Employment Training Act and bad debts. The Annual Financial Report
for 1980 shows numerous transfers from the Capital Improvement
Fund for the planning commission, development district, and other
purposes; but these are not listed as general government expenditures. The Annual Financial Report for 1979 shows no special revenue expenditures for general government through May 31, 1979.

[b]Includes parks ($604,262); recreation ($234,420); and transfers
from Capital Improvement Fund to Community Recreation Center
($10,000) and English Park ($194,395).

[c]Public safety includes police ($2,016,272); fire ($1,649,611);
and transfer of $100,000 from Capital Improvement Fund to Police
and Firemen's Retirement Fund.

[d]Listed as sanitation.

[e]The General Fund total includes more than the selected functions listed above.

Sources: City of Owensboro, Kentucky, Annual Financial Report (1979), p. 3; idem, Annual Financial Report (1980), pp. 26-42;
and Owensboro-Daviess County Public Library, Statement of Receipts and Disbursements (July 1, 1978, to June 30, 1979).

TABLE A. 12

Municipal Expenditures by Function in Owensboro, Kentucky,
Fiscal Year 1980
(in dollars)

Selected Functions	Expenditure
General government[a]	822,295
Library	446,058
Parks and recreation[b]	996,128
Public safety[c]	4,105,413
Refuse collection and disposal[d]	1,959,683
General Fund total	11,315,340[e]

Fiscal year = July 1, 1979, to June 30, 1980

[a]Activities included as general government are those listed in the Annual Financial Report as administration—city commission, finance, personnel, and administrative. Omitted from the Owensboro general government listing are public service employment, Comprehensive Employment Training Act (CETA) on-job training, CETA wages, and bad debts. The Annual Financial Report shows numerous transfers from the Capital Improvement Fund for the planning commission, development district, and other purposes; but these are not listed as general government expenditures. It furthermore shows a special revenue expenditure of $3,517 for general government, but this is from community development funds—a category excluded from general government for purposes of this study.

[b]Includes parks ($778,814); recreation ($208,083); and a transfer from Capital Improvement Fund to Community Recreation Center ($9,231).

[c]Public safety includes police ($2,139,607); fire ($1,804,849); and a transfer of $160,957 from Capital Improvement Fund to Police and Firemen's Retirement Fund.

[d]Listed as sanitation.

[e]The General Fund total includes more than the selected functions listed above.

Note: The city of Owensboro shifted its fiscal year with the 1979-80 year and reported 13-month expenditures. Therefore, reported expenditures were reduced by one-thirteenth for this table.

Sources: City of Owensboro, Kentucky, Annual Financial Report (1980), pp. 3, 26-42; and Owensboro-Daviess County Public Library, Statement of Receipts and Disbursements (year ended June 30, 1980).

Municipal Expenditures by Function in Chapel Hill, North Carolina,
Fiscal Year 1979
(in dollars)

Selected Functions	Expenditure
General government[a]	602,786
Library	277,482
Parks and recreation	421,114
Public safety[b]	1,909,609
Refuse collection and disposal[c]	567,465
General Fund total	6,370,577[d]

Fiscal year = July 1, 1978, to June 30, 1979

[a]Activities included as general government are those listed in the Budget as mayor/council, town manager, personnel, elections, finance, revenue collections, town clerk, and legal.

[b]The police department provides animal control services in addition to more traditional services and includes two animal control officers. The special costs associated with animal control were not identified in the budget and therefore have not been excluded. The town also operates a public safety officer (PSO) program, based in the fire department, with two PSOs in fiscal year 1979.

[c]The town operates a landfill that generates revenues in excess of expenditures. Total landfill expenditures are not reported. Only landfill use fees paid as part of the town's solid-waste-collection activity are reported, along with other collection expenditures.

[d]The General Fund total includes more than the selected functions listed above.

Note: Neither Capital Improvement Fund expenditures nor general revenue-sharing expenditures, also commonly used for capital improvements or major equipment acquisition, are reported in this table. Specific uses of the two funds for fiscal year 1979 were not reported in the material obtained from Chapel Hill. Expenditures for equipment maintenance, fuel, and tires in Chapel Hill are consolidated in a single activity and are not reported for the selected functions. The director of finance and administrative assistant in the public works department provided the following expenditure estimates for these items, which have been incorporated into the figures reported in this table: general government, $600; library, $1,300; parks and recreation, $9,000; public safety, $56,000; and refuse collection and disposal, $66,000.

Sources: Town of Chapel Hill, North Carolina, Adopted Budget (1981-82); and information from the Chapel Hill director of finance.

TABLE A.14

Municipal Expenditures by Function in Chapel Hill, North Carolina
Fiscal Year 1980
(in dollars)

Selected Functions	Expenditure
General government[a]	645,036
Library	319,466
Parks and recreation	505,252
Public safety[b]	2,310,735
Refuse collection and disposal[c]	623,236
General Fund total	7,268,011[d]

Fiscal year = July 1, 1979, to June 30, 1980

[a]Activities included as general government are those listed in the Budget as mayor/council, town manager, personnel, elections, finance, revenue collections, town clerk, and legal.

[b]The police department provides animal control services in addition to more traditional services and includes two animal control officers. The special costs associated with animal control were not identified in the budget and therefore have not been excluded. The town also operates a public safety officer (PSO) program, based in the fire department, with two PSOs in fiscal year 1980.

[c]The town operates a landfill that generates revenues in excess of expenditures. Total landfill expenditures are not reported. Only landfill use fees paid as part of the town's solid-waste-collection activity are reported, along with other collection expenditures.

[d]The General Fund total includes more than the selected functions listed above.

Note: Neither Capital Improvement Fund expenditures nor general revenue-sharing expenditures, also commonly used for capital improvements or major equipment acquisition, are reported in this table. Specific uses of the two funds for fiscal year 1980 were not reported in the material obtained from Chapel Hill. Expenditures for equipment maintenance, fuel, and tires in Chapel Hill are consolidated in a single activity and are not reported for the selected functions. The director of finance and administrative assistant in the public works department provided the following expenditure estimates for these items, which have been incorporated into the figures reported in this table: general government, $600; library, $1,400; parks and recreation, $11,000; public safety, $71,000; and refuse collection and disposal, $77,000.

Sources: Town of Chapel Hill, North Carolina, Adopted Budget (1981-82); and information from the Chapel Hill director of finance.

TABLE A. 15

Municipal Expenditures by Function in Greensboro, North Carolina,
Fiscal Year 1979
(in dollars)

Selected Functions	Expenditure
General government[a]	3,255,776
Library[b]	1,602,005
Parks and recreation[c]	3,635,543
Public safety[d]	14,292,118
Refuse collection and disposal[e]	2,696,114
General Fund total	36,123,103[f]

Fiscal year = July 1, 1978, to June 30, 1979

[a]Includes General Fund expenditures for legislative, executive (except human relations), personnel, finance, and law ($3,255,776). General revenue-sharing expenditures designated for maintenance and operations in the finance department ($215,595) and antirecession expenditures in the finance department ($98,000) were primarily reallocated for street maintenance and contributions to nonprofit agencies and were excluded from this figure. No funds from these sources were actually used for finance department operations, according to the finance director. Manpower Consortium Fund expenditures also are excluded.

[b]Library includes General Fund expenditures ($1,533,740) and general revenue sharing expenditures for maintenance and operations ($50,339).

[c]Includes parks and recreation department, with the exception of Gillespie golf course ($83,444); Bryan Park golf course ($390,775); Natural Science Center and zoo ($272,200); and Memorial Stadium ($106,521), which are excluded for the sake of intercity comparability, and also includes general revenue-sharing expenditures for parks and recreation, excluding capital outlay ($10,330).

[d]Public safety includes the General Fund expenditures for the public safety, police, and fire departments, with the exception of the Emergency Management Assistance Agency—civil defense ($13,653,974), and the general revenue-sharing expenditures for police and fire, excluding capital outlay ($638,144).

[e]Includes sanitation administration, waste collection, and solid waste disposal—city.

[f]The General Fund total includes more than the selected functions listed above.

Sources: City of Greensboro, North Carolina, Annual Budget (1980-81); and information from the Greensboro finance director.

TABLE A. 16

Municipal Expenditures by Function in Greensboro, North Carolina,
Fiscal Year 1980
(in dollars)

Selected Functions	Expenditure
General government[a]	3,384,173
Library[b]	1,967,599
Parks and recreation[c]	3,976,549
Public safety[d]	15,470,197
Refuse collection and disposal[e]	2,877,820
General Fund total	39,430,580[f]

Fiscal year = July 1, 1979, to June 30, 1980

[a]Includes General Fund expenditures for legislative, executive, personnel, finance, and law ($3,384,173). General revenue-sharing expenditures designated for maintenance and operations in the finance department ($401,475) and antirecession expenditures in the finance department ($22,028) were primarily reallocated for street maintenance and contributions to nonprofit agencies and are excluded from this figure. No funds from these sources were actually used for finance department operations, according to the finance director. Manpower Consortium Fund expenditures also are excluded.

[b]Library includes General Fund expenditures ($1,897,580) and general revenue-sharing expenditures ($50,000) for maintenance and operations.

[c]Includes parks and recreation department, with the exception of Gillespie golf course ($91,868); Bryan Park golf course ($418,480); Natural Science Center and zoo ($302,794); and Memorial Stadium ($77,312), which are excluded for the sake of intercity comparability.

[d]Public safety includes the General Fund expenditures for the public safety, police, and fire departments, with the exception of the Emergency Management Assistance Agency—civil defense ($14,891,472); and also includes general revenue-sharing expenditures for police and fire, excluding capital outlay ($578,725).

[e]Includes sanitation administration, waste collection, waste disposal, and solid waste disposal—city.

[f]The General Fund total includes more than the selected functions listed above.

Sources: City of Greensboro, North Carolina, Annual Budget (1981-82); and information from the Greensboro finance director.

TABLE A.17

Municipal Expenditures by Function in Upper Arlington, Ohio,
Fiscal Year 1979
(in dollars)

Selected Functions	Expenditure
General government[a]	581,701
Library[b]	886,225
Parks and recreation[c]	690,803
Public safety[d]	3,248,532
Refuse collection and disposal[e]	736,809
General Fund total	6,737,976[f]

Fiscal year = January 1, 1979, to December 31, 1979

[a]General government includes city council ($9,331); city clerk ($45,379 + $15,995 = $61,374); finance administration ($203,474 + $27,101 = $230,575); city manager, including purchasing and personnel ($139,570 + $33,866 = $173,436); city attorney ($65,234 + $17,777 = $83,011); civil service expenses and legal advertisements ($4,411); and a portion of deductions by county auditor ($19,563). Not included from Upper Arlington's general government listing are mayor's court, city engineer, lands and buildings, portions of other administrative, and workmen's compensation.

[b]Library expenditures are reported separately from the General Fund. Not reported, for purposes of this study, are substantial debt-service expenditures ($206,150) in fiscal year 1979.

[c]Parks and recreation includes parks ($438,190 + $71,444 = $509,634); recreation ($140,984); and cultural activities ($35,991 + $4,194 = $40,185).

[d]Public safety includes general law enforcement ($1,018,541 + $237,593 = $1,256,134); fire prevention and control ($1,465,600 + $305,009 = $1,770,609); communications ($74,788 + $25,068 = $99,856); and police and fire pension reserve ($121,933).

[e]Refuse collection and disposal is listed as garbage and refuse collection ($592,159 + $144,650 = $936,809).

[f]The General Fund total includes more than the selected functions listed above.

Note: The city of Upper Arlington reports city expenditures for employee retirement contributions and group insurance in an account separate from departmental totals. The city's retirement contribution in 1979 was 13.95 percent of payroll. The cost of group insurance was $189,278 for coverage for the city's approximately 246 employees, or approximately $775 per employee. Expenses for stationery and supplies; gasoline; equipment rental and maintenance; training, travel, and conferences; telephones; and vehicle maintenance are also reported as citywide totals, amounting to a grand total of $407,416. For purposes of this report, these consolidated expenses have been reallocated to selected functions based upon payroll (retirement) or upon the percentage of total city employment represented by a given department. These reallocated expenses appear as the second figure within the parentheses in the footnotes to this table.

All federal revenue-sharing expenditures in fiscal year 1979 were for equipment and capital outlay. Those expenditures are not reported for purposes of this study.

Source: City of Upper Arlington, Ohio, 1981 Budget.

Municipal Expenditures by Function in Upper Arlington, Ohio,
Fiscal Year 1980
(in dollars)

Selected Functions	Expenditure
General government[a]	662,046
Library[b]	1,093,756
Parks and recreation[c]	560,639
Public safety[d]	3,343,136
Refuse collection and disposal[e]	881,752
General Fund total	7,203,026[f]

Fiscal year = January 1, 1980, to December 31, 1980

[a]General government includes expenditures and encumbrances at year end for city council ($9,439); city clerk ($40,668 + $16,925 = $57,593); finance administration ($227,296 + $30,234 = $257,530); city manager ($124,426 + $30,139 = $154,565); purchasing and personnel ($25,930 + $7,662 = $33,592); city attorney ($80,991 + $20,263 = $101,254); civil service expenses and legal advertisements ($9,010); a portion of deductions by county auditor ($34,363); and new equipment for these activities ($4,700). Not included from Upper Arlington's general government listing are mayor's court, city engineer, lands and buildings, portions of other administrative, and workmen's compensation.

[b]Library expenditures are reported separately from the General Fund. Estimated 1980 expenditures, as listed in the 1981 Budget, are reported in this table.

[c]Parks and recreation includes expenditures and encumbrances at year end for parks ($271,909 + $83,234 = $355,143); recreation ($150,478); cultural activities ($47,913 + $4,673 = $52,586); and new equipment for parks and recreation—cultural arts ($2,432).

[d]Public safety includes expenditures and encumbrances at year end for police division ($975,876 + $254,321 = $1,230,197); juvenile-community-relations program ($84,689 + $21,261 = $105,950); fire division ($1,448,655 + $349,938 = $1,798,593); communications division ($75,260 + $27,700 = $102,960); police and fire pension reserve ($103,936); and new equipment—police ($1,500).

[e]Refuse collection and disposal includes expenditures and encumbrances at year end for sanitation division ($644,375 + $166,814 = $811,189) and new equipment—sanitation division ($70,563).

[f]Includes expenditures and encumbrances at year end. The General Fund total includes more than the selected functions listed above.

Note: The city of Upper Arlington reports city expenditures for employee retirement contributions and group insurance in an account separate from departmental totals. The city's retirement contribution in 1980 was 13.95 percent of payroll. The cost of group insurance was $233,997 (expended or encumbered at year end) for coverage for the city's approximately 246 employees, or approximately $951 per employee. Expenses for stationery and supplies; gasoline; equipment rental and maintenance; training, travel, and conferences; telephones; and vehicle maintenance are also reported as citywide totals, amounting to a grand total of $473,376 (expended or encumbered at year end). For purposes of this report, these consolidated expenses have been reallocated to selected functions based upon payroll (retirement) or upon the percentage of total city employment represented by a given department. These reallocated expenses appear as the second figure within the parentheses in the footnotes to this table.

All federal revenue-sharing expenditures in fiscal year 1980 were for equipment and capital outlay. Those expenditures are not reported for purposes of this study.

Sources: City of Upper Arlington, Ohio, The Finance Director's Annual Report of Receipts and Disbursements for Period Ending December 31, 1980; and idem, 1981 Budget.

TABLE A.19

Municipal Expenditures by Function in Oak Ridge, Tennessee,
Fiscal Year 1979
(in dollars)

Selected Functions	Expenditure
General government[a]	470,186
Library	297,249
Parks and recreation[b]	650,155
Public safety[c]	1,903,805
Refuse collection and disposal	677,161
General Fund total	4,872,714[d]

Fiscal year = July 1, 1978, to June 30, 1979

[a]General government includes city council ($26,097), elections ($3,494), city clerk ($24,267), city manager ($51,282), administrative management ($30,468), legal ($26,716), budget officer ($10,801), data processing ($50,515), personnel ($53,476), finance supervision ($25,987), stationery stores ($42,909), general accounting ($38,451), business office ($10,557), tax and license administration ($42,688), purchasing ($4,168), and community services control ($28,310). Among the excluded activities are planning, city court, warehousing, insurance, and economic development.

[b]Parks and recreation includes gross expenditures for recreation supervision ($64,772), playgrounds ($22,018), swimming pools ($122,732), community centers ($219,470), athletics ($54,646), parks ($98,675), concessions ($5,038), Senior Center programs ($54,157), and federal revenue-sharing expenditures at the Recreation Center ($6,419) and the Senior Center ($2,228).

[c]Public safety includes gross expenditures for police ($968,900) and fire ($934,905). Excluded is civil defense ($12,861).

The General Fund total includes more than the selected functions listed above. The reported total, however, excludes the General Fund appropriation to local schools.

Sources: City of Oak Ridge, Tennessee, Budget Nineteen Eighty-One; and idem, Annual Financial Report for Fiscal Year Ending June 30, 1979.

TABLE A.20

Municipal Expenditures by Function in Oak Ridge, Tennessee,
Fiscal Year 1980
(in dollars)

Selected Functions	Expenditure
General government[a]	545,767
Library	330,627
Parks and recreation[b]	718,051
Public safety[c]	2,107,016
Refuse collection and disposal	730,210
General Fund total	5,258,095[d]

Fiscal year = July 1, 1979, to June 30, 1980

[a]General government includes city council ($31,210), elections ($79), city clerk ($25,929), city manager ($50,937), administrative management ($33,741), legal ($30,771), research and budget supervision—General Fund ($14,547), budget officer ($13,261), data processing ($66,985), personnel ($55,619), finance supervision ($27,510), stationery stores ($39,627), general accounting ($33,663), business office ($11,750), tax and license administration ($35,975), purchasing ($9,808), community services control ($33,948), and special funds for research and budget supervision ($30,407). Among the excluded activities are planning, city court, warehousing, insurance, and economic development.

[b]Parks and recreation includes gross expenditures for recreation supervision ($72,476), playgrounds ($21,820), swimming pools ($119,971), community centers ($211,484), athletics ($102,236), parks ($136,074), concessions ($9,537), and senior center programs ($44,453).

[c]Public safety includes gross expenditures for police ($1,110,327) and fire ($996,689).

[d]The General Fund total includes more than the selected functions listed above. The reported total, however, excludes the General Fund appropriation to local schools.

Sources: City of Oak Ridge, Tennessee, 1982 Budget; and idem, Annual Financial Report for Fiscal Year Ending June 30, 1980.

TABLE A.21

Municipal Expenditures by Function in Austin, Texas,
Fiscal Year 1979
(in dollars)

Selected Functions	Expenditure
General government[a]	9,686,636
Library[b]	4,107,651
Parks and recreation[c]	8,495,653
Public safety[d]	27,347,250
Refuse collection and disposal	3,828,675
General Fund total	82,425,256[e]

Fiscal year = October 1, 1978, to September 30, 1979

[a]Includes mayor/council ($165,434), city manager ($216,642), city clerk ($354,196), management services ($187,926), data systems ($1,119,813), city attorney ($906,637), personnel ($896,994), public information ($577,544), internal auditing ($112,699), finance ($1,116,350), purchases and stores ($1,094,645), research and budget ($368,161), auditing ($140,355), election cost ($87,678), and tax ($2,341,562).

[b]Deductions for Central Texas Library System, health sciences, and others reduce net expenditures to $3,589,234.

[c]Does not include auditorium and coliseum department ($737,986) or golf courses ($721,670). Deductions for expense refunds reduce net expenditures to $7,996,352.

[d]Includes fire ($10,350,957 gross), police ($16,984,395 gross), and firemen's pension system expense ($11,898).

[e]The General Fund total includes more than the selected functions listed above.

Source: City of Austin, Texas, 1980-81 Approved Annual Budget.

Municipal Expenditures by Function in Austin, Texas,
Fiscal Year 1980
(in dollars)

Selected Functions	Expenditure
General government[a]	10,910,598
Library[b]	4,153,143
Parks and recreation[c]	10,235,990
Public safety[d]	31,188,086
Refuse collection and disposal	4,332,442
General Fund total	95,630,092[e]

Fiscal year = October 1, 1979, to September 30, 1980

[a]Includes mayor/council ($219,472), city manager ($199,124), city clerk ($399,670), management services, excluding energy conservation and renewable resources ($268,267), data systems ($1,500,074), city attorney ($1,066,812), personnel ($906,379), public information ($579,484), internal auditing ($283,306), finance ($1,257,008), purchases and stores ($790,411), research and budget ($461,241), auditing ($342,534), election cost ($39,468), and tax ($2,597,348).

[b]Deductions for Central Texas Library System, interdepartmental charges, and others reduce net expenditures to $3,436,154.

[c]Does not include auditorium/coliseum ($847,339) or golf courses ($782,585). Deductions for special revenues, interdepartmental charges, and others reduce net expenditures to $8,737,282.

[d]Includes fire ($12,174,626 gross), police ($18,995,104 gross), and firemen's pension system expense ($18,356).

[e]The General Fund total includes more than the selected functions listed above.

Source: City of Austin, Texas, 1981-82 Proposed Annual Budget, Charter Volume.

TABLE A.23

Municipal Expenditures by Function in Richardson, Texas,
Fiscal Year 1979
(in dollars)

Selected Functions	Expenditure
General government[a]	736,006
Library	509,328
Parks and recreation[b]	1,175,826
Public safety[c]	4,019,421
Refuse collection and disposal[d]	1,265,927
General Fund total	11,527,768[e]

Fiscal year = October 1, 1978, to September 30, 1979

[a]Includes mayor/council ($62,539), general government
($150,155), audit ($31,303), legal ($12,547), data processing
($83,140), finance ($138,541), personnel ($63,001), and tax
($194,780). Of a substantial expense category entitled "General Ex-
penditures" ($222,711), only the audit and legal expenses noted
above are reported for purposes of this study. Other items in that
category are not clearly associated with the functions considered to
be general government.
[b]Includes parks and recreation—administration ($163,356),
pools ($189,709), tennis center ($13,906), recreation program
($259,360), park maintenance ($497,099), greenhouse ($26,372), and
older adult program ($26,024). Does not include golf ($297,499).
[c]Includes police ($2,346,731), fire ($1,577,555), and fire
marshal ($95,135). Does not include emergency services.
[d]Includes sanitation—residential collection ($962,751) and sani-
tation—commercial collection ($303,176).
[e]The General Fund total includes more than the selected functions listed above.

Sources: City of Richardson, Texas, 1980-81 Budget; and
idem, Annual Financial Report: 1978-79.

TABLE A.24

Municipal Expenditures by Function in Richardson, Texas,
Fiscal Year 1980
(in dollars)

Selected Functions	Expenditure
General government[a]	769,647
Library	586,991
Parks and recreation[b]	1,448,913
Public safety[c]	4,906,126
Refuse collection and disposal[d]	1,778,372
General Fund total	14,725,455[e]

Fiscal year = October 1, 1979, to September 30, 1980

[a]Includes mayor/council ($40,010), general government ($179,264), audit ($31,640), legal ($16,309), printing, binding, and copying ($12,103), data processing ($87,636), finance ($154,612), personnel ($75,133), and tax ($172,940). Of a substantial expense category entitled "General Expenditures" ($291,694), only the audit; legal expenses; and printing, binding, and copying noted above are reported for purposes of this study. Other items listed in that category are not clearly associated with the functions considered to be general government.

[b]Includes parks and recreation—administration ($189,760), pools ($230,357), tennis center ($19,714), recreation program ($354,213), park maintenance ($590,249), greenhouse ($35,048), and older adult program ($29,572). Does not include golf ($360,276).

[c]Includes police ($2,932,743), fire ($1,866,655), and fire marshal ($106,728). Does not include emergency services.

[d]Includes sanitation—residential collection ($1,181,552) and sanitation—commercial collection ($596,820).

[e]The General Fund total includes more than the selected functions listed above.

Sources: City of Richardson, Texas, 1981–82 Budget; and idem, Comprehensive Annual Financial Report for the Fiscal Year Ended September 30, 1980.

TABLE A.25

Municipal Expenditures by Function in Newport News, Virginia,
Fiscal Year 1979
(in dollars)

Selected Functions	Expenditure
General government[a]	2,667,934
Library[b]	827,861
Parks and recreation[c]	1,899,772
Public safety[d]	9,090,997
Refuse collection and disposal[e]	3,034,892
General Fund total	46,164,003[f]

Fiscal year = July 1, 1978, to June 30, 1979

[a]Includes city council ($48,489 + $2,160 = $50,649), city manager ($155,316 + $31,083 = $186,399), budget and evaluation ($81,543 + $13,207 = $94,750), city attorney ($198,644 + $39,224 = $237,868), city clerk ($34,658 + $3,494 = $38,152), city auditor ($62,359 + $11,167 = $73,526), external auditor ($26,500), administrative—management services ($47,668 + $10,217 = $57,885), data processing (net expenditure of less than zero owing to service charges, reported as $0 for purposes of this study), personnel ($122,872 + $21,940 = $144,812), real estate assessor ($261,601 + $49,896 = $311,497), purchasing ($127,747 + $23,143 = $150,890), print shop ($63,148 + $4,782 = $67,930), mail service ($6,664 + $1,407 = $8,071), finance administration ($326,164 + $47,579 = $373,743), retirement administration ($35,976 + $5,735 = $41,711), city treasurer ($322,305 + $58,045 = $380,350), commissioner of revenue ($340,634 + $57,565 = $398,199), board of equalization ($3,500 + $210 = $3,710), and memberships ($21,292). Not included are central warehouse, risk management, workman's compensation claims agent, economic development, community development, planning, graphic services, and commonwealth attorney (a prosecutor function common to county governments).

[b]Total for library ($724,253 + $103,608 = $827,861) includes law library ($21,798 + $1,180 = $22,978).

[c]Includes administration—recreation/parks ($118,320 + $17,929 = $136,249), program—recreation/parks ($316,932 + $56,054 = $372,986), operations—recreation/parks ($818,176 + $133,499 = $951,675), maintenance—recreation/parks ($360,950 + $59,495 = $420,445), and public works building maintenance—recreation buildings ($18,417). Does not include museum or golf course.

[d]Includes police, with the exception of water patrol ($4,451,866 + $1,217,878 = $5,669,744), and fire, with the exception of emergency medical service—ambulance ($2,708,876 + $712,377 = $3,421,253).

[e]Includes administration—solid waste ($54,081 + $9,266 = $63,347), collection—residential ($1,476,805 + $198,430 = $1,675,235), collection—commercial ($578,026 + $41,898 = $619,924), disposal—incinerator ($544,697 + $81,802 = $626,499), and disposal—landfill ($42,781 + $7,106 = $49,887).

[f]The General Fund total includes more than the selected functions listed above, including such uncommon General Fund activities as sewer operations and the sheriff's department. The reported total, however, excludes the General Fund appropriation to local schools.

Note: The FY 1981 Budget indicates calendar year 1980 fringe benefits for social security amounting to 6.13 percent of wages applied to earnings up to $25,900; for retirement amounting to 11.02 percent of wages for general employees and 20.41 percent for police and fire employees; for life insurance at $0.64 per $1,000 per month; and for health insurance at $468 to $789 per employee per year. All expenditures for fringe benefits are reported by the city of Newport News in accounts separate from departmental totals. For purposes of this study, approximate fringe-benefit costs (assuming 1979 benefits were similar to 1980 benefits) have been distributed to the various municipal activities by multiplying personal services in each by 22 percent for general employees and by 32 percent for police and fire employees (exception: city council and board of equalization multiplied by 6 percent for social security only). Estimated fringe-benefit costs are reflected in the footnotes as the second entry within the parentheses.

Source: City of Newport News, Virginia, FY 1981 Approved Budget.

TABLE A.26

Municipal Expenditures by Function in Newport News, Virginia,
Fiscal Year 1980
(in dollars)

Selected Functions	Expenditure
General government[a]	2,926,900
Library[b]	905,003
Parks and recreation[c]	2,369,718
Public safety[d]	9,451,745
Refuse collection and disposal[e]	2,758,478
General Fund total	49,860,753[f]

Fiscal year = July 1, 1979, to June 30, 1980

[a]Includes city council ($57,474 + $2,160 = $59,634), city manager ($174,921 + $33,514 = $208,435), budget and evaluation ($94,288 + $18,175 = $112,463), management/legislative services ($27,965 + $5,291 = $33,256), city attorney ($233,567 + $45,936 = $279,503), city clerk ($41,938 + $5,566 = $47,504), city auditor ($61,085 + $13,089 = $74,174), external auditor ($32,503), data processing/microfilm ($13,725 + $74,862 = $88,587), personnel ($123,742 + $22,682 = $146,424), real estate assessor ($279,145 + $50,876 = $330,021), purchasing ($134,490 + $24,262 = $158,752), print shop ($40,168 + $5,161 = $45,329), mail service ($6,596 + $1,209 = $7,805), finance administration ($337,480 + $50,458 = $387,938), retirement administration ($37,190 + $6,175 = $43,365), city treasurer ($361,391 + $61,585 = $422,976), commissioner of revenue ($369,578 + $62,388 = $431,966), board of equalization ($3,500 + $210 = $3,710), and memberships ($12,555). Not included are central warehouse, risk management, workman's compensation claims agent, economic development, community development, planning, and commonwealth attorney (a prosecutor function common to county governments).

[b]Total for library ($793,635 + $111,368 = $905,003) includes law library ($22,661 + $1,301 = $23,962).

[c]Includes administration—recreation/parks ($107,908 + $16,188 = $124,096), program—recreation/parks ($347,688 + $60,234 = $407,922), operations—recreation/parks ($872,596 + $139,581 + $1,012,177), maintenance—recreation/parks ($512,964 + $81,791 = $594,755), public works building maintenance—recreation buildings ($20,374), and parks and recreation revolving fund expenditures ($210,394) for fee-supported arts and crafts, after-school programs, and other activities. Does not include museum or golf course.

[d]Includes police ($4,466,411 + $1,186,446 = $5,652,857) and fire, with the exception of emergency medical service—ambulance ($2,992,072 + $806,816 = $3,798,888).

[e]Includes administration—solid waste ($89,425 + $17,072 = $106,497), collection—residential ($1,334,008 + $182,369 = $1,516,377), collection—commercial ($463,558 + $38,061 = $501,619), disposal—incinerator ($455,028 + $76,285 = $521,313), and disposal—landfill ($104,369 + $8,303 = $112,672).

[f]The General Fund total includes more than the selected functions listed above, including such uncommon General Fund activities as sewer operations and the sheriff's department. The reported total, however, excludes the General Fund appropriation to local schools.

Note: The FY 1981 Budget indicates calendar year 1980 fringe benefits for social security amounting to 6.13 percent of wages applied to earnings up to $25,900; for retirement amounting to 11.02 percent of wages for general employees and 20.41 percent for police and fire employees; for life insurance at $0.64 per $1,000 per month; and for health insurance at $468 to $789 per employee per year. All expenditures for fringe benefits are reported by the city of Newport News in accounts separate from departmental totals. For purposes of this study, approximate fringe-benefit costs have been distributed to the various municipal activities by multiplying personal services in each by 22 percent for general employees and by 32 percent for police and fire employees (exception: city council and board of equalization multiplied by 6 percent for social security only). Estimated fringe-benefit costs are reflected in the footnotes as the second entry within parentheses.

Sources: City of Newport News, Virginia, Approved Budget FY 1982; and idem, FY 1981 Approved Budget.

TABLE A.27

Municipal Expenditures by Function in Roanoke, Virginia,
Fiscal Year 1979
(in dollars)

Selected Functions	Expenditure
General government[a]	3,574,032
Library[b]	790,737
Parks and recreation[c]	1,130,084
Public safety[d]	8,157,992
Refuse collection and disposal[e]	1,835,365
General Fund total	54,743,094[f]

Fiscal year = July 1, 1978, to June 30, 1979

[a]Includes city council ($78,122 + $2,244 = $80,366), city clerk ($85,392 + $14,177 = $99,569), city manager ($247,509 + $34,246 = $281,755), city attorney ($200,443 + $26,072 = $226,515), city information services ($530,710 + $39,704 = $570,414), purchasing and materials control ($388,556 + $32,199 = $420,755), personnel ($147,145 + $16,505 = $163,650), director of finance ($286,551 + $47,958 = $334,509), commissioner of revenue ($237,691 + $41,336 = $279,027), city treasurer ($216,917 + $38,213 = $255,130), assessment of real estate ($261,553 + $39,313 = $300,866), division of billings and collections ($266,163 + $44,292 = $310,455), municipal auditor ($99,013 + $18,804 = $117,817), independent auditing ($34,950), electoral board ($74,079 + $2,416 = $76,495), and board of equalization ($21,562 + $197 = $21,759).

[b]Libraries ($677,382 + $91,361 = $768,743) plus law library ($20,553 + $1,441 = $21,994).

[c]Parks and recreation expenditures include those reported in the parks and recreation activity ($612,117 + $83,772 = $695,889), parks maintenance (estimated at $360,000, based upon allocations for grounds maintenance in 1981-82 and consideration of fringe benefits), and special purpose grant projects ($74,195). Reported expenditures do not include civic center operations and promotion or the armory, stadium, and athletic field activity, which is separate from the athletic programs of the parks and recreation department.

[d]Includes director of administration and public safety ($50,251 + $8,778 = $59,029), fire ($3,341,172 + $672,193 = $4,013,365), police, excluding estimated costs for animal control, based upon 1980 ratio ($3,571,000), communications (included within the street-maintenance activity in fiscal year 1979 but estimated for purposes of this study at $420,000, a figure derived by reducing the fiscal year 1980 expenditures for communications [adjusted for fringe benefits] by 10 percent and reducing that product by 10 percent to account for non-public-safety communications, as estimated by a budget and systems department official), and special purpose grant projects in the police department ($94,598). Does not include court or sheriff's operations.

[e]Refuse collection ($1,627,947 + $207,418 = $1,835,365) includes capital outlay of $205,868 reported within the activity.

[f]The General Fund total includes more than the selected functions listed above, including such uncommon General Fund expenditures as the sheriff's department and transfers to the Sewage Treatment Fund. The reported total, however, excludes the General Fund appropriation to local schools.

Note: The city of Roanoke reports employee fringe benefits in an account separate from departmental totals. The city's costs for fringe benefits in fiscal year 1979 were approximately 12.91 percent of personal services for retirement (no differential between public safety and general employees), 6.13 percent for social security, 1.01 percent for life insurance, and $12 per month per employee for health insurance. For purposes of this study, fringe-benefit costs have been assigned to activities at 21.25 percent of the basic expenditure for personal services. The fringe-benefit cost appears as the second figure within the parentheses in the footnotes to this table.

Sources: City of Roanoke, Virginia, Department of Finance, Supplement to the Annual Financial Report (July 1, 1979, to June 30, 1980); idem, Supplement to the Annual Financial Report (July 1, 1978, to June 30, 1979); and idem, Resource Allocation Plan: Adopted Budget for Fiscal Year 1981-82.

TABLE A.28

Municipal Expenditures by Function in Roanoke, Virginia,
Fiscal Year 1980
(in dollars)

Selected Functions	Expenditure
General government[a]	4,041,472
Library[b]	869,351
Parks and recreation[c]	1,147,290
Public safety[d]	9,716,137
Refuse collection and disposal[e]	1,910,568
General Fund total	56,529,234[f]

Fiscal year = July 1, 1979, to June 30, 1980

[a]Includes city council ($113,692 + $2,237 = $115,929), city clerk ($96,909 + $16,820 = $113,729), city manager ($307,617 + $52,465 = $360,082), city attorney ($183,904 + $29,218 = $213,122), city information services ($576,583 + $48,936 = $625,519), management services ($19,261 + $3,820 = $23,081), purchasing and materials control ($389,686 + $34,207 = $423,892), personnel ($180,266 + $23,448 = $203,714), director of finance ($327,546 + $57,964 = $385,510), commissioner of revenue ($261,427 + $45,731 = $307,158), city treasurer ($224,747 + $40,218 = $264,965), assessment of real estate ($273,158 + $45,021 = $318,179), division of billings and collections ($351,967 + $59,888 = $411,855), municipal auditor ($110,400 + $20,398 = $130,798), independent auditing ($29,888), board of equalization ($25,259 + $196 = $25,455), and electoral board ($85,794 + $2,802 = $88,596). Not included are board of zoning appeals, Comprehensive Employment Training Act program agent, and human resources.

[b]Libraries ($740,027 + $103,165 = $843,192) plus law library ($24,744 + $1,415 = $26,159).

[c]Parks and recreation expenditures include those reported in the parks and recreation activity ($618,959 + $94,956 = $713,915, which includes senior citizens programs), parks maintenance (estimated at $429,000, based upon allocations for grounds maintenance in 1981-82 and consideration of fringe benefits), and parks study (HCRS) ($4,375). Reported expenditures do not include civic center operations and promotion or the armory, stadium, and athletic field activity ($70,575 + $3,787 = $74,362), which is separate from the athletic programs of the parks and recreation department.

[d]Includes director of administration and public safety ($42,919 + $7,405 = $50,324), fire ($3,902,283 + $755,821 = $4,658,104), police, excluding animal control ($3,769,976 + $656,545 = $4,426,521), communications ($467,000, based upon adjustment for fringe benefits and budget and systems department official's estimate that approximately 90 percent of the communications expenditures are related to public safety functions), and special purpose grant projects in the police department ($114,188). Does not include court or sheriff's operations.

[e]Refuse collection ($1,675,946 + $234,622 = $1,910,568) includes capital outlay of $143,953 reported within the activity.

[f]The General Fund total includes more than the selected functions listed above, including such uncommon General Fund expenditures as the sheriff's department and transfers to the Sewage Treatment Fund. The reported total, however, excludes the General Fund appropriation to local schools.

Note: The city of Roanoke reports employee fringe benefits in an account separate from departmental totals. The city's costs for fringe benefits in fiscal year 1980 were approximately 12.91 percent of personal services for retirement (no differential between public safety and general employees), 6.13 percent for social security, 1.01 percent for life insurance, and $15 per month per employee for health insurance. For purposes of this study, fringe-benefit costs have been assigned to activities at 21.25 percent of the basic expenditure for personal services. The fringe-benefit cost appears as the second figure within the parentheses in the footnotes to this table.

Sources: City of Roanoke, Virginia, Department of Finance, Supplement to the Annual Financial Report (July 1, 1979, to June 30, 1980); and idem, Resource Allocation Plan: Adopted Budget for Fiscal Year 1981-82.

APPENDIX B

QUESTIONNAIRES

CITY MANAGER/CHIEF EXECUTIVE QUESTIONNAIRE

Survey of Full-Service Cities with High-Quality Performance

I. Please rank the problems or issues in the following list as they affect your local government. Place a "1" beside the most pressing issue, a "2" beside the second most pressing, and so forth through "10" for the least pressing issue.

_____ capital improvements
_____ community relations
_____ economic development
_____ intergovernmental relations

_____ labor relations
_____ productivity improvement
_____ public safety

_____ quality of life
_____ staff development
_____ the "fiscal crisis"

II. Do you have the flexibility to reward exceptional administrators for productivity improvements beyond what is granted to average administrators?

_____ Yes   _____ No

If "yes," please indicate the type of reward available:

_____ Extra step(s) in pay range advancement beyond the norm
_____ Total flexibility to adjust pay levels anywhere within a specified range without regard to structured pay steps
_____ One-time bonus
_____ Nonmonetary recognition
_____ Other (please specify) _____

III. How is the productivity improvement effort structured in your organization?

_____ Basically, it is unstructured. Improvements occur as opportunities arise.
_____ Productivity improvement efforts are decentralized. Department heads are held accountable for improvements on a regular basis.
_____ Primary productivity efforts are given a centralized focus through the following office or unit with responsibility for serving as a catalyst for organizationwide productivity improvement (please

(continued)

263

identify your city's productivity unit, if this response is marked):

_____ Other (please specify) _____

IV. Does your city contract for services from a private company or another government entity in any of the following functions? (Please check the space for any function for which you obtain contractual services for actual service provision. In such instances, please indicate whether the contractual services supplement city forces or perform the function entirely, by circling the appropriate parenthetical response.)

_____ Street construction   (supplementary/primary service provider)
_____ Street maintenance   (supplementary/primary service provider)
_____ Park maintenance   (supplementary/primary service provider)
_____ Recreation services   (supplementary/primary service provider)
_____ Police   (supplementary/primary service provider)
_____ Fire   (supplementary/primary service provider)
_____ Library   (supplementary/primary service provider)
_____ Refuse collection   (supplementary/primary service provider)
_____ Legal services   (supplementary/primary service provider)
_____ Planning services   (supplementary/primary service provider)
_____ Custodial services   (supplementary/primary service provider)
_____ Other (please specify) (supplementary/primary service provider)

V. If you believe that your city has operations that have unusually productive features that would be of interest in this study, we would be delighted to have a brief description or documentation. If magazine or journal articles have been written in the last decade about any aspect of your city's operation, please send us a copy or the appropriate citations so that we may look them up.

Respondent: _____

City Manager

Thank you for completing this questionnaire. Your cooperation is sincerely appreciated.

PERSONNEL DIRECTOR QUESTIONNAIRE

Survey of Full-Service Cities with High-Quality Performance

I. Please place an "X" in the appropriate spaces for any of the following employee incentives in use by your city and available to specified employee groups. (An incentive available to ALL employees would have four "X's." An incentive available only to recreation department employees, for example, would have only an "X" in the space for "Other City Employees.")

Police Employees	Fire Employees	Public Works Employees	Other Employees	Incentive
___	___	___	___	Educational Incentives—involve monetary or nonmonetary rewards designed to encourage employees to take certain types of training or continue their education.
___	___	___	___	Attendance Incentives—involve monetary or nonmonetary rewards designed to induce employees to improve attendance (e.g., reduce lateness, absenteeism, sick leave abuse, etc.)
___	___	___	___	Variation in Working Hours—modification of work hours to accommodate employees or improve performance (commonly, "flextime," four-day workweek with 10-hour days). If applicable, please describe:
___	___	___	___	Safety Incentives—monetary or nonmonetary rewards to encourage employees to improve their safety records.
___	___	___	___	Task Systems—usually involves clearly specified activities whose completion constitutes a "fair day's work." Under such system, an employee completing the task

(continued)

265

PERSONNEL DIRECTOR QUESTIONNAIRE (continued)

Police Employees	Fire Employees	Public Works Employees	Other Employees	Incentive

early can go home and still be paid for a full day. Please indicate any activities in the city with "task systems":

Job Enrichment—formal processes designed to motivate employees by making their work more intrinsically interesting and making the work place more challenging, humane, and satisfying (commonly, "team efforts," "increased participation," "job rotation," "job redesign"). If applicable, please describe:

Suggestion Awards—designed to encourage ideas for improving municipal operations.

II. Does your city have formally recognized employee unions for bargaining purposes, informal employee associations, or no such organizations in the following service functions? (Please place an "X" in the appropriate space.)

	Formal Employee Union	Informal Employee Association	No Permanently Organized Effort	Please identify association or union by name, if applicable
Police				
Fire				
Office workers				

Public works _____

Any other _____

III. What is the length of your city's standard workweek?

_____ 40 hours   _____ 35 hours

_____ 37.5 hours   _____ Other (please specify) _____

IV. In your opinion, does your city make a special effort—beyond that of the average city—to improve the productivity of departments and employees? (Please see footnote. Absolute candor is essential.)

_____ Yes

_____ No, nothing special

*If "yes," would you say that your city's approach to productivity improvement is more "behavioral" (e.g., organizational development, job enrichment, employee motivation, etc.) or more of an "industrial engineering" nature (e.g., work measurement, job simplification, procedures improvement, etc.)?

_____ Mostly "behavioral"

_____ Mostly "industrial engineering"

_____ Approximately equal amounts of each

_____ Neither

_____ Don't know

V. Please ESTIMATE the percentage of department heads in your city in each of the following formal education categories. (Precise figures would be excellent, but simply your "best guess" would be sufficient. Please see footnote. Absolute candor is essential.)

_____ Percentage with less than high school education

_____ Percentage with high school diploma, but no college

_____ Percentage with high school diploma, some college, but no college degree

_____ Percentage with college degree, but no graduate degree

_____ Percentage with graduate degree

100% Total

267

(continued)

PERSONNEL DIRECTOR QUESTIONNAIRE (continued)

VI. Does your city utilize volunteers in any of the following services? (Please check the space for each department using volunteers and indicate in such instances, by circling the appropriate parenthetical response, whether you believe the use to be less than average, average, or greater than average in most other municipal operations of similar size and function.)

____ Library   (less than average/average/greater than average)

____ Fire department   (less than average/average/greater than average)

____ Police department   (less than average/average/greater than average)

____ Recreation   (less than average/average/greater than average)

____ Parks   (less than average/average/greater than average)

____ Other (please specify):   (less than average/average/greater than average)

VII. What was the starting salary for an entry-level clerk-typist in your city on January 1, 1979? $ _____

What was the starting salary for an entry-level clerk-typist in your city on January 1, 1980? $ _____

_____

*Replies to questions IV and V will remain anonymous with responses reported only as grouped data or as associated with "City A," "City B," etc., rather than using actual city names.

Thank you for completing the questionnaire. Any supplemental information you care to provide on any of these topics (e.g., incentives, special productivity efforts, volunteerism) would be helpful. Your cooperation is sincerely appreciated.

Respondent _____   Title _____

ASSISTANT CITY MANAGER/ASSISTANT CHIEF EXECUTIVE QUESTIONNAIRE

Survey of Full-Service Cities with High-Quality Performance Profile of Organizational Characteristics

INSTRUCTIONS: On the lines below each organizational variable (item), please place an "X" at the point that, in your experience, describes your organization at the present time. Treat each item as a continuous variable from the extreme at one end to that at the other. All responses will remain anonymous and will be linked only to pseudonyms (e.g., "city A," "city B," etc.) rather than to cities identified by actual name. Your complete candor is very important.

Organizational Variable				Item No.

1. Leadership processes used

Extent to which superiors have confidence and trust in subordinates

Have no confidence and trust in subordinates | Have condescending confidence and trust, such as master has in servant | Substantial but not complete confidence and trust; still wishes to keep control of decisions | Complete confidence and trust in all matters

Item No. 1

2. Character of motivational forces

Manner in which motives are used

Fear, threats, punishment, and occasional rewards | Rewards and some actual or potential punishment | Rewards, occasional punishment, and some involvement | Economic rewards based on compensation system developed through participation; group participation and involvement in setting goals, improving methods, appraising progress toward goals, etc.

Item No. 2

(continued)

Organizational Variable					Item No.
Amount of responsibility felt by each member of organization for achieving organization's goals	Personnel at all levels feel real responsibility for organization's goals and behave in ways to implement them	Substantial proportion of personnel, especially at higher levels, feel responsibility and generally behave in ways to achieve the organization's goals	Managerial personnel usually feel responsibility; rank and file usually feel relatively little responsibility for achieving organization's goals	High levels of management feel responsibility; lower levels feel less; rank and file feel little and often welcome opportunity to behave in ways to defeat the organization's goals	3

3. Character of communication process

Organizational Variable					Item No.
Direction of information flow	Downward	Mostly downward	Down and up	Down, up, and with peers	4
Extent to which downward communications are accepted by subordinates	Generally accepted, but if not, openly and candidly questioned	Often accepted but if not, may or may not be openly questioned	Some accepted and some viewed with suspicion	Viewed with great suspicion	5
Accuracy of upward communication via line	Accurate	Information that boss wants to hear flows; other information may be limited or cautiously given	Information that boss wants to hear flows; other information is restricted and filtered	Tends to be inaccurate	6

4. Character of interaction-influence process

Amount of cooperative teamwork present

| None | Relatively little | A moderate amount | Very substantial amount throughout the organization |

7

5. Character of decision-making process

At what level in the organization are decisions formally made?

| Decision making widely done throughout organization, although well integrated through linking process provided by overlapping groups | Broad policy decisions at top, more specific decisions at lower levels | Policy at top, many decisions within prescribed framework made at lower levels but usually checked with top before action | Bulk of decisions at top of organization |

8

Are decisions made at the best level in the organization as far as the motivational consequences are concerned (i. e., does the decision-making process help to create the necessary motivations in those persons who have to carry out the decision?)

| Decision making contributes little or nothing to the motivation to implement the decision, usually yields adverse motivation | Decision making contributes relatively little motivation | Some contribution by decision making to motivation to implement | Substantial contribution by decision-making processes to motivation to implement |

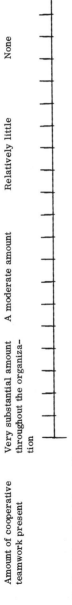

9

(continued)

Organizational Variable					Item No.

6. Character of goal setting or ordering

Manner in which usually done	Except in emergencies, goals are usually established by means of group participation	Goals are set or orders issued after discussion with subordinates of problems and planned action	Orders issued, opportunity to comment may or may not exist	Orders issued	10

7. Character of control process

Extent to which control data (e.g., accounting, productivity, cost, etc.) are used for self-guidance or group problem solving by managers and nonsupervisory employees, or used by superiors in a punitive, policing manner.	Used for policing and in punitive manner	Used for policing coupled with reward and punishment, sometimes punitively; used somewhat for guidance but in accord with orders	Used for policing with emphasis usually on reward but with some punishment; used for guidance in accord with orders; some use also for self-guidance	Used for self-guidance and for coordinated problem solving and guidance; not used punitively	11

Respondent _____   Title _____

Thank you for completing this questionnaire. Your cooperation is sincerely appreciated.

CITY CLERK/SECRETARY QUESTIONNAIRE

Survey of Full-Service Cities with High-Quality Performance

I. How many permanent citizen boards and commissions are appointed by the _____ city council?

Number of boards and commissions: _____ ESTIMATED total membership (your "best guess" will be fine) _____

II. How many ad hoc citizen advisory groups are appointed in a typical year? (please check the appropriate space)

_____ None   _____ 1 to 3   _____ 4 to 6   _____ 7 or more

III. In what year was _____ incorporated?   Year: _____

IV. The Municipal Year Book: 1979 reports that _____ has _____ city council members.

Is that number correct?   _____ Yes   _____ No.   The correct number is _____

Certain background information on council members is needed for this study. No names are necessary; only grouped data and city pseudonyms ("city A," "city B," etc.) will be reported for this question, thereby protecting anonymity. Please complete the following table to the best of your knowledge (your "best guess" will be fine). One line is provided for each council member (council member #1, council member #2, etc.).

Council Member	Occupation of Council Member (check one) (In the case of a homemaker, please check "homemaker" and also check the occupation of spouse. If retired, check "retired" and indicate occupation prior to retirement.)							Maximum Attainment in Formal Education (check one)							Years on Council (round to nearest half year —e.g., 2 yrs., 2.5 yrs., 3 yrs., etc.)
	Executive, Proprietor, Manager, Professional, Administrator	Small Businessman, Clerk, Salesman, Teacher, Technician, etc.	Skilled, Semiskilled, Unskilled Employee (blue collar)	Other (please specify)	Home-maker	Retired	Unknown								
#1															
#2															
#3															
#4															
#5															
#6															
#7															
#8															
#9															
#10															
#11															
#12															

SELECTED BIBLIOGRAPHY

Adam, Everett E., Jr., James C. Hershauer, and William A. Ruch. "Developing Quality Productivity Ratios for Public Sector Personnel Services." Public Productivity Review 5 (March 1981): 45-61.

Advisory Commission on Intergovernmental Relations. Changing Public Attitudes on Governments and Taxes, 1982. Washington, D.C.: U.S. Government Printing Office, 1982.

_____. Payments in Lieu of Taxes on Federal Real Property. Washington, D.C.: U.S. Government Printing Office, 1981.

Alford, Robert R., and Harry M. Scoble. "Political and Socioeconomic Characteristics of American Cities." In The Municipal Year Book 1965, vol. 32, pp. 82-97. Washington, D.C.: International City Management Association, 1965.

Ammons, David N., and Joseph C. King. "Productivity Improvement in Local Government: Its Place among Competing Priorities." Public Administration Review 43 (March-April 1983): 113-20.

Ardolini, Charles, and Jeffrey Hohenstein. "Measuring Productivity in the Federal Government." Monthly Labor Review 97 (November 1974): 13-20.

Balk, Walter L. "Technological Trends in Productivity Measurement." Public Personnel Management 4 (March-April 1975): 128-33.

_____. "Toward a Government Productivity Ethic." Public Administration Review 38 (January-February 1978): 46-50.

_____. "Why Don't Public Administrators Take Productivity More Seriously?" Public Personnel Management 3 (July-August 1974): 318-24.

Barbour, George P., Jr. "Key Factors Influencing Productivity of State and Local Government Activities." Public Productivity Review 4 (September 1980): 273-82.

_____. "Measuring Local Government Productivity." In The Munici-
pal Year Book 1973, vol. 40, pp. 38-46. Washington, D. C.:
International City Management Association, 1973.

Barkdoll, Gerald L. "Type III Evaluations: Consultation and Consensus." Public Administration Review 40 (March-April 1980):
174-79.

Baumol, William J. "Macroeconomics of Unbalanced Growth: The
Anatomy of Urban Crisis." American Economic Review 57
(June 1967): 415-26.

Bernstein, Samuel J., and Leon Reinharth. "Management, the Public Organization and Productivity: Some Factors to Consider."
Public Personnel Management 2 (July-August 1973): 261-66.

Bingham, Richard D. The Adoption of Innovation by Local Government. Lexington, Mass.: D. C. Heath, Lexington Books, 1976.

Bradford, D. F., R. A. Malt, and W. E. Oates. "The Rising Cost
of Local Public Services: Some Evidence and Reflections."
National Tax Journal 22 (June 1969): 185-202.

Burkhead, Jesse, and Patrick J. Hennigan. "Productivity Analysis:
A Search for Definition and Order." Public Administration Review 38 (January-February 1978): 34-40.

Campbell, Donald T. "Reforms as Experiments." Urban Affairs
Quarterly 7 (December 1971): 133-71.

Carter, Steve. "Trends in Local Government Productivity." In
The Municipal Year Book 1975, vol. 42, pp. 180-84. Washington, D. C.: International City Management Association, 1975.

Committee for Economic Development. Improving Productivity in
State and Local Government. New York: CED, 1976.

Cordtz, Dan. "City Hall Discovers Productivity." Fortune 84 (October 1971): 92-96, 127-28.

Dalton, Melville. "Conflicts between Staff and Line Managerial Officers." American Sociological Review 15 (June 1950): 342-51.

Downs, George W., Jr. Bureaucracy, Innovation, and Public Policy.
Lexington, Mass.: D. C. Heath, Lexington Books, 1976.

Drucker, Peter F. "The Deadly Sins in Public Administration." Public Administration Review 40 (March–April 1980): 103–6.

Dye, Thomas R., and John A. Garcia. "Structure, Function, and Policy in American Cities." Urban Affairs Quarterly 14 (September 1978): 103–22.

Ervin, Osbin L. "A Conceptual Niche for Municipal Productivity." Public Productivity Review 3 (Summer–Fall 1978): 15–24.

Fainstein, Norman I., and Susan S. Fainstein. "Innovation in Urban Bureaucracies." American Behavioral Scientist 15 (March–April 1972): 511–31.

Fisk, Donald, Herbert Kiesling, and Thomas Muller. Private Provision of Public Services: An Overview. Washington, D.C.: Urban Institute, 1978.

Florestano, Patricia S., and Stephen B. Gordon. "Public vs. Private: Small Government Contracting with the Private Sector." Public Administration Review 40 (January–February 1980): 29–34.

Fosler, R. Scott. "State and Local Government Productivity and the Private Sector." Public Administration Review 38 (January–February 1978): 22–27.

Fox, William F. Size Economies in Local Government Services: A Review. Department of Agriculture Rural Development Research Report no. 22. Washington, D.C.: U.S. Government Printing Office, 1980.

Frendreis, John P. "Innovation Characteristics as Correlates of Innovation Adoption in American Cities." Midwest Review of Public Administration 12 (June 1978): 67–86.

Fukuhara, Rackham S. "Productivity Improvement in Cities." In The Municipal Year Book 1977, vol. 44, pp. 193–200. Washington, D.C.: International City Management Association, 1977.

Gellerman, Saul W. "In Praise of Those Who Leave." Conference Board Record 11 (March 1974): 35–40.

General Accounting Office. State and Local Government Productivity Improvement: What Is the Federal Role? Washington, D.C.: U.S. Government Printing Office, 1978.

Gissler, Sig. "Productivity in the Public Sector: A Summary of a Wingspread Symposium." Public Administration Review 32 (November–December 1972): 840–50.

Golembiewski, Robert T., and Carl W. Proehl, Jr. "Public Sector Applications of Flexible Workhours: A Review of Available Experience." Public Administration Review 40 (January–February 1980): 72–85.

Gotbaum, Victor, and Edward Handman. "A Conversation with Victor Gotbaum." Public Administration Review 38 (January–February 1978): 19–21.

Greiner, John M. "Incentives for Municipal Employees: An Update." In The Municipal Year Book 1980, vol. 47, pp. 192–209. Washington, D.C.: International City Management Association, 1980.

Greiner, John M., Harry P. Hatry, Margo P. Koss, Annie P. Millar, and Jane P. Woodward. Productivity and Motivation: A Review of State and Local Government Initiatives. Washington, D.C.: Urban Institute, 1981.

Guyot, Dorothy. "What Productivity? What Bargain?" Public Administration Review 36 (May–June 1976): 340–43.

Haggerty, Patrick E. "Productivity: Industry Isn't the Only Place Where It's a Problem." Forbes 107 (February 1, 1971): 43–45.

Hall, John R., Jr. Factors Related to Local Government Use of Performance Measurement. Washington, D.C.: Urban Institute, 1978.

Hamilton, Edward K. "Productivity: The New York City Approach." Public Administration Review 32 (November–December 1972): 784–95.

Hatry, Harry P. "Issues in Productivity Measurement for Local Governments." Public Administration Review 32 (November–December 1972): 776–84.

_____. "Performance Measurement Principles and Techniques: An Overview for Local Government." Public Productivity Review 4 (December 1980): 312–39.

_____. "The Status of Productivity Measurement in the Public Sector." Public Administration Review 38 (January-February 1978): 28-33.

Hatry, Harry P., Louis H. Blair, Donald M. Fisk, John M. Greiner, John R. Hall, Jr., and Philip S. Schaenman. How Effective Are Your Community Services? Procedures for Monitoring the Effectiveness of Municipal Services. Washington, D.C.: Urban Institute, 1977.

Hatry, Harry P., and Donald M. Fisk. Improving Productivity and Productivity Measurement in Local Governments. Washington, D.C.: Urban Institute, 1971.

Hayes, Frederick O'R. Productivity in Local Government. Lexington, Mass.: D. C. Heath, Lexington Books, 1977.

Hayes, Frederick O'R., and John E. Rasmussen. Centers for Innovation in the Cities and States. San Francisco: San Francisco Press, 1972.

Hayward, Nancy S. "The Productivity Challenge." Public Administration Review 36 (September-October 1976): 544-50.

Hayward, Nancy, and George Kuper. "The National Economy and Productivity in Government." Public Administration Review 38 (January-February 1978): 2-5.

Herzberg, Frederick. Work and the Nature of Man. Cleveland: World, 1966.

Hirsch, Werner Z. "The Supply of Urban Public Services." In Issues in Urban Economics, edited by Harvey S. Perloff and Lowdon Wingo, Jr., pp. 477-525. Baltimore: Johns Hopkins University Press, 1968.

Holzer, Marc, ed. Productivity in Public Organizations. Port Washington, N.Y.: Kennikat Press, 1976.

Holzer, Marc, David Tatge, and John Jay. "Educating and Training for Productivity." Public Productivity Review 2 (Fall 1977): 3-9.

Horton, Raymond D. "Productivity and Productivity Bargaining in Government: A Critical Analysis." Public Administration Review 36 (July-August 1976): 407-14.

Institute for Local Self-Government. Alternatives to Traditional Public Safety Delivery Systems: Civilians in Public Safety Services. Berkeley, Calif.: Institute for Local Self-Government, 1977.

Joint Financial Management Improvement Program. Implementing a Productivity Program: Points to Consider. Washington, D.C.: U.S. Government Printing Office, 1977.

Katzell, Raymond A., and Daniel Yankelovich. Work, Productivity, and Job Satisfaction: An Evaluation of Policy-Related Research. New York: Psychological Corporation, 1975.

Keevey, Richard F. "State Productivity Improvements: Building on Existing Strengths." Public Administration Review 40 (September-October 1980): 451-58.

Kellar, Elizabeth K., ed. Managing with Less: A Book of Readings. Washington, D.C.: International City Management Association, 1979.

Kendrick, John W. "Exploring Productivity Measurement in Government." Public Administration Review 23 (June 1963): 59-66.

_____. Understanding Productivity: An Introduction to the Dynamics of Productivity Change. Baltimore: Johns Hopkins University Press, 1977.

Kuhn, James W. "The Riddle of Inflation: A New Answer." Public Interest 27 (Spring 1972): 63-77.

Kull, Donald C. "Productivity Programs in the Federal Government." Public Administration Review 38 (January-February 1978): 5-9.

Levine, Charles H. "More on Cutback Management: Hard Questions for Hard Times." Public Administration Review 39 (March-April 1979): 179-83.

_____. "Organizational Decline and Cutback Management." Public Administration Review 38 (July-August 1978): 316-25.

Lewin, David. "The Prevailing-Wage Principle and Public Wage Decisions." Public Personnel Management 3 (November-December 1974): 473-85.

Lewis, Carol W., and Anthony T. Logalbo. "Cutback Principles and Practices: A Checklist for Managers." Public Administration Review 40 (March–April 1980): 184–88.

Likert, Rensis. The Human Organization: Its Management and Value. New York: McGraw-Hill, 1967.

Lineberry, Robert L., and Edmund P. Fowler. "Reformism and Public Policies in American Cities." American Political Science Review 61 (September 1967): 701–17.

Lipsky, Michael. Street-Level Bureaucracy: Dilemmas of the Individual in Public Services. New York: Russell Sage Foundation, 1980.

Lucey, Patrick J. "Wisconsin's Productivity Policy." Public Administration Review 32 (November–December 1972): 795–99.

_____. "Wisconsin's Progress with Productivity Improvements." Public Administration Review 38 (January–February 1978): 9–12.

McGregor, Douglas. The Human Side of Enterprise. New York: McGraw-Hill, 1960.

Malkiel, Burton G. "Productivity: The Problem behind the Headlines." Harvard Business Review 57 (May–June 1979): 81–91.

Mark, Jerome A. "Meanings and Measures of Productivity." Public Administration Review 32 (November–December 1972): 747–53.

_____. "Measuring Productivity in Government: Federal, State and Local." Public Productivity Review 5 (March 1981): 21–44.

_____. "Progress in Measuring Productivity in Government." Monthly Labor Review 95 (December 1972): 3–6.

Methé, David T., and James L. Perry. "The Impacts of Collective Bargaining on Local Government Services: A Review of Research." Public Administration Review 40 (July–August 1980): 359–71.

Morgan, David R. Managing Urban America: The Politics and Administration of America's Cities. North Scituate, Mass.: Duxbury Press, 1979.

Morris, Thomas D., William H. Corbett, and Brian L. Usilaner. "Productivity Measures in the Federal Government." Public Administration Review 32 (November-December 1972): 753-63.

Multi-Agency Study Team. "Report to the National Productivity Council, November 1979." Public Productivity Review 4 (June 1980): 167-89.

Mushkin, Selma, ed. Public Prices for Public Products. Washington, D. C.: Urban Institute, 1972.

Mushkin, Selma J., and Frank H. Sandifer. Personnel Management and Productivity in City Government. Lexington, Mass.: D. C. Heath, Lexington Books, 1979.

National Center for Productivity and Quality of Working Life. Employee Attitudes and Productivity Differences between the Public and Private Sector. Washington, D. C.: U. S. Government Printing Office, 1978.

_____. Improving Governmental Productivity: Selected Case Studies. Washington, D. C.: U. S. Government Printing Office, 1977.

_____. Total Performance Management: Some Pointers for Action. Washington, D. C.: U. S. Government Printing Office, 1978.

National Commission on Productivity and Work Quality. Employee Incentives to Improve State and Local Government Productivity. Washington, D. C.: U. S. Government Printing Office, 1975.

_____. Improving Police Productivity: More for Your Law Enforcement Dollar. Washington, D. C.: U. S. Government Printing Office, 1975.

National Productivity Council. Federal Actions to Support State and Local Government Productivity Improvement. Washington, D. C.: National Productivity Council, 1979.

Newland, Chester A. "Personnel Concerns in Government Productivity Improvement." Public Administration Review 32 (November-December 1972): 807-15.

Newstrom, John W., William E. Reif, and Robert M. Monczka. "Motivating the Public Employee: Fact vs. Fiction." Public Personnel Management 5 (January-February 1976): 67-72.

Ostrom, Elinor. "Multi-Mode Measures: From Potholes to Police." Public Productivity Review 1 (March 1976): 51-58.

Ostrom, Elinor, Roger B. Parks, Stephen L. Percy, and Gordon P. Whitaker. "Evaluating Police Organization." Public Productivity Review 3 (Winter 1979): 3-27.

Peterson, Peter G. "Productivity in Government and the American Economy." Public Administration Review 32 (November-December 1972): 740-47.

Petrovic, William M., and Bruce L. Jaffee. "The Use of Contracts and Alternative Financing Methods in the Collection of Household Refuse in Urban Areas." Public Productivity Review 3 (Summer-Fall 1978): 48-60.

Poister, Theodore H., James C. McDavid, and Anne Hoagland Magoun. Applied Program Evaluation in Local Government. Lexington, Mass.: D. C. Heath, Lexington Books, 1979.

Poole, Robert W., Jr. Cutting Back City Hall. New York: Universe, 1980.

Price Waterhouse. Productivity Improvement Manual for Local Government Officials. New York: Price Waterhouse, 1977.

Public Technology. Improving Productivity and Decision-Making through the Use of Effectiveness Measures: Literature and Practice Review. Washington, D.C.: U.S. Department of Housing and Urban Development, 1979.

Quinn, Robert E. "Productivity and the Process of Organizational Improvement: Why We Cannot Talk to Each Other." Public Administration Review 38 (January-February 1978): 41-45.

Rainey, Glenn W., Jr., and Lawrence Wolf. "Flex-Time: Short-Term Benefits; Long-Term . . . ?" Public Administration Review 41 (January-February 1981): 52-63.

Ridley, Clarence E., and Herbert A. Simon. Measuring Municipal Activities: A Survey of Suggested Criteria for Appraising Administration. Chicago: International City Managers' Association, 1943.

Robinson, Barbara M. "Municipal Library Services." In The Munic-
    ipal Year Book 1979, vol. 46, pp. 63-84. Washington, D. C.:
    International City Management Association, 1979.

Rogers, David. Can Business Management Save the Cities? The
    Case of New York. New York: Free Press, 1978.

Rogers, Everett M. , and F. Floyd Shoemaker. Communication of
    Innovations: A Cross-Cultural Approach. New York: Free
    Press, 1971.

Ross, John P. , and Jesse Burkhead. Productivity in the Local Gov-
    ernment Sector. Lexington, Mass.: D. C. Heath, Lexington
    Books, 1974.

Savas, E. S. "Intracity Competition between Public and Private Ser-
    vice Delivery." Public Administration Review 41 (January-
    February 1981): 46-52.

_____. "Service Levels for Residential Refuse Collection." In The
    Organization and Efficiency of Solid Waste Collection, edited
    by E. S. Savas, pp. 67-78. Lexington, Mass.: D. C. Heath,
    Lexington Books, 1977.

Savas, E. S. , and Sigmund G. Ginsburg. "The Civil Service: A
    Meritless System?" Public Interest 32 (Summer 1973): 70-85.

Simon, Herbert A. Administrative Behavior. New York: Free
    Press, 1957.

Skogan, Wesley G. "The Validity of Official Crime Statistics: An
    Empirical Investigation." Social Science Quarterly 55 (June
    1974): 25-38.

Smith, Russell L. , and William Lyons. "The Impact of Fire Fighter
    Unionization on Wages and Working Hours in American Cities."
    Public Administration Review 40 (November-December 1980):
    568-74.

Stanley, David T. Managing Local Government under Union Pressure:
    Studies of Unionism in Government. Washington, D. C.: Brook-
    ings Institution, 1972.

Staudohar, Paul D. "An Experiment in Increasing Productivity of
    Police Service Employees." Public Administration Review 35
    (September-October 1975): 518-22.

Steiss, Alan Walter, and Gregory A. Daneke. Performance Administration: Improved Responsiveness and Effectiveness in Public Service. Lexington, Mass.: D. C. Heath, Lexington Books, 1980.

Stevens, Barbara J. "Scale, Market Structure and the Cost of Refuse Collection." Review of Economics and Statistics 60 (August 1978): 438-48.

Stevens, John M., Thomas C. Webster, and Brian Stipak. "Response Time: Role in Assessing Police Performance." Public Productivity Review 4 (September 1980): 210-30.

Stillman, Richard J., II. The Rise of the City Manager: A Public Professional in Local Government. Albuquerque, N. Mex.: University of New Mexico Press, 1974.

Stone, Harold A., Don K. Price, and Kathryn H. Stone. City Manager Government in the United States. Chicago: Public Administration Service, 1940.

Swidorski, Carl. "Sample Surveys: Help for the 'Out of House' Evaluator." Public Administration Review 40 (January-February 1980): 67-71.

Taylor, Frederick W. Principles of Scientific Management. New York: Harper & Row, 1911.

Thayer, Frederick C. "Productivity: Taylorism Revisited (Round Three)." Public Administration Review 32 (November-December 1971): 833-39.

Thomas, John S. "Demand Analysis: A Powerful Productivity Improvement Technique." Public Productivity Review 3 (Spring 1978): 32-43.

_____. So, Mr. Mayor, You Want to Improve Productivity. Washington, D.C.: U.S. Government Printing Office, 1974.

Turner, Wayne C., and R. J. Craig. "Productivity Improvement Programs in the Public Sector." Public Productivity Review 3 (Spring 1978): 3-22.

Usher, Charles L., and Gary C. Cornia. "Goal Setting and Performance Assessment in Municipal Budgeting." Public Administration Review 41 (March-April 1981): 229-35.

Van Meter, Donald S., and Carl E. Van Horn. "The Policy Implementation Process: A Conceptual Framework." Administration and Society 6 (February 1975): 445-86.

Vickery, Edward, Sally Plotecia, Lois MacGillivray, and Philip Coulter. "Operational Productivity Measures for Fire Service Delivery." In The Municipal Year Book 1976, vol. 43, pp. 173-78. Washington, D.C.: International City Management Association, 1976.

Vough, Clair F. Productivity: A Practical Program for Improving Efficiency. New York: Amacom, 1979.

Walker, Jack L. "The Diffusion of Innovations among the American States." American Political Science Review 63 (September 1969): 880-99.

Washnis, George J., ed. Productivity Improvement Handbook for State and Local Governments. New York: John Wiley & Sons, 1980.

Williams, Oliver. "A Typology for Comparative Local Government." Midwest Journal of Political Science, May 1961, pp. 150-64.

Williams, Oliver P., and Charles R. Adrian. "Community Types and Policy Differences." In City Politics and Public Policy, edited by James Q. Wilson, pp. 17-36. New York: John Wiley & Sons, 1968.

Wilson, James Q. "Innovation in Organization: Notes toward a Theory." In Approaches to Organizational Design, edited by James D. Thompson, pp. 193-218. Pittsburgh, Pa.: University of Pittsburgh Press, 1966.

Wilson, O. W., and Roy Clinton McLaren. Police Administration. New York: McGraw-Hill, 1972.

Wise, Charles R. "Productivity in Public Administration and Public Policy." Policy Studies Journal 5 (Autumn 1976): 97-107.

Wood, Robert C. 1400 Governments: The Political Economy of the New York Metropolitan Region. Cambridge, Mass.: Harvard University Press, 1961.

Wright, Deil. "The City Manager as a Development Administrator."
In Comparative Urban Research, edited by Robert Daland, pp.
203-48. Beverly Hills, Calif.: Sage, 1969.

Yates, Douglas. The Ungovernable City: The Politics of Urban Problems and Policy Making. Cambridge, Mass.: MIT Press, 1979.

Yin, Robert K., Karen A. Heald, and Mary E. Vogel. Tinkering with
the System: Technological Innovations in State and Local Services. Lexington, Mass.: D. C. Heath, Lexington Books, 1977.

Young, Dennis R. "Institutional Change and the Delivery of Urban
Public Services." Policy Sciences 2 (1971): 425-38.

Zaltman, Gerald, Robert Duncan, and Jonny Holbek. Innovations and
Organizations. New York: John Wiley & Sons, 1973.

INDEX

ABOUT THE AUTHOR

DAVID N. AMMONS is an assistant professor of public administration at North Texas State University in Denton, Texas. Previously, he served in various administrative capacities in the municipal governments of Fort Worth, Texas; Hurst, Texas; Phoenix, Arizona; and Oak Ridge, Tennessee.

Dr. Ammons's primary research interests are municipal administration and productivity improvement. He has authored or co-authored articles in such journals as <u>Administration and Society</u>, <u>American Review of Public Administration</u>, <u>Municipal Management: A Journal</u>, and <u>Public Administration Review</u>.

Dr. Ammons holds a B.A. in government from Texas Tech University, a Master of Public Administration degree from Texas Christian University, and a Ph.D. in political science from the University of Oklahoma.